CHEF'S TALES

BY
MICHAEL SAXON

Published by

MELROSE
BOOKS

An Imprint of Melrose Press Limited
St Thomas Place, Ely
Cambridgeshire
CB7 4GG, UK
www.melrosebooks.com

FIRST EDITION

Copyright © Michael Saxon 2008

The Author asserts his moral right to
be identified as the author of this work

Cover designed by Dave Tupper
Book illustrations by Jimmy Loh, Art Revo Studio

ISBN 978-1-906050-74-0

FSC
Mixed Sources
Product group from well-managed
forests and other controlled sources
Cert no. SGS-COC-2953
www.fsc.org
© 1996 Forest Stewardship Council

Printed and bound in Great Britain by:
CPI Antony Rowe, Chippenham, Wiltshire

To
My parents for their unstinting support in helping me through years of catering school. Also to my wife, Beatrice, and my two daughters, Alycia and Jessica, for their endless dedication, support and love.

Many thanks to the Eastern & Oriental Hotel for their invaluable contribution towards the publication of this book.

EASTERN & ORIENTAL HOTEL
10 Lebuh Farquhar, 10200 Penang
Malaysia
Tel: +(6) 04-222 2000 (General Line) / +(6) 04-222 2199 (Direct Line)
Fax: +(6) 04-261 6333
E-mail: michael.saxon@e-o-hotel.com
E-mail: reservations@e-o-hotel.com (Suite Reservations)
Website: www.e-o-hotel.com

Thanks are also due to *Flavours* magazine for publishing some of the new stories featured in this book.

Michael Saxon
General Manager
Eastern & Oriental Hotel

With lots of fond memories to share,
I share with you this book.

Mike
Penang

CONTENTS

IT'S A COOK'S LIFE ...

I ALWAYS WANTED to be a chef – I don't know why – it just happened that way. But realising my ambition was never going to be easy. I was 14 years old when I really began to think about my career in earnest. Being a cook in England was seen as a girl's job. I had to endure taunts of 'queer', 'sissy' and all the rest, when I decided to take the Home Economics course on offer at my school.

Even the teacher did not want a 'stupid' boy in her class 'causing trouble'. However, it only took a few sessions cooking up a storm to change their minds, and I was eventually left to get on with it. I was even given my own apron, or 'pinnie' as the bullies called it, signifying my acceptance on the course.

Although I was set on catering, I had no idea that it might lead to an international career and a multitude of adventures – both good and bad – that would change my whole life and shape my personality. Being a chef has provided me with experiences that money could never buy, and memories that time can't erode. I've worked with people from across the globe, and come to understand and appreciate the religions and cultures of the many countries I've worked in and visited. As a result I would like to think this has made me a more tolerant and open-minded person who can adapt and fit in just about anywhere.

The hotel business is a very transient one; where people just become, well, people, and customers are good customers so long as they pay the bill. To offer a good international range of food, a hotel has to have a mix of staff from different countries. Working in harmony with other foreign nationals is imperative. You have to be able to work under enormous stress, in a small area, often in very hot conditions, and get by without killing your fellow workers. Everyone relies on each other to keep the machine rolling smoothly, so colour, race and religion become secondary to working together and getting the job done.

Living in foreign countries, and seeing and doing things that you could never properly explain to your friends and family back home, make the gap between your old life and your new one widen as time goes by.

How can you possibly explain to the folks back home, who may never have strayed from their backyards, what it feels like to stand on the Great Wall of China in the middle of winter when it's covered in a blanket of snow? I felt a very long way from home, taking in the sheer size of that man-made structure and knowing that so many people had worked and died while building it. I felt it even more acutely as I began to realise that everyone around was staring at me because I was the only 'round eye' to be seen, and also the only person wearing a colour that was not blue, green or grey.

Would my friends back in Yorkshire even want to know how much water actually flows over Niagara Falls, how crowded the streets are in Hong Kong, or what the poverty in Indonesia or the Philippines is really like? How to explain the experience of being in the middle of a huge lake in north America, completely iced over in the middle of winter, not being able to see land in any direction, and watching the ice glow at sunset, reflecting the most amazing firestorm of orange and red hues. Then, a short time later, standing in awe as the full moon rises and the scene turns into a magical glow of bright light, so dazzling it seems like daytime again. Most of us need to see these things with our own eyes in order to fully appreciate them, and I am no exception.

I first visited China before it really opened up, and I have never been the same person since. The country left a profound impression on me and I have always felt since that if only everyone could witness at first hand the lives of those who are less fortunate than themselves, we could all live together rather better than we do now.

It is said that most hoteliers care little about where they work, only that they are working at all. Often workaholics, they do a job which normal people would consider lunacy yet enjoy every minute of it. It's a way of life. There is no way you could tolerate the thankless, endless days that come with the territory, not to mention working through Christmas, New Year's Eve, weekends and every other major holiday, if you didn't enjoy it.

Can you imagine the pressure of catering for a young couple about to get married and relying on you to make sure it's a day they will always remember with pleasure rather than one to forget? Hoteliers, and more especially restaurateurs within the hotel industry, are a breed on their own, living a strange lifestyle that only they can fully understand and appreciate. Of course, hoteliers would not exist without their guests, and they, too, form part of my rich store of treasured memories as an international chef. To all these people I dedicate this book and share my reminiscences, hoping that one day we will all have the opportunity to work and live alongside people from other cultures, and so enjoy the sort of priceless experiences that have been my daily life for the last twenty years.

About the Author

Michael Saxon is the General Manager of the Eastern & Oriental Hotel, effective from 1 September 2006. Mr Saxon first joined the Eastern & Oriental Hotel in July 2001 as Food & Beverage Manager, and having left to gain more experiences, he returned to take up the position of Executive Assistant Manager in September 2004. Prior to this appointment, Mr Saxon held the position of Hotel Manager since December 2005.

[Since its establishment by the Sarkies Brothers in 1885, E&O Hotel has charmed travellers from near and far, creating a reputation to match its sister hotels – Raffles, Singapore and The Strand in Rangoon - also founded by the Sarkies. Lone Pine Hotel is the oldest beach hotel, established in 1948, along Penang Island's famed tourist strip of Batu Ferringhi. With these 2 uniquely-positioned properties as its foundation, The E&O Group is set to expand its portfolio of hotels and resorts.]

Mr Saxon has more than 30 years experience in the hospitality industry, with experience in both operational and managerial positions. Mr Saxon started his career in 1981 as Chef de Partie with The Windsor Arms Hotel, Canada. Since then, he has traveled the world over as a hotelier and worked with renowned hotels in Canada, the Bahamas, Hong Kong, Taiwan, Indonesia, Singapore, Philippines and Malaysia – which includes the Four Seasons Yorkville Hotel (Canada), Resorts International Hotel & Casino (Paradise Island, Bahamas), the Regal Riverside Hotel (Shatin, Hong Kong) and the Taipei Hilton Hotel (Taiwan).

A member of a cooking team in Food Asia, Mr Saxon had won several awards for his creativity in designing culinary dishes. He was also responsible in overseeing hotel refurbishments and introducing fresh, new restaurant concepts during his stint with The Grand Plaza Parkroyal Kuala Lumpur, as well as The Royal Holiday Inn Crowne Plaza (Singapore).

Mr Saxon holds a culinary diploma from Harrogate College, Yorkshire, England.

I

WELCOME TO THE ZOO!

PUTTING MYSELF THROUGH hotel school was only possible because I had supportive parents who helped me financially, but pocket money and practical experience were in short supply so I decided to take a part-time job as a waiter in a top hotel in my home town – Harrogate in England. Nothing could have prepared me for this wake-up call to the profession I had chosen. Walking through the back door of the hotel after clocking-in was like walking into a totally different world – a world of lunacy and endless stress that no one of sound mind would possibly want, and yet I loved it! I was 16, wet behind the ears and the wolves were waiting for me.

The first time I walked into the kitchen was a harrowing experience. I had been waiting for a well-done sirloin steak ordered a few minutes earlier and I wanted to enquire how much longer it was going to take. Big mistake! This rather odd-looking guy in a tall white hat screamed at me at the top of his voice, yet nobody looked the least bit surprised, or stopped working. I was more than a little disconcerted. My father had never shouted at me like that. Who was this horrible man?

If you have ever seen the typical saloon scene in a western movie, where the piano player stops playing and everyone glances around waiting for the quick draw, and with it the instant death of the slower sharpshooter, well, this was an action replay. All of a sudden everyone looked up, mouths open, waiting for the imminent bloodbath.

"Since you're new here," smiled the chef, "I will cut you some slack, son … You can come and pick up your order in two minutes."

So off I went, feeling pleased with myself and already visualising my role as the chef's newest protégé. When I came back two minutes later as instructed, the chef told me to take the newly grilled steak he had set out on the plate. As I grabbed the plate with my bare hands, I instantly realised that the plate had been heated savagely to the point of being white hot. It was now galvanized to my hand and although I tried to let it go, it was stuck. I could smell burning flesh as I screamed in pain. To this, the chef coolly turned round and said, "Oh, is the plate hot, son? Sorry about that, but welcome to the zoo!"

After that I had a clearer idea about where the best job was, and that was in the kitchen, 'inside' the show. Unfortunately, I had to do my time as a waiter to get an introduction to the business, and also do a spell of room service. Now that really was an eye-opener for a 16-year-old greenhorn.

I remember walking into a bedroom after being told to come in, and a woman was shouting from the bathroom, "Please bring it here." I walked in and to my amazement she was sitting completely naked in the bath, and had not made any effort to use even a few soap bubbles to cover her modesty. As I held out the bill for her to sign, her naked body presented just too much of a sight for my young nerves to take, and I dropped it into the bath. She just giggled, said it was cute that I was shy, signed the dry part of the bill, and gave me a great tip. Really, the money was a bonus.

Another time I knocked on a door and entered to find a couple in the missionary position with one of them pointing to the table, telling me where to place the tray and asking for the bill, as if it was half-time at the match and they were stopping for a pie and a Bovril. Here I was, a young lad, trying hard to grasp what the heck was going on and wondering what I was going to see next, but I was not yet familiar with a classic saying in the business: 'When you think you have seen it all, something else is coming'.

A few weeks later I was back in the restaurant again waiting on some customers when the general manager strutted in. "Good evening, sir," I exclaimed politely.

"Don't 'good evening' me, young man. Where's my dog?"

"I'm always glad to see that the senior managers in this hotel have their priorities in order," whispered a senior waiter, before sending me off to housekeeping to fetch some clean tablecloths.

I was surprised to find the housekeeping department's door closed when I arrived and all the lights turned off. I enquired of a passing colleague where the light switch was, and was advised that it was at the back of the storeroom and that I would have to cross the room in the dark and turn it on myself. I was a little more wary by now, so I thought about it for a second, then set off slowly across the storeroom one step at a time. CRUNCH! What was that? CRUNCH! CRUNCH! I hastened my steps in a hurry to get to the light switch and, as I did so, I found the floor apparently moving about. At least, at first glance, it looked that way. It was, in fact, a sea of huge, black cockroaches, which scared me half to death as they scurried about trying to find a safe haven from being squashed like their less lucky counterparts. As I screamed in horror, I heard the sound of giggling outside, as if a bunch of school kids were listening to the show. Didn't the staff in this hotel have anything better to do?

Arriving back at the restaurant somewhat shaken, I was surprised to find the 'naked lady' from room service seated at a table in my station. She called me over to place her order, and I was relieved to see that she had at least made an effort to put some clothes on. Demure enough to begin with, the lady finished up true to form. On finishing her dessert, she scribbled her room number down on a piece of paper, passed it to me, and told me to come and see her upstairs if I needed anything. What could she possibly mean? I was here to serve her; what could I possibly give her other than attentive table service? What can I say? I was only 16.

After finishing work that night, I happened to pass through the kitchen to find a bunch of chefs filling a huge soup pot, big enough to bathe in, with all kinds of goodies. From leftover gravy to food colouring, eggs, flour and baked beans. The only thing missing from their disgusting brew was the feathers. As I wondered what was going to happen next, they grappled a young chef to the ground and dragged him off, dumping him head first into the brimming pot of kitchen waste, turning him into a sort of human soup. I guess that was intended to be his birthday treat. The very next day, when I arrived at work, I asked at personnel if personal details were kept private, or whether they were available to all and sundry. I wanted to know if it was possible that they could be leaked to certain characters who may be waiting to give this particular new kid a celebratory dip of his own.

In the hotel industry, the people who do the pot washing are often treated pretty badly by the young chefs who are always playing tricks on them. In this particular hotel, the banquet kitchen was one floor higher than the main kitchen and was connected by an escalator. The young chefs, after finishing a large banquet, would send all the dirty pots and pans down the escalator, unaccompanied, sitting them on the steps to be taken off by the pot washer below.

One night, one of the chefs was at the top of the escalators, smiling strangely as he placed the first pot on the step. The pot washer that evening was an old chap with a war wound of some kind which made him walk with a limp. The chef placed the pots on every tenth step or so, giving just enough time for our limping labourer to pick up a pot, walk over to the sink, place the pot in it and be back to pick up the next pot in line. The process continued at a steady pace, but as time went by I saw the chef upstairs lining up another prank. He placed the pots on every eighth step, making the war hero move just a little bit quicker. The pot washer, realising what was going on, glanced upstairs and shouted, "Don't even think about it!"

That was it, the challenge was on. The pots were gradually placed at more and more frequent intervals until the pot washer had to run back and forth, so as not to be outdone by the young 'un. Eventually the chef upstairs would have to run out of dirty pots, right? Wrong. This had been a busy night and the pots were endless. As they started to pile up at the bottom of the escalator, the pot washer began shouting, "Turn off the bloody escalator, you idiot." But the chef was having too much fun watching him struggling back and forth, limp and all. Finally, as the pot washer arrived to pick up yet another load, two of the pots collided, spilling leftover soup all over the escalator and the floor below. The pot washer slipped on it, flew three feet into the air and landed backside first in cold crab bisque.

"Excuse me, is my steak ready yet?" I dared to enquire in the midst of this melee, but the chef was laughing so loudly he completely ignored my temerity.

The next day I saw the same chef with a huge red blister on the back of his head and I enquired what had happened. He explained that when his back was turned, the pot washer had taken a baked potato out of the oven and cut open the tin foil, allowing some of the hot steam to be released, but not all of it. He had then crept behind the chef and, in an act of calculated and well-planned revenge, slapped it, still steaming hot, onto the back of his bare head. Hence the third-degree burn, shaped exactly like a baked potato, stencilled into the back of the chef's head. Another lesson learned in the kitchen. Revenge isn't always a dish best served cold.

Some time later I was finally trusted to serve silver service at a banquet in the ballroom. As I had not done this type of service before, I was given a crash course – five whole minutes before the party started. Everything seemed to be going fine until the main course, when I was presented with the biggest, hottest platter of roast beef and Yorkshire pudding I had ever seen. How was I going to carry it all the way to the ballroom, much less hold it for goodness knows how long, while serving the food with a spoon and fork, in a style which I just learned to do only a few minutes ago? I decided to give it my best shot and as I carried my platter out, the last thing the chef said to me was, "Don't spill anything. Not a single drop!"

"Right, boss!" I announced confidently. It would take a bloody miracle, I thought, but off I went on the long walk to the ballroom which seemed to last forever. My arm was already getting tired when I overtook a young waitress whose arm was obviously in a state worse than mine – her platter was on the slant. Before I could spring to her rescue, all twelve portions of beautifully roasted, medium-rare, juicy beef slid off her platter, as if in slow motion, onto the carpet. Just thinking about the prospect of having to tell the chef what had happened made her start to cry. I felt so sorry for her, but not sorry enough to offer my tray! Maybe because she was a girl, the chef would cut her some slack, I told myself. And off I galloped.

After serving my main course I arrived back in the kitchen to find the chef yelling at the sobbing girl, while his staff were busy washing the same beef that had been on the carpet and adding some new gravy as camouflage. The platter was returned to her, and she was sent on her way again. I wondered why they thought that she could make it this time when she had been so short of the finishing line the first time …

Back at room service, one of the full-time staff had been fired so I was sent to help out. On my arrival, I asked why the other guy had been dismissed and was told the story. Apparently, he had been called to a room and, so he alleged, a female guest had made a pass at him. Although he had declined her offer, the guest, feeling slighted, had complained to the management with her own version of the event, and the guy was gone. Just as I was thinking to myself what I might have done to handle such a situation, the room service phone rang. It was the same woman ordering dinner!

Since I was the only waiter on duty, I was now going to have the chance to find out if my way of dealing with this tricky task would fare any better. Drumming up all my courage and the thin reserves of experience I had gained during the past few weeks, I set off upstairs.

The ride in the lift went all too quickly, and before I could put together anything resembling a master plan I had arrived at her door.

"Room service," I announced hesitantly. From inside, I could hear a far more sheepish voice. "Come in," she replied gently. So this was the sound of the 'great seducer'.

As I entered the room I could see that she was standing up in a rather skimpy see-through nightie. This was not fair! When was this job going to cut me a little slack, I wondered. It had been non-stop action from the start and it wasn't about to let up now.

As she leaned forward to sign her bill, I got the proverbial 'eyeful', but as she handed over the slip of paper I suddenly realised that it looked like I was going to make it out in one piece. Relief met naïvety. "Would there be anything else, madam?" I swallowed heavily, nearly choking on my own words. I could not believe that I had just said that. What had I done?

"No thank you, you're not my type," she replied with a cheeky grin.

In the lift going down my relief was palpable, but perversely I could not help but wonder just why I wasn't her type. What was so good about the other fellow anyway? He was no stud. But what the heck, I concluded, even if she had asked me I would probably not have known what to do anyway, and would very likely have beaten a rapid retreat.

Downstairs, the manager asked me what had happened, so I explained the whole story, about her trying to seduce me, and me resisting for professional reasons … telling her in the most courteous manner that I was working, and that regrettably I could not oblige.

Coolly, the manager replied, "So what you are trying to say is that she was not interested?"

"Yes, that's right," I said sheepishly. What was he, a mind-reader?

Strangely, this hotel used the floor with the best view – its top floor – for the staff quarters, defying all commercial logic. This floor had a reputation for being a den of wild parties, sleepovers, gossip, fighting, stealing, gambling and other sterling qualities. It was impossible to keep track, for example, of who was dating whom, as they all seemed to change partners so often. Most new waitresses and housekeeping staff who arrived from out of town and were put up in the staff quarters would fall victim to one of the male staff sooner or later. Luckily, I just lived down the street from the hotel so I stayed at home and, for once, was happy to do so.

The live-in staff used to 'borrow' hotel equipment to use in their rooms, such as glasses, cutlery, plates, and so on. Of course, there are always a few who will take it to the extreme, and after a while would be discovered with full sets of silver and bone china tea services in their rooms. Eventually, the hotel would begin to run short of equipment and the general manager or chief of security would come scurrying upstairs to go through the staff rooms to recover the borrowed items.

During one of these forays, I was told to accompany the boss with a trolley, in order to collect and carry the loot back to the restaurant. As we went through the staff rooms, the general manager began to get angrier and angrier with the sheer scale of the equipment borrowing, not to mention the state of the whole staff floor, especially the rooms. As we reached the final door we noticed a shoe box on the floor in the middle of the corridor with his name written on it. We knew the staff were aware of this spot check, so I was intrigued to know what was the little 'gift' they had left for him. The general manager started shouting at the security boss, asking him why his department was not doing its job and stopping the staff from taking all this equipment in the first place.

Winding up his right leg like a football striker, he bellowed, "And clean this shit up!" With this, he swung his left foot and kicked the box so hard David Beckham would have been proud. Unfortunately, his words proved prophetic. The box had been filled with human waste – both solid and liquid – which sprayed all over the walls and up his trouser leg. Stunned, the general manager could only mutter, "What's wrong with these people? I don't understand them at all. I'm leaving!" And he was gone, never to inspect the staff quarters first-hand again.

And when the zookeeper's away …

II

IF YOU CAN'T STAND THE HEAT ...
GO FISHING

WISE WORDS, BUT I did not listen to them.

After finding out I had passed my catering exams, I decided to apply to live and work in Canada. Various people I had spoken to told me how hard it was to be granted 'landed immigrant' status, and that you had to have a lot of money in the bank to achieve this, as well as have a job to go to. I applied anyway, and heard nothing for a few months before eventually receiving a letter inviting me for an interview in London.

This was a four-hour train ride away, and everyone told me that I was wasting my time and money. Yet there I was, sitting on the train, with no proper clothes to wear for the interview, no money and no job, wondering what the heck I was doing. At Canada House, I was scared to death and feeling very foolish, half expecting the interviewer to look at my application and laugh.

When I was eventually called for my interview, I walked in, sat down and just looked at the floor. As my head came up slowly to take in the scene, I noticed the interviewer was wearing sunglasses and holding his head with a look of real discomfort on his face. He explained to me that the annual staff party had been held the night before and that he had drunk far too much. There was a glass of water with a just-added Alka Seltzer on his desk doing its usual jig – the one which gives you hope that you are going to feel better when you have that morning-after feeling.

Without even giving me a glance, he said, "I think people eat with their eyes, you know. What the food looks like is as important as how it tastes."

I hesitated for a second and replied, "Yes, I agree, sir." He had still not looked in my direction, or properly at my application, but, nonetheless, he told me to see the secretary outside.

As I reached the door to leave his office, he said to me, "I hope you have some good winter clothing!"

The entire 'interview' lasted but a single minute.

Speaking to the secretary, she told me I had been accepted and that I would be receiving the papers in the post within the next few weeks. From that day to this, I do not know if it was pure luck that the man had been distracted by a hangover, or if they had somehow decided before I went into the interview that they were going to accept me. I was told later that at the time I had applied they needed qualified chefs rather badly as tourism in Canada was booming, and many new hotels had opened or were under construction and there were not enough good chefs to go around. Timing, it would seem, was on my side.

So off I went to live in Toronto, with my aunt initially, never to return to the life I had once known or to be the same person that first set out on this journey.

I was soon lucky enough to get my first job as a chef. In those days you had to virtually pay the hotel to learn the trade, and I was only awarded a minimal salary, just enough to buy one small chef's knife every week and to leave me a little bit of pocket money to spend. I was lucky my parents did not ask me to send them any money as so many people working overseas have to do.

I found myself working eighty hours a week, which was double the norm, and everyone thought this was not only crazy but totally against the law. I knew this, but it was the only way I was going to learn my trade and develop my skills. I worked initially at a small, privately owned French hotel where the kitchen was run by a couple of old-school French chefs. These guys seemed to believe that all young people were a waste of space and that they had personally been placed on Earth blessed with God-given skills and knowledge. They also thought they were above the law and did not care about matters such as labour rules. What did the government know anyway, they thought, especially about the hotel industry!

Despite the cavalier attitudes which prevailed in the kitchen, I did gain a good understanding of what being a chef was really about, and how hard it was to work in an industrial kitchen, producing meals at 1,000 mph. Kitchen hygiene was just one of the topics which came high up the agenda, and not always to the positive. On one occasion, when I was indulging myself in some of the many menial jobs you have to tolerate when you first start out, like peeling potatoes, chopping onions, washing lettuce, and so on, I felt something tugging at my trousers and thought it was one of the other chefs playing the fool.

Trying to act experienced, and as if it wasn't disturbing me, I decided to ignore it. But the tugging and pulling continued until I became really irritated and glanced down. To my horror, there was a big rat, chewing at the brand new chef's trousers

that I had proudly bought with my first pay cheque. Did this lousy rodent not realise how hard I had worked to save the money for these trousers, and how thrilled I was to have finally been able to buy something with my own money?

As I shook my leg to try to get rid of the beast, it ran further up my trousers and I started to scream while gripping my trousers at the knees to avert any further travel plans it might have had. One chef was howling with laughter, while the top guy came running out shouting, "Don't let it go! I've been chasing that sucker for weeks."

He was brandishing a meat cleaver like some maniac out of a horror movie, and there I was, shaking my leg, hoping the rat was going to drop off before chef began his attack.

All of a sudden the furry rodent dropped off and scurried across the floor with a so-called professional chef chasing him, swinging the cleaver back and forth, screaming, "I'm gonna kill you, I'm gonna kill you!" As it happened, he didn't catch it, and on his return I was held personally responsible for its escape. For my sins I had to stay back late and wash a mountain of dirty pots which were stacked messily all the way to the ceiling.

Pots were, sadly, a major feature of my life at this time. I had been working solidly each day and evening for a week and was totally exhausted. On leaving the kitchen one night, I said a weary goodnight to the chef, whose response was: "Yes, you can go home as soon as you have finished washing the pots." I went back round the corner like a somnambulist, and on seeing another mountain of pots, I remember thinking it was time to call it quits and walk out. But I wanted to be a chef so badly I spent another couple of miserable hours washing the burnt-on pots. These, mind you, were not just pots with mere food residue caught at the bottom. There was half an inch of thick, burnt-on yuck firmly attached to these pots. Were these French fellows chefs or food destroyers? I often wondered. Sometimes I was not so sure. But I did know that complaining was not going to help me.

As I was polishing my last gleaming masterpiece, the phone rang. It was the front office manager telling the chef that some guests had called to say they could not sleep due to a couple of cats apparently rummaging around in the rubbish area in the backyard, and could he chase them off? The chef agreed, and he went out with a bucket of cold water to try to scare them away. After a few seconds I heard him groan, "Arh, help!" Thinking he was being murdered or something, I ran out and immediately encountered two huge rats frolicking in the kitchen rubbish. These were surely the mother, and indeed, the father of all rats, and I ran back into the kitchen, grabbed a large spoon and a cooking pot, and in sheer panic ran outside, banging the spoon against the pot and shouting at the top of my voice. This, I was mightily relieved to see, succeeded in scaring the rats away.

Chef and I went back into the kitchen to have a beer and talk about our heroism, only to find the front office manager waiting to tell us that he had just called the police. He had apparently told them that there were two lunatics in the backyard, wreaking havoc, and the hotel needed help. Not only that, but by now a number of the guests had been woken up and were extremely annoyed. What shall we do now? chef asked. And together we decided our plan of action.

When the police turned up, the manager sent them out to the backyard, where the chef and I were putting on a great performance of running around looking for these nutcases whom we had, of course, already chased off! The next day all the guests heard the story and congratulated us on our efforts. Which reminds me of another hotel that used to have a sign on the wall of the entrance to its public area which read, 'Smile, You Are on Stage'. It's always show time when you are dealing with guests.

Another of the characters in this kitchen was Guido, an Italian chef who thought he was Pavarotti. He really did have a good voice and used to break into song any time, delivering operatic arias as we cooked, and as the executive chef was also Italian and loved opera, it all made perfect sense, right? But one day, when Guido had just finished one set and was feeling pretty good about himself, he decided to have a cigarette while filleting some fish. While doing this, he casually looked out of the window only to see, with horror, the public health inspector peeping in from outside. Before the inspector could come running in to catch him in this thoroughly unhygienic course of action, Guido ran into the cold store, picked up a single piece of white asparagus, stuck it in his mouth and threw away his cigarette in the pig bin (I'll explain about the pig bin later).

So when the inspector ran in, saying, "Now I've caught you," his guilty target whined, "OK! you got me, but please don't tell my boss or he will kill me." The inspector now began to take in that the object in his mouth was not quite what he thought it was, and Guido explained that it was white asparagus and very expensive too. He elaborated that the executive chef had ordered him not to nibble on it, as he was eating away at the profits!

"Oh man, that's such a crock!" said the inspector. "I saw you smoking through the window." The inspector looked around in vain for any evidence, got frustrated and stormed out. As he reached the door he turned round, looked at me and said, "Every time I catch him I can never find the evidence. Who does this guy think he is? Houdini?"

"Actually, Pavarotti!" I declared, and at that moment Guido broke out with his own rendition of 'Che Gelida Manina', which sounded great, by the way.

Ah yes, the pig bin. This is the place where every kitchen puts its wet rubbish, or leftover food items from buffets or unfinished meals. I once heard that this amounts to so much food that if every food outlet in North America alone could save the wasted food from a single day, it could go some way towards feeding the starving poor of Africa for a year. It just goes to show that there is sufficient food to feed the world, but what is lacking is the political will to redistribute it. Anyway, the food in the pig bin is collected from all the hotels and restaurants and sent to a factory where

11

they boil it forever, to an incredible temperature, which is supposed to make it fit for animal consumption.

I say 'supposed' because it is a good job they do all that boiling since what I have seen going into the pig bins would make your flesh crawl. For example, when a chef has had a night of heavy drinking and cannot even make it to the toilet, he's liable to vomit into the bin. I've seen one of the top chefs, having been bought 'a couple' of beers to thank him for a great meal, take a leak into the bin rather than risk falling down the stairs he would have had to negotiate to get to the toilet. So the pig bin and its contents are a highly dubious affair, to say the least, and to be treated with the utmost caution by both man and beast, if truth be told.

Getting back to the rough jobs that I had to do as a rookie chef, one night I was yet again washing the pots when the chef put a cauldron of what I thought was dirty water next to the sink. I hastily poured the dirty water down the sink and wondered why the pot was so easy to wash. As I did so, the chef came back and asked me in his French accent, "Verre eez may consommé?" Now, anyone who knows how to make consommé would know how the chef felt when I told him it was halfway to Lake Ontario. He immediately started to scream at the top of his voice and proceeded to lunge at me, forcing me out into the car park and chasing me like a madman, around and in-between the parked cars.

Finally, when he ran out of breath, he leaned forward with his hands on his knees and in an exasperated tone told me, "Come here and turn round." As I did so, he gave me a sharp kick on the backside and told me if I ever did that again he would kill me. I didn't think he was joking either. When we got back to the kitchen, the front office manager was waiting, looking totally frustrated, and told us that if just one guest complained about the noise, he was personally going to kick us both where it would hurt. Not a good day. Whatever next? I thought.

I had been waiting for my big moment to finally cut, or chop, something for once. The chef lined me up with a very sharp knife, showed me how to cut potatoes and then let me have a go. I did it, but of course cut my finger instead of the potato. It was a very deep gash and blood was spurting all over the potatoes. Chef was shouting at me, and the other cooks were laughing, so I took the best possible course of action – I fainted. As I came round, the chef was leaning over me with a glass of brandy. "Drink this," he said. I took a big swig and remember not feeling so dizzy anymore, but instead feeling sick as hell. Of course, the possibility of going home to nurse my wound was out of the question; there was still work to do.

And that reminds me about a tale involving windows. The same one the public health inspector looked through was right next to a stove where the chefs used to make sauces. One day, the chef asked me to make a basic sauce and, as I finished the job, I was feeling rather proud of myself. The chef came over, tasted it and smiled. I remember how great that felt, until he shouted a few choice obscenities at me, then bent over and tossed the whole pot of my wonderful creation right out through the open window.

I went dolefully outside to retrieve my pot and saw a metal plaque on the floor that said, 'Green Boy's Pot Wash Corner', and there was a little hose with running water and a scrubbing brush ready for me to do the necessary clean-up job. I must have gone in and out to the green boy's corner a dozen times that day. It was the most disheartening and sickening thing you could imagine, but somehow considered an essential part of making me a real chef.

The chef had wrapped my cut finger up with some Band-Aid plaster, the sort that looks like a roll of Sellotape. It had started to throb and hurt like hell by the time I was due to go off duty. I mentioned to the chef that I did not feel so good and he told me to go and have a few beers. Ah yes, the answer to all problems, I thought.

Ignoring this sterling advice, I took myself off to the hospital. On arrival I filled out a registration card and explained to the nurse that I wanted to have someone take a look at my finger.

Along came the doctor who observed my wrapped finger, shook his head and stared at me with amazement and, it seemed, some disgust. He asked me if it was Florence Nightingale who had attended to me in such a caring manner. Without further ado, he ripped off the plaster, and, I recall, huge chunks of my skin. The next thing I remember was coming round and looking up at the doctor as he was inserting numerous stitches. I heard myself saying, "No brandy for me, please, I've already had too many beers!"

The next day I went to work with a giant condom on my finger and thankfully was reduced to washing lettuce. This was alright, as the full-time lettuce washer was smarter than me anyway, and I thought some of his wisdom might rub off. I prepared a couple of salads for an order and sent them out to the restaurant and about five minutes later saw the chef strolling towards me.

"Washing lettuce is an easy job, isn't it?" he said, holding one of my salads in his hands. I looked at the bowl and tried to imagine what my response should be.

"Yes," I replied hesitantly, "but I am still learning the fine art, and only under your expert guidance will I eventually master it."

The chef looked at me, clenched his fist and told me, "kiss my arse". He then tossed the bowl onto the table beside me and walked off. Wanting to know what the problem was, I quickly excavated the salad to find a pocket of dirt, about the size of a small coin, buried within it. As I studied it, the chef returned and announced that he had now calmed down, but that if I ever served lettuce like that again, he would stuff it down my throat, dirt and all.

After a few months working at the hotel I was asked to go and help out at a party at the owner's house. He lived in a very expensive part of downtown Toronto. When all the food had been served and the party was in full swing, the owner finally began to relax and came into the kitchen to say thank you to the staff and give us some champagne for our efforts. I remember drinking mine on an empty stomach and later roaming around outside, mingling with the guests. The owner had told me that the best way to have a successful party was to make sure that there was a 'free flow' of continuous alcohol, great food and good company, and on that night he certainly had the formula mastered.

Everyone was totally plastered but having a great time, and the DJ was going crazy, jumping around and directing the fun. Hailing from an English working-class background, working at five-star hotels had opened my eyes to luxury bordering on decadence, but this was in a class of its own. Caviar, goose liver, vintage wines and champagnes, endless other luxury food and beverages, and – sadly – a total disregard for waste.

The DJ was now really rocking, and decided to jump up onto his console and start doing a striptease while the owner was outside in the garden. As he got down to his undies, he promptly dropped them but hid his wedding tackle with his hands. At that very moment, the owner looked through the huge windows to see this bare back-side jiggling and shaking to an Elvis Presley number. He ran in frantically, shouting, "The neighbours, the neighbours!" The DJ climbed down, apologised and decided to get 'a game' going instead. He said he wanted everyone to get on the dance floor first, before the game started, and he looked over and shouted, "You too, big guy!"

I turned round, wondering who he was talking to, and realised it was me. I glanced at the owner and he gave me the nod of approval so over I went to the dance floor, still in my chef's whites, and awaited further instruction. By this time, the champagne I had drunk was starting to send the whole room spinning, and I knew that this was not a good idea at all.

The DJ announced that he was going to play a tune and we should all start danc-ing. When the song stopped, everyone had to exchange a piece of clothing with the person standing nearest to them. My gut instinct told me that I did not want to be a part of this situation, so I began to make a run for it. At that moment, a wonderfully dressed, very sexy-looking woman grabbed me, looked into my eyes and told me that she'd always wanted to wear chef's clothes. I was in this game whether I liked it or not.

I walked out of that house wearing a frilly shirt, a bra, panties, a hat with feath-ers, high-heeled shoes and lipstick! I never did get my uniform back, but then neither did the owners of those assorted items. The next day, the owner told me I could go to his parties any time I liked. In fact, the guests had asked him to provide me with a special open invitation. I just remember thinking what a crazy evening it had been, but how normal it seemed to them.

Let's get back to my more usual habitat, the hot and sweaty kitchen. At one stage I was having a hard time fitting in with the other staff, and there was a North American Indian named Joe, whose job it was to wash lettuce and such like. This guy was actually pretty smart, but he much preferred to do the easy, no-stress jobs. I confided in him that the other chefs did not seem to like me, and I asked him why he thought that was. He closed his eyes for a second to think about my question and then said, "If there are ten people working with you, nine think you are a good person and one thinks you are a pain in the neck. The chances are you are a good person. If five think you are a good person and five think you are a pain in the neck, you could be either. However, if one thinks you are a good person and nine think you are a pain in the neck, the chances are you are a pain in the neck." He gave me a very direct look and said, "Which one are you?"

Not quite the response I was expecting. Was this man insinuating something? That really made me angry. The next day I went to work ready to do battle with the whole hotel, but one look across at Joe, the lettuce washer, and I found myself walking around and apologising to everyone for being such a pain in the neck.

That night a group of us decided to go to a lounge for a game of pool. We had a pile of coins on the table, and as I was leaning over the table taking one of those shots you would rather forget forever, I heard a voice ask, "Is there any chance of a game?" I looked down at the floor and saw a pair of sneakers; as my gaze moved upwards I took in the designer jeans, a nice casual shirt and ... blow me, if it wasn't Dustin Hoffman, the actor, standing right in front of me. I was just getting ready to show whoever it was my pile of coins and to tell them to come back in two hours, but now I found myself telling Dustin Hoffman to help himself. This was the first time I had ever met a superstar and we played pool all night. He explained he was in town to promote his new movie and had a little spare time. I can tell you, he was a thorough gentleman, and it was a pleasure to meet him.

Our executive chef came to work with a hangover most of the time and it usually took him until lunchtime to get himself 'balanced', so one day we decided to teach him a lesson for all the shouting he had subjected us to. He happened to have huge feet, and his shoes looked like canoes. We placed teaspoons inside the toes of his canoes and watched him limp around for two hours until, in his hungover state, he finally realised something was wrong. He reached into a shoe, pulled out a spoon and graced us with another of his inimitable 'English language classes'.

That night Joe, the lettuce washer, asked me if I wanted to go somewhere with him the next day. As my social calendar was not exactly filled with other exciting happenings, I agreed. The next day Joe picked me up in a large van and we drove for a while before parking in a large open field. He suggested we climb onto the roof of the van because we could get a better view from there. "A better view of what?" I enquired. There were by that time hundreds of other people packing into every available space in this makeshift parking lot, and I asked him again what was going on. Joe just smiled and said I would soon see. A few minutes later, he announced, "It won't be long now," and at that moment everyone started screaming and cheering. Joe looked up to the sky and pointed, "There, look," he said. I turned round to see a huge jumbo jet, flying very low and sounding extremely loud. To my astonishment, it was carrying the NASA space shuttle on its back.

I had mentioned to my new friend a few weeks earlier how the space programme fascinated me and how much I loved to watch each of the take-offs live on television. He had remembered this exchange and had gone to the trouble of bringing me to see this once-in-a-lifetime event. It felt incredible to be so close to the shuttle, almost being able to touch it, and to feel part of something special. It disappeared behind some clouds before reappearing for one last circle around before it was gone. I looked back at my friend and he was smiling. He had a solitary tear welling up in his eye, and at that moment I would have given anything to know what he was thinking. How could I possibly thank him for organising and sharing this special moment with me? I pondered. That afternoon we drove back to the hotel without speaking. The whole experience had overwhelmed us both.

Later that same evening, Joe was getting behind with his work and the chef started to shout at him and call him names. I became upset and angry on his behalf and felt terribly sorry for this fine man. When the chef left, I asked him how he managed to stay so calm when being insulted and why he did not lose his temper. He explained why intelligent people should not get angry when insulted: "When insulted, if it is not true, why would you become angry? If it is true, then you listen and turn it into positive criticism. Only you can make yourself angry. If you are in control of your own mind, nobody can force you to become angry or irritated."

I went home thinking about what he had taught me that day and decided that the next day I was going to offer him my deepest thanks and appreciation. I was on the morning shift and he was due on the afternoon shift, but he never showed up to work that day, or the next, and I never saw him again. He just disappeared from my life, but he will never disappear from my mind or my heart. I have always kept my friend's words in mind and, whenever the chef would berate me with his trademark, 'You will never make a chef as long as you have a hole in your arse!', his nasty comments did not bother me any more because I knew, and believed, otherwise.

It used to amaze me that the waiters and chefs would argue and fight, even during service. They would call each other names, threaten each other with violence, say the most hateful things in the heat of the moment and yet when it was all over, more often than not, go out together for a drink. One night when it was extremely busy, I found I could not handle all the orders which were coming in, seemingly at the same time. The stress really was too much. To add to it, a waiter came in and said, "Hey there, chef, why don't you pull your thumb out your arse and give me my salad?" What was this thing these people had about arses? I just couldn't understand it at all, so I looked up at him and said, "You're a waiter, right? So bloody well wait, then!" I was obviously getting the hang of things in the zoo by now.

Stress is an inherent part of the job and it can affect people in different ways. We once had a food and beverage manager who had been busy for an extended period without any time off. One hectic night we could not find him anywhere, and knew it was not like him to disappear during service and keep the guests waiting. At the end of the night, we went looking for him and found him sitting in a corner on the floor, drunk and crying to himself. What a terrible thing it was to see a grown man crying simply because of excessive stress. Is any job really worth that kind of misery? Fortunately, in this case, the hotel manager forced him to take two weeks' leave and, on his return to service, he was back to normal. Of course, no one ever mentioned that night again in his presence.

Anyway, back to the waiting waiter. Remembering my own time as a waiter, I told the chef in the hot kitchen what this one had said and he told me not to worry. About fifteen minutes later, the cloth-less waiter picked up a piping-hot plate, and, predictably, let out one hell of a scream. As he did so, I leaned forward and said, "Welcome to the zoo."

Wow! That felt great, until I realised that I had actually hurt the guy pretty badly and recalled how it had hurt me before. So I apologised and bought the guy a couple of drinks after work to ease my guilt. But did my soft feelings mean I would never make a good chef? After all, I had a conscience. I thought about this for a while and determined that it actually meant I would become an even better one ... even if I did have a hole in my arse!

There is, unfortunately, a tendency for chefs, especially those in the hotel industry, to drink a little too much, due to the constant stress of running a twenty-four-hour, fully operating kitchen. The easy availability of alcohol, ostensibly for cooking, does not help either. A few of the chefs I have worked with have been angels at seven o'clock in the evening and total monsters by ten, due to customers buying them drinks as a way of saying thanks for a lovely meal. It sometimes gets so serious that they are not balanced when they wake up in the morning, until they have a drink to start the day.

In this particular Toronto hotel, the kitchen was very hot, all of the time, and the cooks were each given a couple of cans of soft drinks daily, in accordance with the union rules. I would occasionally see cooks looking wobbly, and even fall down while preparing dishes, but in my naïvety I always thought it was because the floor was slippery. One day, I picked up the wrong can of Sprite and took a big gulp, only to immediately feel very wobbly at the knees, and just about everywhere else. Whoever was drinking this particular can of Sprite had spiked it with whisky from the supposedly locked liquor cupboard. It was so strong it tasted like 90 per cent whisky and 10 per cent Sprite. I was worried to death in case the chef smelt my breath and I would be the one in trouble through no fault of my own, so I went to get a drink of that time-honoured camouflage – freshly brewed coffee.

There were a couple of happy-go-lucky chefs in the hotel. One was Italian, the other second-generation Canadian. I was getting changed at work one day when the Italian chef was taking a shower before going home. He seemed a little worried and upset, so I asked what was wrong. He looked at me and said, "Here, check out this shit!" At which point he undid his shirt and literally flapped a huge lump of fat on his shoulder. I had never seen anything like it and asked what it was. "Cancer, my friend, cancer," he replied.

I was totally horrified but was somehow unsure whether he was joking or being serious. The answer came only a few weeks later, when the executive chef attended his funeral on behalf of the hotel. I found it hard to believe that such a strong and alert man could disappear so quickly.

A couple of weeks later, the Canadian chef did not show up for work and since nothing was heard from him for a couple of days, the executive chef went to his apartment to see what had happened, only to find him dead in bed. The chef also went to his funeral, where he and the priest buried him with no one else in attendance. I remember thinking at the time, how lonely his life must have been if not a single person cared enough about his death to bother to attend his funeral. Since then, one of my biggest fears has been that I might grow old alone, and I've always thought that loneliness must be just about the biggest curse anyone could face.

I was put in charge of organising a vast fruit display for a huge function to be held in the ballroom where all the guests would be vegetarians. The display involved a virtual mountain of fruit emerging from huge wicker baskets. I lost count of how many cases of different types of fruit had been carried out of the kitchen. There were literally thousands of pieces in the luscious display.

As I watched the guests mingle, I glanced around the room and saw someone who looked and dressed exactly like Mr T, the television and movie actor, coming towards me. At that time, the film *Rocky III* had just been released and it was a great box office success, so I thought this person must be another Mr T wannabe, but as he got closer I realised that I was in fact face to face with the man himself. I could not believe that Mr T actually walked around dressed just like his character in the *A-Team* – dangling with gold chains. Since his role was very much one of being the real tough guy, as he approached I tried to imagine what he was going to say to me. "Hey, sucker, give me some of those bananas before I rip your face off!" Or, "If you ain't got what I want, all you're gonna feel is pain." But before I could imagine any more, he asked me in the most polite and gentle voice for some apples, and then he was gone.

A minute later, while I was still trying to get over the fact that I had just met the big guy, a guest came over and asked me if we had any grapes. I looked at the mountain of fruit and realised that she had managed to find just about the only fruit fit for human consumption that I did not have in this gargantuan display. "What, no grapes!" she proclaimed in disgust, obviously upset at the prospect of her whole evening being ruined by the absence of the grapes. So off I went, looking for the elusive fruit.

In the kitchen, the chef told me that there were no grapes and that I should go to the hotel next door and borrow some. "By the way," said the chef, "while you are there, ask the kitchen team if we can borrow some chicken lips." Next door, they readily gave me the grapes, but when I asked for the chicken lips, the chef looked at me incredulously. He told me that since I was so gullible, he wanted to sell me some choice land he had in his possession for a bargain fee! These guys had an indefatigable sense of humour and were forever sending rookies like me on wild goose chases, looking for tartan icing, a soufflé pump, a lobster gun and the world-famous chicken lips, to mention just a few.

I got back to my function as quickly as I could, washed the grapes and then walked around the near-2,000-strong crowd, looking for the 'grapes lady' to give her the desired fruit. When I did finally locate her to offer up my grapes, she said, "Oh my goodness, red grapes. I only like green ones … but I guess they will suffice. Of course, they had better be seedless," she added for good measure.

At that moment, I found myself thinking, well maybe the seeds will be so big you'll choke on one, madam! But when I opened my mouth, I felt my lips mutter the words, "We offer only the finest quality, madam. Only these can possibly equal the quality of your good self." It's show time, I thought to myself.

Just as I was thinking how smart I was, I heard another young chef scream as he dropped a lit Sterno onto the new carpet. Sterno is used to keep the food in the warming dishes hot. It's a gel-like substance that when lit is placed under a container of water and subsequently boils the water to keep the food hot. There was now a pile of Sterno in flames on the carpet, so up stepped Superman to the rescue – me! I stomped on the pile of Sterno, thinking I could extinguish the fire, only to see it spread all over the place. Now there were dozens of smaller piles, all on fire, on the carpet. Thanks to my valiant efforts, we had many more small burn marks than the single one that we would have had if I had just stood and watched.

One of the other things you learn fast in an international kitchen is that if something is not nailed down or under lock and key, it will go missing. Pilfering is a huge problem in many large kitchens and most young chefs use a hot iron to burn their names into the wooden handles of their knives, much like branding a cow. It's miserable to work hard all week only to find someone else has appropriated your expensive tools. Of course, the thief cannot use the knives in the same kitchen for fear of being caught, so usually sells them off to a chef in another hotel for a fraction of what you paid for them.

There is a crude but commonly used term in hotel life that defines the situation of having too many á la carte orders coming through at the same time and not being able to cope. This is when stress levels reach a peak and I remember the first time it happened to me. I was very nervous, trying to get all the orders out at the same time and with some quality that I could be proud of, when up limbered the chef.

"Are you in the shit, Saxon?" he said. I remember looking down at the floor to check if I was standing in something, and wondered what he was talking about.

"In what shit, chef?" was my nervous, puzzled response. Afterwards, the guys explained that the chef was actually just asking if I needed any help. Apparently, when you can't handle your orders and you start to get behind, making the guests wait, the choice description given to this is that you are 'in the shit'.

19

There was a spiral staircase in the hotel lobby with a thick wool carpet on the treads. It was often used for photo sessions, or as a platform for the children's choir at Christmas time, and for other special occasions. One night a Japanese businessman was running up the spiral staircase like a frolicking gazelle, when suddenly he slipped and fell, banging his head on the soft carpet – thank goodness it was not the more usual cold marble flooring. Despite the carpet, he still knocked himself unconscious. Worryingly, when he came round he could not remember his own name. He was apparently staying at another hotel, which he also could not recall, and he had failed to carry any form of identification. The upshot was that he stayed with us for a few weeks, while the Japanese embassy tried to trace his family and organise sending him home. The hotel, of course, footed the bill, and we took care of him for longer than anyone expected. We became quite fond of our 'long-staying guest'. For months afterwards, he continued to write to us, keeping in touch and expressing his gratitude.

It's always difficult when new senior staff start in any job and the kitchen is no exception. When you are used to working with one boss and he or she leaves, you always wonder about the newcomer. Soon after our Japanese friend found his way home, our executive chef left and the staff were all waiting in anticipation to see what his replacement was going to be like.

The day his replacement was due to start, I was scheduled to be on the breakfast shift, starting at five-thirty – not the best of shifts when you are young and single, and like to go out at night to have some fun! One of the worst things about being on the breakfast shift is frying eggs at six o'clock in the morning, when you have a hangover and are feeling tired and sorry that you had that last drink. Telling yourself 'never again' does not seem to help at all, especially when you're looking at all the oil in the pan, and the egg yolk is leaking out of the broken 'over easy' that you're supposed to be preparing.

Fortunately, on this particular morning, I arrived at five-thirty, feeling good as I had not been out the night before. It was a cold wintery morning, around minus 20°C. There were little flurries of snow in the air and it was lovely and quiet. I arrived at the loading dock – the point of entry where suppliers deliver their goods – and saw some homeless guy taking a leak off the top of the dock. I remember being impressed that he could perform this task in such cold temperatures. The steady stream and the hot steam rising made me feel sorry for the guy, out in such bad weather with nowhere to go. Being homeless in a hot climate must be bad enough, but being homeless during a Canadian winter must be pure hell.

I went on into the hotel to change and set to work on my eggs. Before long, the senior chef asked me to come and meet the new executive chef, and I was surprised to hear that he was in at work so early on his first day. As I entered the office, I was staggered to see it was the same guy I had seen taking a leak off the dock. I knew straightaway that working with this guy was going to be a ride that I would never forget, and I was not far wrong.

He was already shouting at everyone on his very first morning, that is, until the union representative came to speak to him about the staff complaints that had already been received about his behaviour. The new guy's favourite saying was, 'I'm not here to shit on anyone's roses, I'm just here to help you learn.' I wondered how many times I was going to hear that line before I could use it myself. Another was, 'Why would anyone drink when there is guzzling available?' That just about summed up the way this guy lived his life. Fittingly, he was soon nicknamed 'Fred Flintstone'.

Of course, karma always hits this kind of person and during the next few months numerous unfortunate things happened to him. He cut his hand so badly one day that I almost fainted looking at it. There was blood everywhere. I remember how he looked at me and shouted, "Saxon, get me Pernod!" What was he talking about? I was a chef not a barman, and in any case that seemed like the last thing he needed. Nonetheless, after giving him the drink we called a taxi to take him to hospital. An hour later, he was back, with seven stitches in his hand, and carried on working like nothing had happened. Only after years of working as a chef myself do I understand how he could do that. Cutting or burning yourself is part and parcel of the job and, after a while, you either become more experienced and don't cut yourself, or you just get used to it. It's really up to you.

A few weeks after that incident, Fred Flintstone finished the building of his dream house on a piece of land which he had bought. However, after a particularly heavy rainstorm, the house started to tilt to one side and he was told that the house had not been built on proper foundations. Apparently, the construction company, on hearing of their impending bankruptcy, had tried to save money on the job by using poor materials. When the chef tried to sue the company, it filed for bankruptcy, and as he had no insurance he lost everything. Not long after that, a woman in the hotel filed a serious complaint against him and he was gone.

So along came a new executive chef – a very nice French guy – who wanted to teach us the fine art of French cuisine. Some of his ideas were great but others troubled me, yet it was all part of me growing into the hotel game. For instance, he taught me how to make soups to order for the fine dining room with no advance preparation at all and, despite this, they tasted great. In this business it is always good to know the right way, as well as the short cuts. The same chef also showed us how to tie a lobster still, so that it stayed straight when cooked. That's right, not only do people want to eat these poor creatures, but they want them to be straight as well.

This chef's favourite saying came up every time the union came to see him. He would say, 'What do you want me to do, drop my pants? Will this make you happy?' This was his unique way of apologising without using more conventional terms. Still, he was another character who taught me that you have to be able to admit when you are wrong, and to be able to say that you are sorry, in whatever way you know how ...

Albert was a great chef, but annoying as hell. One night I was 'in the shit' very badly and he called me to the office. The waiters were all shouting at me for their orders and I was under real pressure, so I shouted to him that I was totally in the shit and that I would come soon. "No, come now!" demanded Albert, and I literally had to drop everything and follow him to his office. When we got there he held up a glossy car magazine, advertising all the latest models. He started showing me the pictures, announcing that he was going to buy a certain model, and asking what I thought about it.

What was wrong with this man? I needed some help right this second, not hindrance. Have you any idea at all what I would like to tell you right now? I thought to myself. I just looked at him and said, "If I am ever lucky enough to land a job like yours and earn as much money as you do, maybe I will be in a better position to make an educated judgement."

He in turn looked at me, reached into his mini bar, pulled out a cold beer and banged the neck of the bottle on the wonderful teak table that he used as his desk, sending the cap flying. The bottle made a chip on the edge of the table, next to the other 500 he had previously made. He then leaned back on his chair, put both feet on the table, and said, "Every time I speak to you, I feel like I'm trying to put ten pounds of shit into a nine pound bag. Why don't you speak English? Does that mean you think it's OK or not?" When he had finished his speech, I wandered slowly back to my area in something of a daze, only to find the service staff waiting for me in droves and by now in a collective state of frenzy.

Later that evening, I was just getting out of the deep hole which the chef had put me into, when a waiter asked me to give him two dozen fresh oysters. Now, these had to be opened on the spot with a special knife designed for the purpose. In short, oysters are a pain in the neck when you are busy as they tend to take too long to prepare, invariably putting you back in the shit. When I finally got them open and gave them to the waiter, along came Albert and grabbed the oysters from the waiter. "Ah dinner!" he proclaimed.

Looking at him, I had just a split second to think about whether I should risk it or not. I knew he had a short fuse, but I also knew that the bomb at the end was fairly small. "Sorry, chef," I responded, "those are for a paying customer and I know it goes against your professional integrity to keep them waiting." He looked at me, then looked at the oysters, then at the waiter, and finally back to me again, before muttering, "Of course, you're right. Serve the guest first."

On another occasion, I was boiling a huge pot of turnips and had overcooked them, turning them to puree. Instead of vegetables, I had a large pot of soup. When the chef saw it, he instructed the sous chef to make me eat the broth daily until it was finished. I ate turnip soup every day for nearly two weeks, until it finally turned sour and I was spared any more of my sickening brew. To this day, I don't eat turnips because they remind me that 'every dog has its day'.

The Aga Khan and Prince Philip came to our hotel on a World Wildlife Fund event to promote a 'Save the Whales' campaign. We had to prepare a dinner for about

250 guests in the ballroom and it was a real drama. The security guards had to have all the staff's particulars. They wanted to look into our backgrounds to check us out, and on the night of the dinner they stood guard in the kitchen, watching our every move. Finally, we were ready to start the function and waited for the VIPs to arrive. At the last moment, the banqueting manager went to get the clean red carpet he had vacuumed and left in the large corridor to air. He was horrified to find the carpet missing and had no idea where it could have disappeared to. The hotel was turned upside down in those few short minutes, but to no avail, and we had to welcome the dignitaries without it. This did not go down at all well and broke the unwritten rule about welcoming royalty. A few days after the function had passed, the general manager went to the new chief of security's office to ask him for help to find the missing carpet, and on walking into the office, was taken aback by what he saw. There in the office was a beautifully laid and impeccably foamed red carpet. The new chief of security on walking down the corridor during his first few days on the job had stumbled upon the drying carpet, and thinking it was long leftover pieces, had jigsaw puzzled the royal carpet to make a nice snug office, which he unfortunately would no longer occupy.

———————◆◆◆◆◆———————

We had a guy, named Paul, working in the kitchen who liked to show off, and who would usually get himself into trouble as a result. For example, one day while we were taking time off visiting a nearby lake, we saw a lot of women sunbathing, water skiing and generally enjoying themselves. Suddenly Paul announced, loudly enough for everyone to hear, that he was going to swim across the lake, and on reaching the other side he would have a drink and then swim back. The lake was not a small one, and in retrospect a one-way swim would itself have been a quite a challenge for a good swimmer. But that was not going to deter Paul. After jumping in and swimming halfway across, he got severe cramp and started to scream, whereby a small speed-boat had to go to rescue him. On another occasion, we went to a gym and because there were women doing their workout routines, Paul decided to pump iron – in this case, well over his capacity – to show them what a man he was. He could not get out of bed for the next three days, having strained his muscles so badly!

I used to make fun of him but, being a skinny guy myself, he would also give me my fair share of insults. It was all done in fun and we never took each other seriously at all. A few months later, Paul went on a break to the mountains and was playing around with a group of his friends. The 'game' they were playing entailed wearing thick outer clothing as protective layers, and then running and jumping into the air, such that they slid along on their bottoms, backs or stomachs on the natural slates. The slates were several layers thick, and moved when rubbed together through friction. You could start yourself in motion in this way and keep sliding for a fair distance.

On this particular day, the guys were apparently playing 'dare' and seeing who could slide on the slates as close to the edge of the mountain as possible. The inevitable soon occurred, and Paul went too far, falling off the side of the mountain and dropping hundreds of feet into a white water river below. He was pulled out from the bottom of the river a few days later. They said that the powerful water had stripped him of his clothing and that he had got stuck under some large logs. He had probably died of a heart attack as he went over the edge, because the shock would have been too much. I felt terrible that I had joked and made fun of him on so many occasions before, but I know deep inside that he always knew we were friends.

Roy was another guy I met. He was an aircraft engineer. I always looked up to him, thinking that a guy with such a job – checking aeroplanes to make sure they were in good order before they went up – deserves some respect. His father was also very proud of him, on account of his time at university where he routinely passed his exams with the highest grades, and invariably ended the year top of his class. I'd often not see him for months at a time as he did shift work, but then out of the blue he would call me to go out with him, and off we would go.

Roy came to pick me up one day in this strange old van with a huge brass cockroach welded on the front, like a trophy. He told me he had resigned his high paying job to become a pest-control man. He later confided that he could not sleep at night while in his former job, with worry that one day he was going to make a serious mistake which could have terrible consequences. He was now happier than ever, he explained, living in his own rented apartment because his father had kicked him out in disappointment over his career decision.

One sunny day as I arrived at the Toronto hotel, I came across a waiter from my restaurant mooching around outside. I asked him what was up, and he told me that he was in trouble over his gambling debts. He was looking around to check if anyone was out there waiting for him in order to collect the money he owed. This guy had always been a happy-go-lucky kind of a guy and, as I had never had contact with these sorts of gambling people, I wondered how he could get himself into such a terrible situation. I said goodbye to him and went into the hotel, not wanting to become accidentally involved.

His problem seemed to have gone away, or at least been avoided, as I saw him later, smiling brightly. He told me he had borrowed money from his family and paid back what he owed. There was another guy whose story did not end so happily. He disappeared from the hotel to re-emerge months later, telling us that his debtors had drilled his kneecaps with a Black and Decker. He had now recovered but would walk with a severe limp for the rest of his life. Theirs, I guess, is a side of life which goes on all the time in international hotels that most people, myself included, would never have an inkling about.

Albert, the bad-tempered French chef, had no hesitation in hiring and firing people when it suited. We entered a cooking competition and started to prepare for it a couple of days in advance. The competition rules stated that we had to prepare hot plated food but serve it cold, coating it with aspic so that it would keep. It would not be eaten but would be judged on its presentation, and recipes were to be provided with the dishes. Our chef entered the pâté and terrine category, and had his pâté prepared and ready in the refrigerator. He was taking everyone in to show off his masterpiece before he took it along to the convention centre for the judging. My own oeuvre was in the same fridge but was not quite ready yet, and, of course, not nearly as good as his.

I hadn't had a wink of sleep in two days due to my efforts and was feeling totally exhausted. As I was putting the final touches to my creation, I sat down to take a closer look and felt something moist and cold on my bottom. I turned round to see what was so cooling, and realised to my horror that I had sat right on top of the chef's pâté. There were now two big buttock shapes imprinted on the top of its shiny finished surface.

I hesitated for a second, contemplating the options. One was suicide, but this seemed a little drastic, although possibly less painful than what would be in store for me when the big guy saw what I'd done. My second option was to resign on the spot, run down to my locker, get changed and try to get through the door before being caught. The last option, as I saw it, was to saunter out of the walk-in fridge, whistling as if butter wouldn't melt in my mouth, and then when the chef found his work destroyed, I would offer to help catch the guilty blighter. But would he not put two and two together when he saw the wet patch on my bottom? I pondered. He'd probably bring in the police to measure my wet patch against the matching dents in his pâté. There seemed to be no way out, except the most dangerous option of all – admit to parking my bottom on his precious creation.

As I walked out of the refrigerator, I met another chef, who asked what was wrong with me. "You look as white as your chef's jacket."

"Listen," I said, "don't tell anyone. I was doing my work and my trousers may have just touched the chef's pâté."

The other chef started to laugh loudly, and then he started shouting, "Hey, everyone, Saxon has sat on the chef's pâté!"

Another chef came over. He was laughing so much he had to hold his stomach. "You must be bloody joking. Let me have a look!" he bellowed.

Suddenly, there was a deadly silence. The executive chef had arrived. "What's all the excitement about, what's going on?" asked the big guy.

"Saxon has something to tell you, chef!" some kind soul declared.

"Oh yes, what's that?" he asked, as everyone looked at me with bated breath. You could cut the atmosphere with a knife.

My whole life and future career passed before me. "Well, it's like this, chef," I hesitated. For a second I was too scared to break the news.

"Yes, yes, what is it?" demanded the chef.

"The truth is, I sat on your pâté, sir, and it's ruined. I cannot apologise enough." I closed my eyes and shrugged my shoulders, waiting for the wrath of his onslaught.

Instead, he looked at everyone and announced, "That's alright, Saxon. I wasn't happy with it anyway. It wasn't my best work."

The other chefs just looked at him, dumbfounded. Some were clearly disappointed that he had not flown off the handle, while others – perhaps earlier victims of his rage – looked relieved.

I thought about it afterwards, and he must have been bitterly disappointed but wanted to get out of the situation with his dignity intact, and he had done just that. His work for that competition was the best I had seen, and yet by announcing that he was not upset and that he was not happy with the quality of his creation, it made him look great. A few years later, I heard that he had been fired from a top job in Vancouver. He had served a dinner comprising marinated mushrooms and had given some important people a bad dose of food poisoning – every chef's nightmare – and that, reputedly, some of the diners had died. Can you imagine living with that? Such a mishap can end a chef's career for good, as it did in his case. Even without such extreme outcomes, finding another job in the industry afterwards is never easy.

Before Albert left our hotel, we had a goodbye drink in his office to send him off. As we were all gathered there, a young chef came to the office, knocked politely on the door and asked if someone could drive him to the hospital.

"I've cut myself," declared the budding Escoffier, as he held out his right hand. In his palm was a cleanly cut-off finger from his left hand.

"For goodness sake!" shouted the chef. "Someone get an ambulance." We wrapped the finger in ice and rushed the young chef and his finger to the closest hospital. He was taken straight into surgery but they were sadly unable to sew the finger back on.

———————•◦✦◦•———————

Like America, Canada has a great love of baseball, which is really a great social gathering, where you eat cholesterol-rich hamburgers and foot-long hot dogs, and drink too much beer. Then there is hockey, or rather ice-hockey. Now that is a gentleman's sport. I fell in love with the game myself, perhaps because of the high-octane action that goes back and forth across the ice rink like a freight train. I used to think that the fighting was all faked nonsense, similar to wrestling, until one night I managed to secure a ticket near the front of the glass perimeter close to the rink, so I could have a better view. About five minutes into the game, there was a huge fight right in front of me. Punches landed left and right, and blood was gushing all over the ice. I was so close, I could see that there was nothing fake about these punches and that every one of them must have hurt like hell. No wonder most professional ice-hockey players have numerous teeth missing.

Another big social event is the 'BBQ'. Calling a few friends over to your house for a barbecue with some beer is big business in Canada. Stereotypically, guys burn the meat and talk nonsense, while the women stay inside to gossip. At one barbecue at a friend's house in Vancouver, I remember something quite wonderful happened. It was almost dusk, the food was finished and we were just sitting around talking quietly. My friend's garden was on the edge of some woods and a beautiful deer just roamed up to have a look at what was going on. The smell of the food must have attracted her attention and my friend told me it happened all the time. "It's no big deal," he said. Well, to me it was a very big deal, and I wanted to buy a house there straightaway. One of the beauties of Canada, I discovered, is that no matter where you live, you are never too far away from nature and wildlife.

Another friend, Pierre, took me way up north to go fishing near to his family's cottage. We finished our night shift around eleven o'clock, threw our fishing tackle in the boot of his car and off we went. Pierre told me it was going to be a four-hour drive and that we were taking no food, just some water. Since we were going to be there for a week, the prospect of going completely hungry did cross my mind, so I was sure hoping that there were fish in the lake and that we were going to catch some of them. About three hours into the journey we were in really thick woods. It was very dark and eerie, and I could not help but think what would happen if the car broke down.

In the end I couldn't stand it any more, so I piped up, "Your car *is* in good health, right?"

"Oh, don't worry, Mike," said Pierre, "anyway, that's not our biggest problem at the moment ... We seem to be lost!" I jumped up in my seat and asked him if he was pulling my leg, but of course he was not.

"The entrance to my family's property is somewhere around here. It's in a small lane and we always cover the entrance to it with some branches. We're not here too often and we don't want strange people breaking into our cottage. I always have this problem, finding the place," declared Pierre.

This announcement did not do too much for my confidence, and I started to have visions of reporters finding two young twits, huddled together in the middle of nowhere, dying of thirst and starving to death.

After another thirty minutes of driving around, he came to a stop and said, "I think this is it." I looked out of the window, saw absolutely nothing and rolled my eyes. He got out of the car and moved a huge bush to reveal a small dirt track.

"What the hell is this?" I asked, "The bloody Batcave?" No wonder he could never find the way in; it was right in front of my eyes and I would not have seen it. We had already driven for over three hours and were still in the middle of nowhere, as far as I could see. After finding the entrance we drove up the lane, replacing the bush behind us, and continued for at least another hour through the dense, black woods. My heart was in my mouth on numerous occasions, and I cannot explain my relief on finally hearing the words, "We're here." I closed my eyes and thanked God.

As I stepped out of the car, all around me was pitch black. You could not see anything, no signs of civilisation whatsoever. Now, when you are not used to that kind of remoteness, it becomes pretty scary, especially when you start to hear all kinds of strange noises from the bushes.

"What would that be, a wolf, I suppose?" I said jokingly.

"No, it's probably a bear or wild boar, something like that," said Pierre, non-chalantly. Naturally that made me feel much better.

In the process of stretching my legs, I wandered a little way from the car, slowly approaching the woods, but Pierre quickly called after me to stand still. "Don't move," he said, "wait just a second."

I stood perfectly still, so scared I could not even blink. For a second, I thought that the huge bear or wild boar had crept up behind me and was just about to have his supper, when at that moment the clouds moved, revealing a full and totally round moon. It was so bright it was like daylight, and everything was white. I looked down at my feet and I was standing on the edge of a small cliff with a ten-foot drop, right into the lake. If I had kept on walking, I would have had a very early morning dip.

Pierre's family's cottage was right on the edge of this wonderful, private and stunningly beautiful lake. There were no people or any other sign of civilisation for miles, and I knew that this was going to be a completely calming little break. I sat on a huge rock overlooking the drop and took in the outstanding view of the entire lake. I listened but I couldn't hear a thing, absolutely nothing. It was so quiet it made my ears ring, and the moon shone on the water creating a mirror effect, revealing a beautiful picture of the clouds overhead and the trees close by. The water was as still as a mill pond, just a huge sheet of polished glass. A pair of water fowl sitting on the water sent gentle ripples out for a few feet before the lake reverted to its perfect stillness.

I went to bed but could not sleep. I was too excited about going out onto the lake in Pierre's boat. I was also hoping that we would catch some lunch. A few hours later, we were out on the water, and hooking fish steadily one after another. When we had half-a-dozen good-sized fish we decided to go back to shore and cook them, as we were pretty well ravenous by this stage. He had his barbecue pit all set up and ready, so we wrapped the fish in leaves and cooked them to perfection. I knew this was going to be my diet for a week, but I did not care at all. It seemed like a kind of meditation, being here on the lake. Very calming indeed.

That afternoon we went out to catch some more fish for dinner but were not having nearly as much luck this time, so we decided to have a nap in the boat instead. After about twenty minutes, the boat started to rock back and forth quite heavily, and I sat up and stuck my head over the side to see what was happening. I screamed with surprise to discover the biggest-looking dog I had ever seen, swimming by our boat on his way to a small island in the middle of the lake. I looked again and realised that the dog was in fact a huge wolf. The wolf swam to the island, crawled onto dry land, shook itself off and stood for a while just looking around, as if he was the king of the castle. After a few minutes, he jumped back into the water, swam back across the lake, shook himself off again and disappeared into the woods.

During these few days of eating fish and drinking bottled water, I really unwound from all the stress of big-city living. We saw many different animals come to the water's edge: deer, bears, moose, skunks and, of course, 'Mr Huff', the wolf.

As we were leaving, I noticed that right in the middle of the tiny island on the lake was a single gravestone. I asked Pierre who it belonged to, and he said that it was there when his family bought the property. I remember thinking there were worse places to be buried than in the middle of this serene, calming piece of heaven.

In Canada, I have seen snow falling in November and the ground remain covered with a coating of white until April. The temperatures can become bitterly cold and the wind-chill factor is an added handicap, making the long winters tiresome and brutal.

Making my way to work on one incredibly cold day, it was just starting to snow as I reached the hotel. Eight hours later, when I stepped out of the door again, I could easily have believed I was in the Antarctic. There was easily three feet of snow settled on the ground, and the wind was howling. I looked up at a huge street thermometer and the reading said −30 °C. My nose was already stinging, so I squeezed it to try to keep it warm. Pain shot down my nose and I realised that the mucus inside had frozen and, by squeezing it, I had cut the inside of my nasal passage. Blood began streaming down my face, so I went back into the hotel, thought about it for a while, then decided to sleep the night in the chef's office.

On my way home in winter I would sometimes see homeless people sitting in the middle of the road on the air vents. Cars would be passing them on either side, some stopping to offer a cigarette and others not giving a second glance. The vents would send warm air out from the underground train stations, in huge clouds of what appeared to be smoke rising in the street, as they sat there and tried to keep warm. I felt hopeless and sad for them. It was not unusual for some of these guys to roam around the park, fall down drunk and freeze to death. Only the fact that I knew there were shelters for them to go to managed to prevent me from weeping to myself in a quiet corner.

During these terrible Canadian cold snaps it can be very hard even to keep your house or apartment warm. My standard joke about my apartment during the winter was to tell my colleagues that I had left the light on, hoping that the non-existent amount of heat it generated would 'keep my cave warm'. Canadians say the only way to survive through these extreme winters is to get involved in some kind of winter sport. This supposedly takes your mind off the weather. I was no good at skating or skiing, so my only choice was ice fishing.

I went to try out this sport with Pierre, the same guy who had introduced me to the great outdoors and the big, bad wolf during the summer months, except this time it was a tad 'cooler'. We arrived at the lake in the morning to see the organiser using a snow ski to drag a large wooden hut out onto the huge body of iced water. Surely, that huge weight was going to go right through the ice and directly to its icy grave, I thought.

I had heard stories of these huts going through the ice and the owners having to wait until the summer, for warmer temperatures and warmer water, before going down to retrieve them. But this hut did not go through and the organiser dragged it out so far that it disappeared from view. He left the hut there and then came back to pick us up. Going out so far onto the ice made me very scared, and by the time we reached the hut, I was freezing half to death, but our guy told us to get out of the snow ski, and walk the last few steps to the hut. As I looked down at the ice, which appeared to be only inches thick, I could see small branches passing under my feet.

The same guy whom we were entrusting with our lives – and about whom we just assumed, or prayed, that he knew what he was doing – took out a huge hand drill and made three holes about a foot in diameter in the ice. The cut pieces of ice were dragged out to reveal themselves to be about four inches thick. Was that thick enough? I wondered. He then dragged the hut over the holes, gave us our fishing gear, a stove for cooking, a kettle and some cold beers.

I literally was *freezing*. The last thing I needed was an ice-cold beer! I felt like saying, "Where's the ice cream?" Shit! What I wanted was a nice powerful heater and a boiling-hot cup of coffee. He then told us he would be back to collect us in ten hours. "Say what? Ten hours? Are you nuts?" I protested. Too late – he was history. I shouted after him, but the noise of the engine on his snow ski drowned my voice.

So there I was with Pierre – freezing cold, hungry, needing to pee and thoroughly unamused at the whole scenario. When I stepped inside the hut, I found Pierre lighting the gas stove and getting ready to fry eggs and bacon. "Hey, wait a second," I shouted. "The stove will melt the ice. It will be summer before they find our bodies."

"Saxon, sit down and shut up, will you? Just relax, man," said Pierre, who had of course done this before – although that did not make me feel any better at all.

As Pierre was cooking our breakfast, he told me to start tying the hooks onto the lines so that we would be ready to fish afterwards. Thank goodness we didn't have to catch lunch today, I thought. My hands were so cold I could barely hold the tiny hooks, so I paused for a second, blowing on my fingers, dreaming it was going to make a difference. Dream on ... although for some strange reason it did start to get warmer inside the hut, almost comfortably so. Pierre quickly assured me – before I asked – it wasn't warm enough to melt the ice. We settled down to some very welcome eggs and bacon, then started to fish. Four hours later, not a single tickle. Nothing. What a waste of time, I thought. Pierre stepped outside and set up a deck chair, leaning back with a cold beer. He looked so comfortable sitting there, as if he was in his armchair at home in front of a log fire, which at that moment in time was where I heartily wished I was.

By now it was midday and the fumes from the stove had given me a terrible headache. This was my dilemma: leave the stove on and have a headache or turn the stove off and freeze to death. What a choice! I met the challenge halfway, sitting in the hut keeping warm until I felt a headache coming on, then jumping outside for a breather until I was near freezing, before returning to the hut to get warm again. I was up and down like a yo-yo all afternoon. And still no fish.

Then it happened. There was a huge sound like a thunderclap from the other side of the lake. I looked at Pierre, sitting back in his deck chair, and asked him, as nonchalantly as I could in the circumstances, "Hey, what was that?"

"That, my friend, is an ice wave and it's coming our way," he boasted. Apparently at midday when it becomes a little warmer, the ice sometimes melts, then refreezes in the afternoon when the temperature dips. The result of which means that there's sometimes too much ice. The ice pushes together and lifts up, causing a domino-like effect across the lake. The dominos then sweep across the ice until they reach the shore.

"So what do we do?" I asked nervously.

"Sit back and enjoy the ride," was his best advice. Just then I turned round to see a wave of ice around two feet high coming towards us at a very fast speed. Seconds later, it hit us and knocked everything four feet into the air. What a scene! Me flying, the hut, Pierre, deckchair, all up in the air as if in slow motion. I pondered whether when we landed, the impact on the ice would push us through. We seemed to be in the air forever and I closed my eyes. We didn't go through but we sure did land with one almighty thud.

So now there I was, cold, scared, in need of urgent medical – if not psychiatric – attention, and I just wanted to go home to my nice cave. I crawled back into the hut and thought the only thing that could save the day was to catch a fish so that we would at least have one story to boast of afterwards.

By late afternoon it was starting to get dark outside and I needed to pee. I stepped out onto the ice to see a sight that I will never forget until the day I die. The sun was going down and the whole sea of ice was a wonderful shade of orange, glowing with shadows glistening all around me. I stood watching and hoping it would last forever. It was genuinely breathtaking and I sat down on the cold, wet ice, feeling nothing but incredible joy. I was mesmerised by the experience and just getting to grips with what I had seen when the full moon started to come up, turning the sea of ice totally white once more. Without a cloud in the sky, this was a superb spectacle.

Here I was, in the middle of a huge body of ice with no land in sight, completely surrounded by my own private, glittering light show. It was ironic: one minute I was eagerly awaiting the journey home and the next, bitterly disappointed to hear the roar of the snow ski coming to pick us up. All the suffering I had gone through that day was suddenly made worthwhile in those few minutes, and I went home feeling wonderfully contented. With no fish, though!

During my time in Canada, I met and cooked food for many famous people: sports stars, heads of state, musicians and actors. Among these were the likes of Prince Philip, the Aga Khan, Charles Bronson, Steven Segal, Glenda Jackson, Wayne Gretzky and John McEnroe.

One cold winter day, I arrived at work to find a small group of screaming girls and a single, lonely photographer outside the hotel. I waited to see who, or what, the gathering was for, and a group of young men arrived, looking very 'out there', so to speak. I asked one of the girls who they were, and she named a young, not well-known but up-and-coming band called Duran Duran.

That night we cooked them dinner, and they gave us a couple of free tickets to go to see their show the following day. Since no one else at the hotel wanted the tickets – in this case, they literally could not be given away – I went along with a friend just to see what was going on. They were playing at a small backstreet kind of pub which could hold no more than 100 people, and there was still plenty of room left. They put on a great show though, and because the venue was so small, you could pat them on the back as they walked by. I stood next to Simon Le Bon as he sang some of their soon-to-be-huge hits. The next day, I saw them in the hotel lobby and told them I was at their show the night before and had enjoyed it a lot. We talked for a while and they left. A few weeks later, I saw their new video on TV and it felt like I was watching old friends.

Soon they were back in town, playing as the opening act for Blondie, another popular band of the time. I saw the guys again and said 'Hi'. I also went along to the concert and thoroughly enjoyed myself. That night they blew Blondie, the main act, right off the stage. Very soon after that, they became the 'overnight sensation' we now know, when they started to play more commercial music, noticeably different from what they had played the first time I saw them in the pub.

When they returned some two years later, they stayed at another Toronto hotel. I was eager to see them play again and queued for hours to try to get a ticket, but to no avail. It just was impossible; there were thousands of fans turned away without a ticket that night, and Duran Duran had sold out a huge sports arena seating tens of thousands. I was very disappointed to think that I was there when no one else wanted to be, and now they were famous I could not beg, borrow or steal a ticket. Despite this, I couldn't help but be pleased for the band on its incredible rise to stardom.

A well-known movie actress also stayed at our hotel. She had starred in various comedy roles but became particularly famous as much because of her more than ample breasts. One night she ordered room service and I thought how lucky I was, being a chef, that I would not have to go to her room with the hot dog she had ordered. When the waiter came down, he was howling and telling everyone that she had given him the best tip ever.

He handed over a Polaroid photograph and I was shell-shocked to see what was on it. After serving the dinner, she had asked her manager to get the camera. She then took off her top, revealing her huge boobs and gave the waiter her permission to bury his face in-between them. The photograph recording his treat was in my hand! There was the waiter, acting as if he was being suffocated, giving her a big hug, with her sporting a look of faked shock. Apparently, she did this to all the people she met in her room as a publicity stunt, and as her boobs were part of her assets and what people paid to see, she did not mind showing them at all. The waiter's photograph hung up in the room service office for quite a time. And I bet it's still there today!

Amongst the others for whom I cooked dinner were ice-hockey star Wayne Gretzky and most of the famous male tennis players of the day. They were all perfect guests, with very polite manners and lovely personalities. Jimmy Connors was a particularly nice guy, but the best one of all, and a real surprise to me, was John McEnroe – given his reputation for notoriously bad behaviour on the tennis court. Maybe that was just his way of winding himself up to play better, but after meeting him in our restaurant and observing his kindness and courtesy, I did not understand it at all.

I met the 'Great One' – if you are a fan of professional ice-hockey, that is – Wayne Gretzky, and he was also a very nice guy, but with him it was different. Everyone knows him as a great guy and a true ambassador for professional sports. I wasn't disappointed. He was everything his professional persona portrayed.

During my last few weeks in the hotel in Toronto, I was winding down, getting ready for my next move, which was to be to Houston in Texas, and I was in the lobby when Stevie Wonder was just leaving, escorted by two burly men, one at either side of him. I instinctively shouted out, "Stevie!" and he turned round to face in my direction, with his signature movement of his head waving left to right.

He spoke out in a wonderful, calming, gentle voice, "Who's that?"

"It's Mike, Stevie," I replied.

"Hi, Mike," he said, and he walked through the lobby to the door and left. The exchange was just a few seconds but it reinforced my impression of him being a gentle, kind man, blessed by God to write songs that make millions of people sometimes laugh, sometimes cry, but always very happy.

I felt the same about my time in Canada, but now it was time to move on.

III

STILL WILD IN THE WEST

"**G**ET DOWN OFF your horse and eat your beans!" What a line. Arriving in Houston for my next challenge was an eye-opener. It was late 1986, and Texas was witnessing a terrible slump in oil prices. Times were extremely tough and people were losing their jobs left, right and centre. There was a real depression in the local economy. I was to be employed in a hotel as sous chef and also placed in charge of an extremely exclusive private club on the top floor which had been made famous by 'Old Blue Eyes' himself. It had once been his favourite hangout when in Houston, and he had dined there many times, turning it into a place to be seen and to rub shoulders with the rich and famous. The local media had quoted him as saying that it had one of the best views he had ever seen. The bar in the centre of the club had huge stained glass windows – and on a clear day you could see for miles – and at night, witness a fantastic, flickering light show all over the town.

To cash buyers, houses were being sold for $10,000 – a fraction of their usual price – and some people were desperate for a quick sale, making this the best time ever to be a buyer.

On my first day in the job, I was introduced to my staff members and knew instantly that things were not going to be easy. The staff were a very rowdy bunch and, excited to meet their new boss, they were getting ready to introduce themselves, one by one, in their own individual way.

As I was by now a Canadian citizen, I arrived at the Texan hotel as a tourist, since my work permit was not quite ready. I felt uncomfortable about starting work without the necessary paperwork. You could cross over the American border at any immigration checkpoint with only a Canadian ID and not need a passport, and stay for up to a year at a time, but you could not work. Being caught working without a proper permit was not such a bad thing for a Canadian, but they could ask you to leave and you might never be allowed to work in the US again. This was a window of opportunity I did not want to close.

When, after about two months at the hotel, its lawyers said the permit application was still 'ongoing' and that I should not worry, I could not help being concerned. This was brought home to me all the more one day when I was sitting in my office and in walked two burly fellows in policeman-like uniforms.

"Are you Michael Saxon?" one of them growled. I swallowed all the way down to my shoes while tilting my head backwards, trying to see the heads at the top of these huge, towering beasts.

"I don't know … Am I? … Who is asking?" I mumbled, already thinking about those American jails with murderers and rapists looking at me amorously, and viewing me as 'fresh meat'.

"Do you have a problem or something, sir?" said one of the brutes. "I just asked you a simple, civil question; all I want is a simple, civil answer. We are from the US Immigration and Naturalisation Service (INS) and need your help on a matter."

My heart was racing a mile a minute, missing the occasional beat. My mind was also working overtime, trying to come up with some sort of answer to dig myself out of the deep hole I had found myself free-falling into. I was absolutely petrified to say the least. These guys were huge and very scary. On top of that, they also had loaded guns and wooden clubs hanging from their belts. I thought about those classic television news reports where police in strange countries are seen hitting rioters on their heads with clubs, and thought how much it would hurt to be clobbered by these two.

When I managed to relax somewhat, I found myself sounding strangely like a lawyer and out popped the rather tortuous line: "I am just here conducting a food promotion to help promote Canadian cuisine to the American public. Only in the great US of A can someone like me be given a chance like this, to share his experiences with others, while picking up new and valuable experiences along the way. Anyway, that is all I am doing here."

"I don't give a shit!" said one of the uniformed hulks. "The front office manager downstairs told me I could find you here." I remember thinking to myself, who was the bozo that had turned me in so easily?

"Anyway, to be blunt, I have come for one of your staff. He's Mexican and an illegal alien. The front office manager said you were in charge of these clowns, so I just wanted to inform you we were taking him in."

"Of course you did," I replied, feeling like I had just put both feet firmly in my mouth. They then waltzed into the kitchen, grabbed my member of staff, handcuffed him and led him to the door.

As they reached the exit, one of the officers turned round and said, "By the way, what were you talking about?"

"Oh nothing," I quickly replied. "I was just playing around."

"I'm sure you were," he said, before giving me one last threatening glance.

My Mexican sauce chef, Pedro, shouted as he was being led away, "See you on Thursday, chef! Have my pay cheque ready, eh?"

What a poor, misguided fool, I thought; he will probably be in the clink by sundown, and back across the border before morning. Another bit of money the hotel had been lucky to save, which would be quickly retrieved by the financial controller on hearing the news, I was sure. Of course, he would not care how we were going to maintain standards without sufficient, or properly trained staff. That was a problem I was paid to solve, would be his view.

On Thursday morning, I was having a coffee in my office, when who should walk in as happy as a lark, but Pedro.

"Morning, chef, what shall I do today? Oh, by the way, where is my pay cheque?"

I was totally intrigued by the whole affair, so I invited him to sit down and explain what the hell was going on. He told me that the INS had kicked him out of the country five times already, and that he had returned with different fake IDs each time. Paying someone to smuggle him right back in again the very next day was just a routine. These people called themselves 'coyotes', as they only smuggle 'clients' over the border under the cover of nightfall. And for a large fee, of course.

As we were finishing our conversation, Jerry, the pastry chef, who I had already decided was trouble, came into my office and asked me if I could come and smell the cake mix he had just made. I followed him into the kitchen where he showed me a huge bowl of uncooked chocolate cake mix.

"Chef, I have mixed this stuff," he said, "but I am not sure if I have added the cinnamon or not. Could you smell it for me and tell me if I have added it already or if I have forgotten?"

I looked at him for a second and asked him if he was joking. A young cook came over, eager to impress me with his smelling talents. He boasted that he could easily tell if it had been added or not, so I passed the task to him. As he bent down and placed his head near the raw mix, the scallywag pastry chef looked at me and winked. He grabbed the young cook by his head and pushed it deep into the raw mix. There was cake mix everywhere. It was in his eyes, ears, nose and all over his uniform. Poor guy, I thought, no wonder there was such a shortage of people wanting to learn how to cook when they are treated like this.

That night the club was very busy and we were all in the 'deepest shit' imaginable. To put it mildly, we were struggling very badly. In the midst of this, I was asked to go outside and speak to two elderly female customers who wanted to meet the new chef-in-charge. I grudgingly obliged. I mean, that was all I needed now, to listen to these fuddy-duddies say how good the last chef was and how they hoped I could live up to his high standards. Here we go, I thought. So I introduced myself and asked, "What may I do for you lovely ladies this evening?"

Off they went. "Good evening, young man. We would like you to make us a special orange sauce to go with our Crêpes Suzette. It's our favourite, you know. The last chef could not make a nice orange sauce if his life depended on it. We could not have been any happier when he left. This is our way of testing to find out if you are worth your weight in coarse sea salt!"

How pleasant, I thought. What a bloody cheek! But naturally I replied, "Of course, ladies, I shall get onto it straightaway. But you understand I cannot divulge my secret recipe, for fear of you learning how to make it yourself, and no longer gracing us with your elegant presence!"

Back in the kitchen, the orders had by now piled up to the ceiling. Everyone else in this exclusive club was completely pissed off with waiting. Ignoring this, I placed one flat pan on the stove, poured in half a litre of fresh orange juice, boiled it and thickened it with cornflour. Adding some fresh orange segments and some sugar to taste, I finished the sauce in three minutes flat and set it aside. Every chef knows a shortcut or two when they are rushed. Around half an hour later, with most of the backlogged orders under control, I decided to step out to see how my two 'golden girls' were doing.

"It won't be long now, ladies. You know great food is the product of love, care and patience."

"We don't mind having to wait for an artist's fine work, chef," they replied.

Five minutes later, I sent out the Crêpes Suzettes and waited for the request for a curtain call. Right on cue, a few minutes later, the head waiter told me that the two elderly ladies wanted to see me, so I put on a clean apron and out I stepped.

The two ladies stood up, clapping and shouting, "Bravo, bravo, chef, bravo!" I conducted myself in the usual manner and gave them a gentlemanly bow. "That was the best orange sauce we have ever tasted, young man. Absolutely first class. Patience has proved to be a virtue yet again."

As I finished my small talk with the ladies, I looked up to see no service staff around at all. The guests were looking at me in annoyance, and pointing at their empty plates, as if to ask what was going on. As I toured around the restaurant, I heard some quiet giggling going on in the storeroom behind the main drinks bar. I quickly rounded the counter and entered the storeroom, where to my amazement all the service and bar staff were being entertained by our Vietnam War veteran, the head barman. He had put a blue movie on one of those old fluttering projectors and was pointing it at one of the blank walls. They had the lights turned down, and a white bed sheet borrowed from the housekeeping department was tacked to the wall. They had planned to watch the movie when the last guest had gone home, but the suspense and excitement were killing them, and being unable to withstand it any longer, they had started the show early.

They totally ignored the fact that the restaurant was still open and decided to have their fun instead. The guys were tickling the girls and everyone was giggling like school kids. I told them that all the guests were waiting and were upset, threatening not to pay, and certainly leaving no tips on their hurried departure. That did the trick. They immediately turned off the projector and the barman shouted, "To be continued later, ladies and gentlemen. On returning to this after-hours orgy, please do not forget to bring your money and your protection. Thank you." Now, this place really *was* a zoo, I thought.

After finishing the service and once everyone had left, they invited me to join the party. I was scared to think what might happen; maybe the next day I would wake up in some strange place, not knowing where I was, but with a tattoo on my bum that read 'Made in England'. After all, there was a free flow of liquor and other drinks during the amorous movie, and some of those waitresses were very sexy. The whole thing spelt trouble to me, so I went home. The next day, I heard that some of the male staff members had got into a fight amongst themselves, trying to pick up the female staff. Apparently, as the gender ratio was uneven, and being aroused by the movie – which had obviously sent much of their blood to the lower regions of their bodies, leaving their brains starved of their usual limited supplies – the inevitable fisticuffs had started.

Of course, the boss had asked everyone to attend a meeting to try and find out what exactly had happened. When asked for my version, everyone stared at me, but I explained that I had no idea as I had already gone home before the would-be action heroes had got it on.

Leaving out the part about the movie show had made me one of the team in the eyes of the staff, and I was trusted much more from that point on. For my part, I considered that if the management were on top of things, when the bar stocks did not balance at the end of the month, they would soon deduce for themselves what had gone on, so why should I be labelled as a 'rat'?

As with any other job, in any other country, a lack of respect from your work colleagues just makes it so much harder to get anything done. A healthy level of mutual respect makes everything move along and happen so much easier. So I contented myself that I had taken the better management decision … at least for now.

The pot washer in this hotel, it was reputed, was a retired general of the Japanese Imperial Army, who was a little hard of hearing due to too many close encounters with exploding ammunition. One day, I bid him a simple 'good morning' and was assaulted with a barrage of old stories about how, when he was younger, he had kicked guys like me in the balls every day. He also made it quite clear that I could expect the same treatment if I liked to think of myself as the 'king shit' of this 'dung heap'.

The staff liked to recount the story of a young chef who had just started and had left a chef's knife in the pot-washing sink full of dirty water. The 'General' had put his hand into the sink to wash the dirty pots and grabbed the knife by the blade, cutting himself quite badly. In double-quick time the budding young chef had resigned, decided to take up carpentry, and walked with a limp for a month! So, all in all,

Mr Teppanyaki, as I began to call him, was a force to be reckoned with, and I was advised that I should treat him with due caution.

I used to see Mr Teppanyaki sitting on his own, sometimes eating pieces of gristly pork crackling with the hottest, take-your-breath-away, chopped chilli smeared all over it. This man was definitely going to be a serious challenge to get anything that resembled respect from, but I felt I had to try. Gonzalez, another of the hotel chefs, told me not to waste my time on him, as he was 'a miserable old goat' and 'good for nothing other than washing pots'. I have always taken the view that everyone is good for something, but that you sometimes have to dig a little to find out exactly what it is. As time went by, I left Mr Teppanyaki alone and he gave me my space, so everything was alright. After all, he was doing a great job, and the last thing I wanted to do was inherit his workload should he resign.

We had a very strict and tough supervisor in the kitchen, who did not tolerate slouches or any laziness. One day, Rosalee, a middle-aged Mexican female member of staff, was caught sleeping in the storeroom and the supervisor wanted to fire her. I took Rosalee to my office and asked her why she was sleeping on the job. She told me that she had just felt very tired and needed a nap, so I told her that this was absolutely against the hotel's policies and generally gave her a good telling-off.

She looked up at me, and a solitary tear trickled down her right cheek. Hey, I'm the boss, I thought, how could you make me feel so guilty for doing my job? This was not fair at all, but I still felt bad anyway.

I told the supervisor to cut her some slack and try to find out why she was sleeping on the job. My intention was to try to help her, and in so doing perhaps get back from her some of that, 'I'll stand by you too' kind of support you need in this job. She did not want to talk about her problems, however, so we left it at that. But a few days later, I decided to pay a surprise visit to her house to follow the matter up personally. After getting her address from the personnel department, I caught a taxi over to what proved to be her truly humble abode.

"Oh man, are you sure you wanna go there, buddy?" the taxi driver asked me.

"Of course," I replied. "One of my staff lives there."

He looked at me over the top of his glasses and said sternly, "Maybe they do, my friend, but you don't."

"Just take me there, please," I said, in frustration. So off we went.

As we arrived in her part of town, I began to wonder if this really was a good idea. I had not seen this side of America before – how the really poor people lived. But now I could see at first-hand the hardships that some people have to grapple with every day. We finally found the right house, or should I say, 'shack', and I knocked on the makeshift door.

When the door opened, I was staggered to see standing in the doorway none other than Mr Teppanyaki himself. I did not know what to say, and I was stammering around trying to find the words to say anything at all. He bowed his head and asked me to enter. I stepped inside to find a tiny living room, sparsely decorated with what appeared to be old second-hand furniture, and an even smaller kitchen, with a portable stove sitting on a table. Bearing in mind that this was Texas and hot as hell, the biggest surprise to me was that there was no electricity in the house, which therefore meant no air conditioning.

Mr Teppanyaki asked me to sit down, which I did, without any comment or attempt at small talk, since I was just plain lost for words. He then disappeared into the darkness and returned a few minutes later with a Japanese tea set and served us both tea. We spoke very quietly for a few minutes, and he explained that Rosalee was actually his wife, and that they wanted to keep their marriage a secret because of their different racial backgrounds. Their respective families, he told me, would not approve and their marriage would likely cause all kinds of family upsets if it were known. So to keep the peace, they had married in secret and were living a secluded life together, in private and in love.

What guts these people have, I thought, but could not help feeling disheartened about how the world sometimes forces people to make such sacrifices in order to live the life they have chosen. I just cannot understand why anyone would even care, much less want to interfere in another person's life choice in this regard, but then I recall the words of Oscar Wilde which seem to sum it up pretty well: 'My own business always bores me to death; I prefer other people's!'

I asked Mr Teppanyaki if Rosalee was around, as I would like to say hello. He put his finger up to his lips and gently said, "Shh!" He led me to the back of the room where there was a blanket hanging from the ceiling, creating a sort of partition, and with it another bedroom for someone to sleep. He slowly pulled back the blanket to show his wife rocking a young child to sleep, and at the same time fanning the child to keep it cool. She had her back to us and seemed unaware of our presence. The area of the room was kept light only by the gentle glow of a solitary candle shimmering in the darkness. So dim was its light that it barely created any shadows to give away our presence. I noticed that as she waved the fan, the fringe of her hair moved back and forth, gently swaying, but discreetly soundless.

Mr Teppanyaki slowly released the blanket and explained to me that to enable the child to get a better night's sleep and thus do better in school, they took turns to stay up all night fanning him to keep him cool. No wonder she was always falling asleep at work, I thought, and that he was eating pork gristle for lunch.

Instantly, the recollection of Rosalee with her solitary tear, as I admonished her, tore me apart, and I felt like some kind of lower life form. I couldn't believe that I had quoted hotel policies and procedures without knowing the whole story, or even the beginning of it. I begged Mr Teppanyaki to tell me how I could ever apologise, or make it up to him and his wife. He graciously told me that I had already done so by appearing at his house. He went on to say that in watching me at work he knew that I had a good heart, and that showing up at the house to find out the real reason for his wife's fatigue, and to see if there was anything I could do to help, served to confirm this opinion. Humbled yet further, that thought helped subdue my guilt, but I vowed to make it up to them somehow.

From that moment on, which I look back upon as a real-life wake-up call, I have always tried to understand and read people; to seek to know why they behave as they do. I have found that there is usually a reason, or reasons, behind most peoples' behaviour, however strange that behaviour may be. Getting to know someone better and understanding their problems can only make it easier for you to get along, thus accomplishing so much more together than you would if you were constantly at loggerheads.

Mr Teppanyaki had shown me that he was a respectful, loving and caring man in a way that I would never have seen or even imagined at work. This underlined my belief that there is good in everyone, only that sometimes it's deep inside, buried under a rubble of past bad experiences or heartaches. It just has to be brought out, or more usually, eased out. Now I had the respect for him that he deserved, and I felt I knew how I could get respect from him in return.

Some weeks after this incident, I was carrying a large ice carving out of the freezer. It was a swan for a wedding dinner that was due to start in the next half an hour. As I placed the ice carving on a trolley, the wheels slipped into a kitchen drainage hole, sending the beautiful carving crashing onto the floor, and smashing it into dozens of small pieces. I was now under enormous pressure, to say the least, to find something to fill its place, and I had no idea what to do or where to start. Even if we salvaged the biggest pieces and managed to locate someone to recarve them, the ice was now only big enough, at best, to carve two small ducks. And on your wedding day, miniature ducks instead of graceful kissing swans somehow just did not make the grade.

I sat on the steps outside my office with my head in my hands, thinking how I had ruined the happy couple's big day, when up stepped my Japanese friend, Mr Teppanyaki.

"What is wrong, Michael san?" he enquired. I explained the story to him and he simply glanced at his watch and said, "Don't worry, I will be back soon."

"Yes, whatever you want," I replied. It was easy for him to say 'don't worry', I thought, but my bloody job was on the line here. The last thing I was actually worrying about at that moment was dirty pots and pans!

I had to come up with something for the happy couple in the next half an hour or else it was crunch time. I busied myself organising the rest of the set-up, including the flowers, the champagne fountain, the wedding backdrop with their names stylishly arranged, and the table centrepieces. I was just gathering my courage to go out and explain my carelessness to the soon-to-be not-so-happy couple, when I started to hear the creaking of what sounded like trolley wheels coming down the corridor. The noise of the oil-thirsty wheels became louder and louder as they got closer to the entrance of the kitchen. As the trolley finally came round the corner and entered the kitchen, there was Mr Teppanyaki with a large beaming smile.

On the trolley were two wonderful, freshly carved kissing swans! I could not believe my eyes. "Michael san," said Mr Teppanyaki, with evident pleasure, "where do you want me to put these?"

"Right this way, sir," I replied, and we went into the ballroom, placing the swans centre stage for everyone to see. I later learned that Mr Teppanyaki had a part-time job as an ice carver, and that he had gone to his other place of work and cut these beautiful swans in ten minutes flat. The guy was obviously a very talented artist and an ice carving genius. It made me wonder all the more what he was doing washing pots for a living. Needless to say, when the full-time kitchen artist left, I persuaded him to take the job so that he could at least get the benefit of the extra revenue.

After a few months working at the Houston hotel, I decided to have an overseas food promotion and chose Spanish cuisine as the theme. Our general manager used to work in Spain and managed to secure the services of a couple of his former chefs to come over to Texas and do their thing. The first night I was with them in the kitchen, it was very tough going. They did not speak English and both were rather quick-tempered, though fortunately without any real bite. Towards the end of the service one evening, the two Spanish chefs started to play around in the kitchen, making the other staff laugh with their big top antics and tricks.

Balancing chef's ladles on their noses and walking around the kitchen with them in that position was not exactly what I had expected from these seasoned and well-travelled professionals, but it made the staff feel good, so I decided not to be a tight-arse and cut them some slack. When service finished that evening, I decided to ask them if they wanted to go out and see a little of what Houston had to offer. On asking the cooks of their whereabouts, they informed me that the chefs had disappeared soon after the last order left the kitchen. Puzzled by this, I went back to my office to finish off some paperwork, when all of a sudden there was a loud drumming sound echoing out of the kitchen, intermingled with what sounded suspiciously like guitar playing.

I ran into the kitchen to see which jokers were creating this melee, only to find my two Spanish friends creating their own Spanish kitchen samba sounds. To cap it, they were dressed up like they were going to the Mardi Gras, or some other carnival where people lose their inhibitions and don't care what they look like.

"What are you clowns doing?" I asked, desperately trying to get a handle on the situation.

"We are going out to entertain the guests, Spanish style," came the response. Then they started the racket again. They were blowing football whistles so loudly that I fully expected the hotel security guards to come running in with a SWAT team at any time.

Here I was with these two hand-picked top-notch chefs, who were ready to party, and with all my Mexican staff dancing and cheering, and the other cooks banging pots and pans with large spoons to add their own 'musical' contribution, when in came one of the hotel security guards.

Instead of challenging me about the racket in the kitchen, he proclaimed in a loud voice, "Do you know that there are two of your staff screwing in the dry store?"

Now close your eyes and picture this zoo-like scene for a second. All I could blurt out in response was, "I'm terribly busy at the moment. I've got to take care of

the Miami Sound Machine here first before I can even think of doing anything else."
As I finished talking with the security guard, I turned round just in time to see all the
staff entering the restaurant, still banging out their blurry cover version of the Conga,
by which time it was too late to do anything at all.

The last cook to enter this top-of-the-line, five-star, exclusive club turned round
and shouted to me, "Come on, boss, let's go."

I managed to brave a faked smile and raise my hand to wave, using only my
fingers in a half-hearted gesture.

"Are you coming or not?" asked the security guard.

"Ahhh, yes," I spluttered. In all the 'excitement and fun' I was having, I had
forgotten about Adam and Eve having their romantic interlude. When I arrived at
the door of the dry store, I found the rest of the kitchen staff – those who presumably
had not fancied themselves as barrack room musicians – listening outside the door,
obviously fancying themselves as voyeurs instead.

The couple's amorous encounter was clearly entertaining everyone, especially
as the moaning and groaning from inside was seeping audibly into the corridor to the
great delight of the gathering staff. I didn't know whether I should be selling tickets
and making myself a bob or two, as more staff were arriving by the second, or starting to organise some crowd control.

Just as I was about to announce that it was time for everyone to go home, the
grunting symphony from the storeroom peaked, and then fell silent. All the staff
outside were by now giggling and waiting in anticipation to see who was going
to step out to take the applause of the cheering fans. A couple of the waiters were
very excited about the possibility of one of the dynamic duo being the beautiful
new barmaid who had just started – thus, no doubt, giving rise to their own private
fantasies.

Everyone started to clap and cheer as the door opened and out stepped Peter.
The cheers and claps completely tapered out as another member of staff, who could
see who was following behind, announced, "Oh, no way, man!"

I was still trying to catch up with what the heck was going on, when out came
the blushing bride. Was it Christine, or Nancy, or that babe Susan? No, it was Paul!
I, in my naivety, had looked inside the storeroom for the blonde-haired babe, that
most of the macho male voyeurs had been envisaging, or more accurately fantasising
about, only to realise that Peter had been getting it on with Paul.

I started to go out a little more at night but actually had no idea where to go. So
I decided to go exploring. On one such excursion, I came across a nightclub about
fifteen minutes from my rented apartment and decided to pop in and have a beer.
I walked in, sat at the bar, asked what kind of beer they had, and in a flicker this huge
African American mountain of a man moseyed on up and replied, "Say what?"

I looked at him and asked again, "I was just wondering what kind of beer
you have."

The big guy leant across the bar, stared right into my eyes, and explained that if I wanted to walk around tomorrow with all my body parts still connected to my body, and in working order, then it might be best that I leave.

I was so scared that my cheeks felt as if they were somehow nailed to the chair, and my legs had turned to jelly. Getting up and leaving, if only for purely practical reasons, was out of the question. Fortunately for me, 'mine host' passed me a beer and asked, "Where y'all from, man?" As I was on my lonesome, I looked around, wondering who the 'y'all' was that he was referring to, and as I did so I saw around sixty people all looking at me, in a surprised manner, and all of them African American.

Hm! I thought, these people must be wondering who is this nutcase that just walked onto our turf? Knowing that this was probably not the time for any of my dry English humour, I decided to keep it very civil, to drink my beer, and wait for the blood to circulate back into my legs before leaving quietly.

"I'm from out of town and just started working here," I murmured.

"No shit!" replied the barman.

"I'm from England," I added.

At which point he loudly pronounced, "It's alright, everybody, he's from the UK." All at once, the other guests started to go about their business and I was left in peace to choke on my beer. The barman went on to explain, "We don't get many white folks coming in here. They're scared."

"Of what?" I asked timidly.

This prompted the barman to throw his head back and let out a huge roar of laughter as he announced to the whole bar, "Look out, folks, there's a virgin in town."

After I finished my beer, I decided to call it a night and, as I was leaving, the big guy called out after me, "Y'all come back now!"

It was about a fifteen-minute walk back to my apartment and I had no idea at the time that I was living in what some would describe as a dangerous neighbourhood. I turned the corner and almost bumped into a middle-aged woman who was built like a World Wrestling Federation champion. She smiled at me and asked, "Are you looking for a lady tonight?"

Well, I was in a humorous mood after escaping from my earlier encounter, so I decided to offer what I thought was a cheeky, harmless joke. I opened my mouth and out it popped.

"Actually, I am, would you have any idea where I could find one?"

I can tell you she swung her handbag like it was her own style of lethal weapon and I only just ducked in time. Then she made a serious lunge with both hands, or should I say talons, at my throat. At that point, I decided to call it quits, and ran like hell. Unfortunately for me, despite her size, she was in better shape than I bargained for and the chase was on. My wits had not deserted me altogether, though; I quickly reasoned to myself that I could not go straight home for fear that on knowing where I lived, she would return with some even bigger, and badder, reinforcements.

So we ran around the street for what seemed, in my frightened state, like five or ten minutes, but was probably more like two or three, until she gave up as the gap between us became too large. When the penny finally dropped that the game was up, she still had one card left to play. She took off her shoe and threw it at me, banging me square on the back of my head, as she yelled what she thought of me, Texas style!

I decided not to take any chances in heading for home too soon after the chase, so I made my way to the local 7-Eleven store to buy some milk for my morning coffee. The overnight guy working in the store was a Somalian citizen, who was in the US putting himself through university with this night job. I had met him a few times previously and got into friendly banter with him. Abby, as I knew him, short for Abiodun, recounted that due to the limited travel experience of many Americans, they were sometimes not so knowledgeable about other countries and people.

"Watch, I'll show you when the next customer comes in," he said, and in walked a customer with whom he proceeded to strike up a conversation.

"Good evening, sir. How are you tonight?" said Abby.

"I'm fine," replied the customer, "how are you?"

"Where are you from?"

"Well, I'm from Dallas. Do you know it at all?"

"Yes, I know it well," replied Abby.

"And where are y'all from?" asked the Texan.

"I am from Somalia. Do you know it?"

"Of course," the customer affirmed. "That's north of Houston, ain't it?"

I was suitably gobsmacked and, after buying the milk and exchanging further pleasantries, I left. As I walked out of the shop, I stood quietly in the doorway for a few minutes to see if my lady friend was still around. Anybody who could throw a shoe with such accuracy and venom, I reasoned, must have once pitched for the local women's baseball team. Not seeing her around, I called it a night.

The next day, I went to work expecting an uproar about the raucous singing chefs, only to discover that they had been a huge hit with the guests, many of whom had joined in. Some had even jumped up and danced on the tables. Who would have thought it? I pondered, not for the first time.

The day was seemingly going steady, without any major setbacks, when the manager of the restaurant asked me if I would go outside into the bar and stop a squabble between two members of staff. I went outside to see what I could do, whereupon the Vietnamese War veteran barman smiled at me and told me to go back inside and mind my own business. Ignoring his advice, I asked him what was going on and suggested that he lightened up a little, saying that maybe later he and I should go for a drink to talk about it.

I, of course, had forgotten a simple truism, that this was not England and that disagreements were sometimes solved in these parts by other methods! As I looked at him, my eyes slowly moved down his arms to see his hands laying palm down on the bar. Under his right hand was a nicely folded crimson napkin and underneath was evidently some kind of handgun, as I glimpsed the barrel pointing out.

I have never been as scared as I was that day. I had heard of how many thousands of weapons had gone missing after the Vietnam War had ended, and wondered if this was his little souvenir. I am not ashamed to say that I went straight back into the kitchen, made my way to my office and locked the door. I stayed there until the shift had finished before I eventually slunk away.

Shaken by the events at work, I decided to have a slow walk home. When I was about halfway, I became aware that there was something above me creating a kind of whirlwind sensation. I looked up to see a police helicopter hovering over my head. They shone a very powerful light on me, and used their loud-speaker to tell me not to move and to stay perfectly still. They had used their radio to call a police car which arrived moments later with all the sirens blazing. I remember thinking, What now? I'm only a bloody chef!

The police officers stepped out of the car and told me to put my hands behind my head, and as I did so, they frisked me. On finding nothing, the officer asked me where I was going. I explained that I was new in town, working at a nearby hotel, that I had just finished work, and as I had not yet got used to the public transport system, I was taking a steady walk home.

I remember the exact words that he used. "Do you have shit for brains, buddy?" They explained that it was extremely dangerous to be downtown after dark and that walking home was sheer lunacy. When I was spotted from the helicopter, they had automatically assumed I was up to no good and had stopped me to check. Apparently, many US cities have become so big, scary and dangerous, that no one wants to live downtown. Most people prefer to live in out-of-town areas, from where they commute to their downtown jobs during the day before retreating to the burbs after dark, fearing for their safety.

After this 'thrilling' experience, I decided to start taking taxis home at night but of course this opened a whole new can of worms. For example, one evening I hailed a taxi outside my hotel, got in and told the driver to take me to my new hangout, so that I could have a nightcap before retiring. I sat in the front seat of the cab without glancing at the driver, and off we sped. I knew that it would only take five minutes or so.

A short while into the journey, I looked up to engage the driver in conversation, only to realise that he was totally naked. I swallowed deeply and decided to act as if this sort of thing happened to me every day. I spoke about the first thing that came to mind which, being British, was of course the very hot weather. This short ride to my local bar felt like I was travelling cross-country. It lasted forever, and it seemed as if we were stopped by every red light.

During these very special moments in life, I sometimes think there is someone, somewhere, laughing like hell, while pushing all the buttons and turning every traffic light red just before you reach it. Then they make the timer that changes it to green take twice as long to change as normal.

On reaching the club, I asked the driver how much I owed him. He just smiled and said, "Good evening, sir," and drove off into the night. Save for his admittedly very unconventional attire, he had otherwise behaved like a gentleman. Most bizarre, but then this *was* America.

There would be other, equally wondrous, close encounters with taxi drivers. One night I was on the way home, and the driver saw someone whose car had broken down, so he decided to stop and offer assistance. The other driver told us his battery was flat and he needed a jump-start. My taxi driver had his own set of jump leads in the boot so he went to get them. He then jump-started the other guy's car, got back in his cab and off we went. After a few seconds, he realised that the other guy had mistakenly gone off with his jump leads, so off we went after him.

Eventually, as we pulled up alongside the driver of the other car, the taxi driver smiled and wound down his window to explain to the other driver that he had mistakenly taken his jump leads and could he have them back, please. The other driver smiled back, raised his hand, giving him the finger, and sped off. We, of course, chased after him. We chased him for ages, all over downtown Houston, often at breakneck speeds. It was like something from an episode of *NYPD Blues*. I just sat there, as one does, meekly having a nervous breakdown.

That night, when I eventually arrived at my 'club', I was introduced to a local celebrity gangster. How nice, I thought. He took pleasure in showing me his personalised, initialled handgun, and for the want of something to say, I made the big mistake of asking him, "How loud is it when it goes off?"

"Come outside and hear it for yourself," he replied.

So we stepped outside and he fired a single shot into the air. It was scary to hear how loud a gunshot is, especially when you are standing so close. Yet surprisingly, this actually made me feel a little better because at night I had sometimes heard shots, and was always scared to death imagining that there was a big shoot-out, or the like, going on and that people were being killed. This little display, silly as it may seem, at least gave me some reassurance that occasionally it was just people messing around with the guns, and it was not always 'end of the world' stuff. In an environment which gives people 'the right to bear arms', at least imagining that people were not pointing them at one another all the time is, I suppose, all one can hope for.

———— ◆•◆•◆ ————

Reading the newspaper one Monday morning, I noticed a reference to a locally well-known and very large old folks' home looking for any type of donations. The feature also stated that once a month they held a birthday party for all the residents who had their birthdays during that particular month. I decided to call them on behalf of the hotel, and offer a large birthday cake for the following month's party.

When I called to make the offer, the nurse who answered the phone told me that it was a very generous gesture and a lovely idea. She then asked me my name, and I told her that I was Michael Saxon, and that I would deliver the cake personally.

I arrived at the old folks' home on the day of the delivery to a resounding welcome. So ecstatic and effusive was the welcome that I could barely believe my eyes. They had all the residents outside to greet me, some were standing and others sitting in their wheelchairs. The nurses were standing and waving. Some of the younger nurses were literally jumping up and down holding makeshift banners reading, 'We love you, Michael'. There were people with cameras, and even what appeared to be the local media.

My first thought on seeing this outpouring was to wonder what would have happened if I had donated a serious amount of money, or something of significant value. What might these nurses have wanted to give me then, I pondered, or rather, fantasised. I mean it was only a birthday cake, for goodness' sake.

As I stepped out of the hotel van, everyone looked at me with such great surprise and evident disappointment, I immediately knew something was amiss. The head nurse came over to me and asked who I was. I told her that I had spoken to a junior staff nurse a few days ago and told her that I would be delivering a cake for the residents today.

"My name is Michael Saxon," I declared.

"Michael who?" she asked, already starting to laugh.

"Michael Saxon," I said once more. "Hey, what the heck is going on?" I asked.

"When you called to say you wanted to deliver the cake, my young nurse thought you said 'Michael Jackson', and we have been planning this event ever since," declared the head nurse.

I have never felt so embarrassed. My attempt at a goodwill gesture had turned into something that disappointed people rather than made them feel better. Yet, on the other hand, I thought, how silly could the young nurse have been to imagine that a worldwide superstar would personally deliver a five-kilo fresh strawberry cream cake to the home? How stingy would he look, with all his fame and fortune, delivering a cream cake?

One member of my culinary brigade, Jung, had arrived in the US from his native Vietnam with a legion of horror stories about his childhood days in his hometown. He told me how it was not unusual for children to play with home-made bombs, guns and live ammunition because of the ready availability of such terrifying items, and the lack of anything else to play with. To them it was a normal everyday occurrence to have target practice, shooting whatever moved in the nearby woods, using the live rounds. Having enough of this dead-end existence, he and his family had decided to buy their places on a small fishing boat that a few people in his local village had secretly built. The master plan was to sail to the 'land of the free' and try to get refugee status and hopefully, later, permanent residence there. Easier said than done, of course, and the reality was more than a little different.

After floating around for weeks, on an overfilled and half-sinking boat, they had to endure, amongst other things, getting hopelessly lost, almost drowning plus unbearable dehydration from the lack of food and water. Surviving miserably long enough to land on a beach somewhere outside Vietnam was itself a harrowing experience. In an effort to try and stem the never-ending influx of uninvited Vietnamese guests, on arrival at the coast of neighbouring South-East Asian countries, some authorities would merely give them food and water before sending them back out into the open sea, hoping that they would wash up somewhere else and become another country's problem.

Recalling that particular fateful day, Jung explained how he and the others experienced such deep emotions on finally arriving on dry land, believing that they had survived such misery, only to be sent back out to relive the nightmare. It was, he recalled, absolutely devastating and soul-destroying. And yet it was an experience they would encounter many times over on their journey to freedom, as they were sent back out to sea numerous times after arriving on so called 'friendly beaches'.

Having endured this harrowing experience once too often, those in the boat finally decided to go for broke. Jung and the others used their makeshift hatchets to carve small holes in the bottom of the boat. Sinking their lifeline to the bottom of the sea, they swam to the shore. On crawling onto the beach, the authorities had no choice but to take them in. The only problem was that they were then kept for months on end in camps specially built to house the 'boat people', which were full of untold crime and corruption, before they were finally given their freedom and allowed to lead normal lives in the world outside.

Jung told me that despite all he had gone through, it still paled in comparison to what he would have had to endure had he chosen to remain in his motherland. His love of America was evident, as were his daily prayers of thanks to his god for helping him get to the land of the free. He told me that the experience now seemed so long ago, and was buried so deep within him, that it felt as if it had all happened in a past life. But to my mind the scars of his experience could never completely heal, and would always lie dormant, waiting to be stirred awake to haunt him.

Despite trying many times to put myself in his shoes and imagine what he had gone through, I knew very well that no matter how hard I tried I could never fully understand his past suffering. My upbringing was within a wonderful loving family, the stuff of Santa Claus, Easter eggs, birthday parties, and the like, and it made me ponder what many of us so readily take for granted, but what is still a million miles from the experience of so many children across the globe.

I had a small tiff one day with the hotel's general manager while he was in the kitchen. It was a minor disagreement, and certainly nothing to write home about.

Yet on hearing about the argument, Jung, my Vietnamese friend, came to see me later that day.

He asked me very matter-of-factly, "Tell me, chef, do you want him dead or alive?"

"Who … what … dead or alive?" I answered, struggling to comprehend what I thought I was being asked.

"The GM, do you want him dead or alive?"

I immediately sat up and went and closed the door. When he asked me this question in a very serious manner, it had scared me, and the thought that he was seemingly wanting, and waiting for, a very serious answer scared me even more. I understood there and then that the scars of his past were not at all healed, and obviously could, at times, be very raw. The thought that he could contemplate such action on my behalf, and in response to such an insignificant occurrence, reinforced for me just how important it is for one's all-round balanced life, to have a normal, healthy childhood!

The following day, I decided that I needed a break from the action, and stayed by the swimming pool in my apartment complex. I put on my swimsuit and settled down by the pool, putting on my Walkman so that I could enjoy the sunshine and not be disturbed. After half an hour or so, I felt a tap on my shoulder which jolted me from my trance, and I sat upright. I took off my sunglasses and looked up to make eye contact with the person trying to talk to me. Despite the glare of the sun almost blinding me, I saw a chap with a girl who looked to me as if she could be his daughter.

He looked at me and asked casually, "Do you want to screw my sister? I want 100 bucks and you can have her for an hour."

The girl looked to be 14 years old at the most and just stood there, looking sad, scared and very lost. She stared at the floor, probably, I thought, praying to any god who would listen that I reject this seriously sick offer. I contemplated how best to answer the man who was obviously either desperate or not of sound mind.

"No, thank you. I am just enjoying the sunshine today, and I'm not feeling particularly well," was the best answer I could muster at short notice.

"Are you trying to tell me that there is something wrong with my sister?" said the man, angrily.

Here we go, I thought, this is where he makes out that I'm the bad guy here and he's just making me a normal, civil offer where, if I refuse, it would appear that I am insulting him and his family.

"No, not at all," I replied. "But I am married and if I play around, my wife will surely know. She has this sixth sense, you see? And I couldn't hide, or live with, this serious breach of her trust."

"Well, could you buy me some cigarettes, then? I'm desperate for a smoke," requested the monster. I jumped up and literally ran to the nearby shop, bought him the cigarettes and handed them over. I wasn't sure who looked the happier, the guy on receiving the smokes or the girl, now knowing that she had got a reprieve.

That night, every time I closed my eyes, I could see the young girl. I could not get her out of my mind and became quite restless. Unable to sleep, I decided to go and say hello to Abby, my Somalian friend at the 7-Eleven, and grab a couple of cold beers while I was there. When I arrived, there was a queue by the cashier's counter and Abby was doing his best to serve everyone as quickly as possible. In line next to me was a large Texan man wearing a cowboy hat, who was evidently becoming more and more agitated with the ensuing wait. Suddenly, another guy ran into the store, shouting obscenities at the top of his voice while brandishing a sawn-off shotgun.

"Give me all the money ... Now!" he demanded.

Abby reached into the till and passed over the bountiful sum of thirty-six dollars. The would-be robber looked at the paltry amount in the palm of his hand, and advised my scared-stiff pal that if he thought that risking the chance of being caught and getting twenty years in the penitentiary for this 'piss pot tea money', he was severely misguided.

"That's all there is, sir," explained Abby. "Every time I have fifty dollars I have to send it to the safe via a magnetic tube. If you look on the door it says that I never have more than fifty dollars in the till at one time."

"Wrong answer!" shouted Billy the Kid, and hit my friend right in the mouth with the butt of his gun. As Abby fell to the ground with his mouth full of blood, Billy the Kid aimed the gun at one of the drinks cabinets and let off one round, blowing the door clean off its hinges and spraying splinters of broken glass everywhere. The crazed gunman then ran out of the store with his loot, shouting, "Yee ha!"

I was so scared throughout this ordeal that I had stood rooted to the spot, unable to move. It was only after the gunman left that I slowly regained my senses, and I saw my friend standing, holding his mouth with the blood seeping through tightly clenched fingers pressed firmly to his face. I placed the beers I had taken from the fridge, which I was still holding, on the counter and asked if I should call the police. Before Abby could answer, the Texan cowboy, who had also silently witnessed the earlier incident, broke his peace to exclaim, "So you gonna serve me, or what? I have been waiting here for five minutes."

What the hell are you talking about? I thought. This man has just been held up at gunpoint and physically assaulted in a terrible manner and needs medical attention immediately. He has probably lost some teeth into the bargain, and all this clown wanted was to pay and go home.

This told me that it was obviously not so rare to see this kind of event, as no one seemed particularly shocked. In fact, Abby said that his shop had been robbed three times in the past month alone. This being the first time he had been hurt in the process made the event a little worse than usual, so he called the police. I stayed back to be a witness, and when the police eventually showed up, around two hours later, all they effectively said was that there was nothing much they could do unless they caught the guy 'red-handed and in the act'. So they bought some coffee and off they went for another cruise around – probably to disturb another poor chef on his way home, I thought.

Another of my interesting taxi experiences occurred towards the end of my time in Houston. I stopped a taxi in the street and before stepping in made sure, of course, that the driver was fully dressed. As everything looked above board, I climbed in and off we went. We were halfway home when, all of a sudden, a guy in a rather expensive-looking suit came running across the road, right into the path of our car. The taxi driver stamped on the brakes, bringing us to an abrupt emergency stop.

I then noticed that the well-dressed man in the street had both hands pointing out in front of him and was holding a handgun, like something akin to Nick Nolte in the movie *48 Hours*. I said to the driver in a quivering voice, "Be careful, big guy. Look, he has a gun!"

"Don't you worry, man," replied the driver, "mine's under the seat, and it's bigger than his!"

Was that supposed to make me feel at ease? I can tell you, the fact that we were also fully armed and just as dangerous as our would-be gunman did not make me feel any more comfortable. Luckily, the gunman ran off in pursuit of someone else, seemingly oblivious to our presence.

Some people, of course, are not so lucky, and instances like that where people become involved involuntarily in incidents, neither of their making or choosing, can sometimes take a wholly different turn, adding real weight to the phrase 'being in the wrong place at the wrong time'.

The prime-time evening news had a regular item on the 'top ten crimes list', which gave information on crime trends in the city. The programme would also give advice on 'do's and don'ts', for keeping yourself out of trouble and out of crime's way. For example, the crime list advice number ten might be, 'Never go down to an underground car park at a shopping centre without the help of a security guard employed by the shopping centre itself.' It was something akin to the Top Ten music charts, only based on the frequency of the crime in question.

Other gems I heard on this prime-time news were, 'When you stop at a red traffic light, you should always look straight ahead, and not to the left or right.' This was to avoid giving someone an excuse to accuse you of staring, which could lead to them getting out of their car and smashing yours, or worse. Also, 'Never stop to assist another driver whose car has broken down', for fear of them faking it and then robbing you; 'Never flag down help if you break down', instead, the advice was to lock your car doors and sleep in the vehicle until morning, and only then stop a tow-truck or police car for help since any would-be good Samaritans might themselves be the very ones who rob you. And again, 'If someone knocks into the back of your car, never get out to observe the damage', went the advice, as the would-be offender may have the intention of stealing it from you.

Every night, at the end of this Top Ten list, the newsreader would add some remarks, presumably intended to make everyone sit up, take notice and stay out of harm's way. Bearing in mind that this was early evening prime-time television, probably with children still watching and, no doubt, sensitive elderly viewers too, I cannot recall the exact words on one particular occasion, but it went something along the lines of: "And remember, ladies, there are monsters out there who will stamp out your life as if you were a cockroach. The only difference is they would not rape the cockroach first."

The coastline off Houston is renowned as very good waters for fishing, and one day, Peter, another chef at the hotel who was a friend of mine, and I decided to go out and try our luck. We arrived at the seafront and found a jagged pile of rocks that jutted way out to sea. Peter suggested we walk out on these rocks towards the end and fish from there, where the water was deeper and where we could hopefully catch bigger fish.

I can tell you, it took forever to get even halfway, as the rocks were very slippery and exceedingly sharp. At one point I slipped and fell, and started to slide in-between two large rocks which were separated by what was obviously very deep water. I stuck out my elbows and they caught the side of the rocks, stopping me from falling in-between. In the process, however, a large amount of the skin was grazed off my arm. Not a good start at all, I thought. As I pulled myself up I realised how crazy we were to be out there at all, and I demanded that we go no further, and that if we must fish, we do it right where we were.

So, we started to fish more or less at that point, and even caught a number of good-sized sea trout, which we tied to a holding rope, leaving them in the water to stay moist while we continued fishing. I had realised by now, that as the sun started to get very hot, there was nowhere to hide from its intensity and a good burning was on the cards. I remarked to Peter that we were going to get burned and he replied, "Yes, I know, the same thing happened the last time I was here."

"You mean you've been here before and didn't tell me to bring some lotion?" I said incredulously.

"No, because I forgot myself," he said, smiling. "Also, you know what else happened last time?"

"No," I said. "Why don't you share it with me. But let me warn you in advance, that if it is not something nice, like you saw a topless mermaid or something, I'm not going to be a happy man."

"No, nothing like that," said Peter. "It's just that a huge oil tanker passed by when we were out here and its wake almost knocked us off the rocks and into the sea. Not only that, but I want to tell you a secret which you must not tell anyone else though, because I am a bit shy about it. But ..."

At which point I cut in, telling him, "Get on with it, and tell me the bloody secret before I lose my cool and do something stupid and maybe drown myself in the process!"

"I can't swim," he declared, with a whisper, while looking to the left and then to the right, just in case someone might be listening, here in the middle of nowhere.

I swallowed deeply and wondered, as a lousy swimmer myself, if anything happened, how on earth I was going to help him, or for that matter, how could he help me? It also dawned on me that the pile of rocks we were standing on had been dumped there to protect the shoreline from the large battering waves it would otherwise receive!

"Let's go back to shore, right now," I demanded, and as we turned to pack up, my eyes almost popped out of their sockets. Some distance away, but very definitely coming in our direction, was the biggest and by far the dirtiest oil tanker I had ever seen.

"Oh, no. Big problem," declared Peter. He always had a knack of stating the obvious but this, I felt, took the biscuit.

"Quick, we have to go … Now! Leave everything," I shouted. Before we had gone but a matter of yards, the first wave hit us, luckily with no force at all. Did that mean the tanker was too far off and that was its best shot, or did it mean that this was the first soft wave and the rest was yet to come? We decided instead to make a stand now before it was too late by getting a good foothold and finding a suitable rock to hold on to.

I shouted, "Find a dry stone to get a grip on." But all the nearby rocks were by now wet and slippery, or worse, covered with damp moss, making it even harder to get a grip. By this time I was very scared, to say the least, and shouted again to Peter to stay still and maybe say a prayer or something because this was it; there was nothing else we could do.

The next wave came in with a bang and was very high. It went right over my head, taking my breath away as I swallowed a mouthful of salty water. Then another, and another; each time making it harder to get my breath back as I struggled to stay calm.

Our prayers must have been heard though, because eventually the waves became less frequent and less fierce, and gradually ceased altogether. I looked around for Peter and he was still there, looking drained and shocked.

"That was the same shit as last time!" he said, putting his hand in his pocket and pulling out a soaked packet of cigarettes. Before I could respond, he then hit me with a further gem. "Hey, where are the trout?"

I looked at him, flabbergasted. "Who gives a monkey about the stinking fish? Don't you realise we could have drowned?"

I started to walk slowly back to the shore; cold, sunburnt, wet and thoroughly fed up. To top it all, as Peter very rarely spent any of his own money, I now faced the prospect of having to *buy* fish from the market for our dinner with *my* money, as our 'catch' seemed to have eluded us.

"Same as last time," he declared.

I was lucky enough to be in a major north American city when one of their sporting teams, the Houston Rockets, won a major championship. In this case, the National Basketball Association (NBA) title. On the night in question, I remember I was watching something else on television, when I heard a lot of shouting and commotion going on outside. Hiding under my bed, fearing the worst, one of my staff knocked on my door. I crawled out from under the bed and answered the door to find one of my chefs standing there.

"Oh man, can you believe it?" he asked joyfully.

"No, I absolutely don't believe it," I replied, still wondering what the hell was going on. "Believe what?"

"The Rockets; they've just won the NBA title," came the ecstatic reply. "Where have you been, Mars?"

"Well, actually, under my bed, fearing for my life and thinking that there must be a riot going on."

"Man, there will be a riot, a big one, if you don't get your skinny arse outside. Let's go."

As we ran outside, it was bedlam, with everyone going wild. We drove around all night in his soft top sports car, with the hood down, screaming at the top of our voices and I didn't even know who the 'Rockets' were. If someone had asked me if I had seen the Rockets, I would probably have made a fool of myself looking to the sky. But it didn't matter as everyone was too far gone. And nobody asked anyway!

After living in Toronto, which had an 80-per-cent-plus occupation ratio of all apartments, driving the rental prices up very high, I was ready when I first came to Houston for a long, hard look at the rental market, before taking the plunge in choosing an apartment which suited my taste and budget. I recall arriving at one apartment complex, which was only fifteen minutes' walking distance from the hotel. I had no expectations at all on asking the supervisor if there were any units available, but was stunned by his reaction.

"Do you mean that you would like to rent a unit?" asked the supervisor.

"Yes, that's right. If there are any available." I could still hear my words hanging around the room, when he came running back to me with a cup of tea and chocolate biscuits. What was going on here, I wondered? This looked very funny, and I began to feel a little uneasy. Maybe the area was dangerous, or the building derelict, or already condemned. Maybe they have huge rats, or maybe it's just downright expensive. I was not sure which, but I knew something was not quite right.

The explanation, as I would learn later, was the terrible market blight, caused by the recession. Quite simply, people were not coming to live in Houston and many were leaving. Hence the excitement at a prospective tenant. It was very much a renter's market, to the extent that some unscrupulous people would rent an apartment, sign the nil-deposit contract and at the end of the month, when the first rent payment was due, disappear in the middle of the night never to be seen, or heard from, again.

People were desperate to rent their units. This was evident, when I was told that if I paid two months' rent in advance, I would receive the third month's rental free. Was this some kind of joke? I thought.

"And by the way," the supervisor added, "since we have problems in getting tenants to pay their rent on time, if you pay early you'll be eligible to enter a lucky draw, and the prize is the next month's rental free."

This all sounded too good to me. However, when the next rental payment was due, I paid two days early just for fun. I had to pay anyway, I reasoned, so what was the difference.

Two days later, there was a knock at the door while I was taking a shower, and I jumped out, dripping wet, wrapped myself in a towel and opened the door.

"Good day, Mr Saxon," started the supervisor. "Since you paid your rent early, we placed your name in the hat, and your name was drawn. Please sign here for your voucher."

I was given another rent-free month. Two months' free rental in less than four months! To round off the story, I later learned that I was the only person in the whole complex of over 600 apartments who had paid the rent on time, never mind early. So the draw must have been a little easier than I had first imagined!

The best, and worst, food concept that was ever conceived and which has gone on to eventually become one of the most universally successful ideas of all time has to be … the buffet. Once in a while there come along some clowns who make you wish that you never had even heard of the concept 'buffet', let alone have one in your hotel.

After cooking up a storm all day to prepare the most extensive spread, we were unfortunately having a very slow night. As I was wondering what I was going to do with all the leftover food and at the same time balance my books, up to the entrance strolled a group of five what can be mostly described as sumo wrestlers.

Here comes trouble, I thought to myself. As soon as they walked through the door (sideways, I might add) it was evident that these people were die-hard buffet eaters, who were the worst possible customers imaginable for this concept. They were going to pay thirty-five dollars and make very sure that they got their money's worth … and more. They would eventually eat you out of house and home and, if they became regulars, would inevitably place you out of business and have you begging in a food line. The word 'bankruptcy' was the first thing that came to mind when I heard one of them say, "Good evening, chef. Would you mind if we had a look at your buffet?"

Trying to talk them out of the buffet was, of course, a waste of time. Trying to convince them to order à la carte, where the portions were controlled to be fair to both parties, was even more a waste of breath. After circling the buffet like a flock of vultures, they stood still for a second while trying to fathom whether it was worth the price. I closed my eyes and chanted, à la carte, à la carte, à la carte, like a mantra of sorts. Then came the depressing and moral gutter-lowering words that would emotionally scar me for years, "I think we will take the buffet tonight."

After this night, I knew that I was going to need some professional counselling, but I tried to hold it together as long as I could for the sake of my staff. I walked over to my cooks, whose heads were already hanging in total despair after hearing the verdict. In trying to lighten the situation that was ready to blow like a powder keg, I whispered to them: "A herd of grazing wildebeest just arrived, and they love the look of your buffet. You'd better tell the other chefs to start cooking before those guys start eating, otherwise you will never be able to keep up! How many people did you cook for tonight?" I asked fearfully.

"Fifty, chef," they sheepishly replied.

"And how many customers did we have before this bunch of twits arrived?"

"Seven, chef."

"Well, the food's not going to be enough, we are in deep trouble tonight."

After the big guys wobbled over to the buffet counter, I was absolutely flabbergasted with the way they went through the buffet like a plague of swarming locusts, devouring everything in sight. We had the chefs inside cooking up a storm and service staff running back and forth trying to keep food on the table, but to no avail. I wandered over to their table to exchange some pleasantries. As I reached their table, they had already started to wind it up. One of them rubbed his very round tummy, and his trousers really looked stressed holding in his mid-section, the buttons were clinging on for dear life. At any time, the buttons were going to give way and go 'twang', shooting across the room like buckshot fired from a gun and maybe take out someone's eye.

"Chef, the food is not as good tonight as it usually is, I think that some of your guys are off their game," said the one in distressed pants.

"You mean to tell me that you have been here before?" I was totally shocked.

"Yes, many times, we are regulars."

I stormed away from the table looking for the manager, and explained to him that actually he should have banned these people from coming here.

"We can't do that, chef. On what grounds can you ban people from a buffet?"

"If you go to any casino," I retorted, "and you continuously win, they ban you. Correct?" I was really trying to make up my own logic to oust these grazing beasts. "What is the difference here?" I asserted. "They beat the establishment every single time they come here by reducing the restaurant to the poverty line, and what is worse, we let them do it without a whimper."

I saw one of the guys motioning for me to go over, so I trotted back to their table. I thought the best way to diffuse the situation was to distract him, so before he started out, I butted in. "Where are you from, sir?" I asked, hoping they were going to announce they were moving to another state.

"Texas," replied the WWF wannabe. "I know that you may be surprised, but I can assure you that I am from here."

I thought to myself, I am not surprised because you are the size of Texas!

"Why don't you try the chicken curry, chef, it is not so good," he said while slurping a small-sized oyster. As he tried to swallow it in one go, he shook his head back and forth like a penguin swallowing a wriggling fish.

"I would love to, but there is none left as you have finished off the whole lot," I said matter-of-factly.

"I beg your pardon!" said the Penguin, spraying dark brown juice from the oyster all over his new John Wayne T-shirt. "There was not much there anyway, just enough for …"

"Fifty people, sir," I interjected.

"I am a growing young man and need to eat properly," he said, defending himself. I could not help but think to myself that he could not possibly want to grow any more and that his buffet-table-sized backside did not need any further encouragement. I rolled my eyes, anticipating a request for a discount. "Actually," he said sheepishly, "I think that the buffet is not value for money."

I called it right – I saw this coming a mile away. There is always one that will start to complain from the start, to build his case to rob you blind like a robber without a gun.

"What is wrong with the food, sir?"

"The buffet is not that good and definitely not worth what you are charging."

"Can you be a little more precise? Is the roast beef overcooked, the seafood not fresh?" I asked, trying to retain my composure.

"No, the whole buffet is no good," was his only assessment.

"Well, we are only charging you thirty-five dollars for the buffet, and you have eaten," I closed my eyes as if ringing it up on a mental cash register, "around fifty-five dollars worth of food!" I then opened my wallet and gave him five dollars.

"What is this for, is it a discount?" he asked with a look of surprise.

"Actually it isn't, I figure if I pay you to go and eat somewhere else I can save us some money." He looked at me astounded for a second, and then he started to howl with laughter.

"Chef, you are the funniest guy I have ever met. Go and eat somewhere else! I have changed my mind. The entertainment is fantastic here, you have just made us customers for life!"

As I walked away from the table, I looked at the manager who was in tears after watching me crash and burn. The worst part was that after I left the table I realised the twit had very discreetly pocketed the money I offered him. Three hours later, when the buffet was destroyed, they moved on to dessert. The only thing that was not consumed was the water from the ice-cream scoop holder. After three gallons of piping hot Italian coffee, they were ready to go and asked for the bill. I told the waiter that I would like to take the bill over myself, to bid them good riddance. I went over to their table, a broken man, devoid of any energy as the battle had taken its toll and wiped me out.

"There, there, chef, you look tired," one of them said emphatically.

"Yes, I surrender, it's over – you win," was all that I could muster. "I have never, ever seen people eat like that before, you guys are record breakers. I will probably loose my job, but what the heck."

"Lose your job? What are you talking about? This is the best dinner we have ever had, we get this size because we like to eat good food. It is a compliment to you and your chefs that there is nothing left and, trust me, the customers tomorrow are going to be happy when all the food that is presented is fresh." I looked at him and reflected on the truth of his words. Big people like to eat and it is a compliment that they choose your place to do so. When considering food cost, overheads, value-for-money factors and recipes, we sometimes overlook that the most important thing to remember is that eating out should be an overall dining experience with good food and service, filled with entertainment and fun. If the overall ambience combined with the food and service is just right, you will always come out on top in the end. So now, before I go out to face that pain-in-the-neck guest, I always remember to think to myself, it's show time!

Living and working in Houston in Texas was an extremely positive and valuable experience, one which I would not trade for all the tea in China. It taught me diligence, self-care, and how to adapt to a very different culture and lifestyle from that which I was used to. Yet after a couple of years there I knew it was time to move on, and I was fortunate to be offered a fabulous position and the chance to move to the Bahamas. I had heard the commercials which declared that 'it was better in the Bahamas' and I wanted to find out for myself.

The day after being offered the position, I went to see the Houston hotel's general manager but he did not want to accept that it was time for me to move on. He started to assume what he thought was the real reason for my wanting to leave, and somehow came to the conclusion that it was to do with the crime and firearms situation in Houston.

"I know you English are not used to the fact that we carry guns here," he went on. "So I am willing to buy you a special gun for protection and to help you feel more at ease."

Ironically, when he said this, it actually served to confirm that it really was time for me to move on. I had enjoyed myself immensely during my time here, but if I had to live with a gun in my pocket, then somewhere else, preferably a white sandy beach with crystal-clear warm water, was calling my name ... loudly!

I gave three months' notice to enable the hotel to find a replacement and do a professional handover, and allow me to make sure that the golden girls still enjoyed their lovely, generations-old recipe, orange sauce. After telling my new friends at the Houston bar, which had become my 'local', of my impending departure, they decided to hold a party to end all parties as my goodbye treat.

When I arrived at the party thrown in my honour, the security guards at the door asked me if I had any firearms. On saying "No," they let me in, and as I passed the cloakroom, I saw a rather large pile of assorted firearms on full view – makes a change from umbrellas, I suppose!

The night was a great affair and the guys really made me feel that I would be missed. I was the only 'gringo' in the whole place, but by then it was already starting to feel completely natural and something that did not really catch my attention any more. By the end of the night, I was a little tipsy, and Walter, the manager who had welcomed me so charmingly on that first night, came to say goodbye in his own heartfelt way. He gave me a hug and asked me to come to the storeroom for one last toast, and said that he also had something to show me. I followed him to the storeroom, not suspecting anything since everyone was acting normally and the whole night had been so lovely.

As we stepped in, he closed the door behind us, locked it, and turned on the light. It was just him and me now, I thought, and I wondered all the more what the heck was going on. Had I offended someone? I pondered. Just then the manager pointed to something and, as I turned round to see what it was, there stood a gorgeous, tall, beautiful woman clad only in underwear, stockings and suspenders.

"She is your goodbye gift, Mike. I want you to know that you can do anything you like as everything has been taken care of," said Walter, with more than a twinkle in his eye. "But first," he added, "I want you to stand next to her so I can take a photo for your future memories."

As I stood next to her for the photo, he was still at it, telling me to do something interesting for the camera. I knew I was really in a terrible position now, as I had no intention of doing anything at all. Nevertheless, I put my arms around her and kissed her on the cheek.

"Oh man, you gotta be kidding," came the immediate response. "I could have taken that shot outside!"

I just stood there, not knowing what to do, and at that moment, my would-be companion grabbed my head and buried my face in her cleavage and the shot was taken. As he left the storeroom the woman started to take off what little she was wearing. I gasped: "Please stop, I just want to talk to you, if that's alright."

"Yeah, man, that's up to you," she said, "since he done paid me already."

We then sat down and talked for about an hour, and I could not understand why this beautiful, intelligent woman was doing this nonsense. One thing I knew for sure though, was that I was not going to risk my life and spoil the night by asking her!

She was even very sweet in offering to save my face on our exit from the room. As we stepped out of the storeroom, everyone began clapping and cheering as she announced what a handful I had been.

"This man is hotter than a handful of Mexican chilli peppers on a midsummer night in Texas … You guys have got nothing in size when it's hanging next to this huge, English blood sausage," she proclaimed, to the whoops and delight of those assembled.

When I was leaving the club, they all slapped me on the back and told me how much they respected me as a man. I smiled and proffered my thanks, but was all the while praying that they were not inclined for me to show them my now famous credentials.

The next morning, I decided to have a last walk around the block before I said goodbye to Houston, and I stopped by the roadside for a cold drink. At the side of the road was a small stream, which grew larger whenever there was a downpour. Just as I was enjoying my final moments in the town, I heard a rather large splash coming from the water.

I strolled over to the stream and saw the largest snapping turtle I had ever seen. Around the large turtle were hundreds of smaller ones, and the water was teeming with other wildlife, such as frogs and lizards. This unexpected sight was in the midst of the downtown area, just a few minutes from my apartment and I'd had no idea it existed during my time there. This was a lovely way to say goodbye to Houston. I gazed at the wildlife for the short time I had left, before departing for the airport and my flight to the Caribbean.

IV

YOU AIN'T GOT NO ARSE!

WORKING IN THE Bahamas was a non-stop merry-go-round of action and everyday dramas. Looking back, some of the incidents were funny, some were very definitely scary, others had a happy side and, as ever, some were sad, but all, I can assure you, are true.

I was fortunate enough to be appointed sous chef of what was then the largest hotel in the Caribbean. It had a total of 1,200 rooms, 12 restaurants, banqueting suites for 800 people, and the capacity to host huge functions in the garden, at the beach and in the banqueting suites – simultaneously, if required.

The hotel had a huge casino, Las Vegas style, to cater for the many Americans who would come across for a weekend of gambling, sand, sea and whatever other kind of fun they hoped for. Bahamians, and those with a resident permit in the Bahamas, were not allowed by law to gamble. And besides, the casino dealt only in US dollars, making it that much more difficult for locals to partake. My guess was that the government was worried about supporting peoples' families in the event of them losing their pay cheques playing blackjack.

Arriving at the hotel, I had a couple of days off before starting work. This enabled me, as the executive chef suggested, to settle into the local lifestyle first. The first night in my new abode I decided to venture downstairs and have a drink at the bar in the casino. It was a very long and elegant-looking bar, made from very expensive carved wood. The first thing that caught my eye, being young, rather naïve, and single, was that the waitresses were dressed in bunny outfits, strutting their stuff in high-heeled shoes and fishnet stockings. What's more, all the drinks served to people playing at the tables were complimentary as long as you gave the girls the customary tip.

Anyway, as I was sitting at the bar, I could not help but be mesmerised by the scene. I had never seen so much action going on under one roof at the same time before. I knew instantly that this place was going to make me grow up in a heartbeat. I also resolved to myself that I would just have to try to relax and enjoy the ride. However, no sooner had I formed this view, than my first jolt of reality came at me like a lightning bolt, reminding me in no uncertain terms of where I was and what the score was in these parts.

I had obviously become used to the very quick pace of the US, where people shout at each other in strange languages through wound-down car windows when stuck in traffic jams, and I had clearly not yet adapted to the slower pace of my new environment. As a result, I was starting to get a little frustrated over the seemingly interminable time it was taking to get my first beer. So I decided to offer my view on the matter to the admittedly huge waiter who was supposed to be attending to me.

"Excuse me there, big guy, is my beer anywhere near ready?" I asked.

"Just one minute, sir. I will be with you shortly," came the reply.

I waited for a couple more minutes and watched him wipe his metal drinks table, at a speed which bordered on going backwards. I had, of course, encountered people who were not in much of a rush before, but this guy was in a near-comatose state, and I thought if I did not remind him a second time, I would either die of thirst or of old age.

"How are you doing there, big guy? Any beer will do," I added, hoping that the hint would be taken. I looked at him and he glanced back, appearing to be just a little rattled as he approached me very slowly, like a bear appearing out of deep hibernation. He leaned forward, crossed his arms, placed both elbows on the bar in front of me and stared right into my eyes.

"Are you on holiday, sir?" he asked, glaring at me with a Mike Tyson-like pre-fight stare. My life passed before my eyes. I couldn't tell him I would be working here for fear of making a very special enemy so early on. I mean, I had only just got there. My bags were not even unpacked.

"Yes, I'm on holiday," I mustered. "I just arrived from Texas."

"Well, heaven forbid that you have to wait five minutes for your beer there, cowboy," came the scarcely veiled, menacing reply. One could by now cut the atmosphere with a knife.

"You're absolutely right," I said, wanting to diffuse the atmosphere. "Five minutes will be fine. In fact, you can take ten if you like. I'm in no hurry at all."

"Now, you just sit there like a good little boy and I will be with you when I can. Is that alright, JR?"

"Yes, fine," I said, knowing full well that I would be lucky to be drinking anything at all now. Nice going, cowboy, I muttered to myself.

So off the barman sauntered to finish wiping and polishing his bar, so nicely in fact that he was able to slowly and accurately comb his hair in the reflection.

A few minutes later, when he had finished doing what he 'had' to do, he managed to locate a clean beer mug and finally went to pull my icy draft beer. But as he pulled the handle, the beer barrel jerked, spitting out nothing but brown foam from the pipes and splashing the barman's newly pressed shirt. The barrel was empty.

I guessed at this point that the beer was just not going to happen. What, after all, were the chances of the barrel finishing just when I wanted mine?

The Tyson lookalike turned to me and winked. He told me that it might take 'a few minutes more' as he did not have a back-up barrel, and would have to go and get another one. I considered offering to go and get the barrel myself, but thought better of it when I relived his not-so-warm stare.

When I did finally get my beer, it was the best I have ever had to wait half a lifetime for! And yet, this eventful first evening was still not through.

Halfway through my long-awaited drink, a lovely, elegant-looking, middle-aged woman came and sat beside me at the bar. She smiled and asked if she could buy me a drink. I laughed and mentioned that I would love a drink but did not think that she could manage the epic feat it might involve.

As she ordered the drinks from the barman, the thought occurred to me, on what basis was she buying this drink? It was too late to say no as the beer was already ordered, although chances were that I could be in my room, fast asleep by the time I would actually get to enjoy it.

Our conversation was going well and I was just starting to relax and lose my paranoia, when she very openly asked me if I would like to entertain her that night. She went on to explain that her husband was a big-time lawyer in Miami and was always too busy to give her the attention which she felt she deserved and needed. Whenever her pleas for attention became too much, her husband would give her a wad of 'green backs' and send her packing, so to speak, to the beach. While there she would usually find some young man to give her the attention she required and on this occasion she had somehow taken a fancy to me sitting there, all on my lonesome.

Being inexperienced as a part-time gigolo, I explained that this would not be possible as I was a member of the hotel's staff and could be fired for less. As I said this, I quickly glanced over to see if the barman was listening, as my not admitting to work at the hotel had spared me earlier in the evening, and I was now fearing that if I told many more 'white lies', I would get myself thoroughly mixed up.

As something of a token face saver, I offered to pay for the drinks that were somewhere on the way. She agreed, and off she went, presumably to hunt another prey, leaving me to finish both drinks, which I had not particularly wanted in the first place.

Well, this *was* a happening place tonight, I thought. I had come close to an altercation for asking for my first beer, and almost been laid in the time it took me to get the second! It was all too much to swallow in such a short time, so I decided to call it a night and try to get back to my room without any further dramas.

Just then the barman re-emerged, looked around for the woman who had been sitting with me, and laughed.

"You're a popular guy tonight," he declared, "a real bundle of chuckles, I must say … Where's your sweetheart? Run off after she smelt your body odour, did she? Here's your bill, Romeo."

And that just about summed up my first night in the Bahamas. Fright, humiliation and ritual embarrassment, all in one evening.

They say in this part of the world that there are two main days of the week, 'payday' and your 'off day'. During your off day you generally try to recuperate mentally and physically, in order to place yourself in good stead to handle the next week, and your pay day was what made it all worthwhile.

Working as a chef in this Bahamas hotel was not easy, if you did not want to play the game by the staff rules. Luckily that was something I did not have to learn the hard way. An example of this was that due to the hot weather and the negotiated union agreement, all staff would be given two cold cans of whatever liquid refreshment they liked … even beer, each day. As a staff member, you could drink it, sell it, or pour it down the sink – the choice was yours. But if, as a manager, you did not give your staff their due drinks, heaven help you.

We had a new French chef who started the same day as me and he decided that since his staff were already paid a salary, they did not deserve the free drinks, especially without any correlation to their effort or need. On making his observations, he announced that starting the next day, drinks would only be given to those staff members whom he decided had performed admirably.

The following day, the executive chef took me along to peep at the French restaurant's kitchen. Lo and behold, there was 'Inspector Clouseau' running around the kitchen on his own, no other staff in sight. Everyone had called in sick to teach him a lesson.

The lock on the drinks cupboard was, of course, promptly reopened and the French chef had to go to the beach to find all his staff and beg them, one by one, to return to work. By which time, of course, the 'price' to settle the argument had increased to three cans instead of the customary two.

Sometimes in this industry, you have to go with the flow, as working against the grain gets you nowhere. Unfortunately, this chef learned the hard way.

My working hours in the Caribbean were typically from three o'clock in the afternoon until 11.30 at night, six days a week. Which day off I took really did not matter, as every day effectively had the same rhythm in this tropical island resort. So every morning I had to make the terrible choice between fishing, snorkelling, sunbathing, or just sitting with a cold drink looking at – well – topless women. Then working exceedingly hard every night, which was followed by going out for a drink, before repeating the whole process again the next day.

The beaches were the nicest, cleanest stretches of sand I had ever seen. Their natural, tropical beauty was the like that I had not seen on television or even in pictures. However, despite the near-paradise quality of the environment, my first day of work brought me down to earth with a very large bump.

No sooner had I stepped into my designated kitchen than I was met with the words, "Hey, whitey, what's up? Man, you're the skinniest white arse I ever saw. We're going to have to do something about that."

I looked at the guy who had greeted me with such refined charm but kept quiet waiting for someone else to jump in. Another person announced, "Hey, Gumbo, you be scaring him, man. He'll be leaving before we can break him in. Leave him alone."

Gumbo looked at my would-be protector and said, "Why don't you get on your hands and knees and kiss my arse. Not on the right side, nor on the left side, but right in the dirty arse middle!"

Then they all started laughing out loud, before drifting off, leaving me standing there, looking like a prized lemon.

The executive chef decided to take me round to introduce me to the crew in the kitchen I would be in charge of and the first guy we came to, as chance would have it, was the already infamous Gumbo.

I looked at him and joked about us already being friends, having been introduced earlier. This must have cut some ice as we did, indeed, go on to develop a good, though jovial, working relationship. He showed me many of the famous Bahamian seafood dishes – the island is abundantly supplied with all types of different fish and shellfish. This, in itself, attracts many tourists who want to try the large conch – the most famous Bahamian shellfish of them all, and the most-often-prepared food in the islands. It is cooked in many different ways: scorched conch, cracked conch, steamed conch, conch chowder, conch salad, conch fritters and even roast conch. They are all delicious.

My mentor was also a great advocate of crawfish, which also appear on many Bahamian menus. They are boasted about as being straight 'from the sea to your table' and are usually as fresh and tasty as they claim to be. Breaded shrimps, grouper fingers and spicy potato salad, all support menus that are healthy and make creative use of the natural resources of the region.

One day, the chef explained to me that we had a very rich Middle-Eastern oil sheik staying at the hotel, and that he was a 'money no object' kind of guy. The situation which followed with the sheik was a quick lesson in what this place was all about.

The sheik had reserved the entire top floor of the hotel, consisting of over forty rooms. Most of the rooms were for the different women from around the world who he had flown in to join him during his stay in the Caribbean. He would also decide, often on the spur of the moment, that he wanted to have a barbecue on the beach, even at four in the morning … And he expected the full works to be laid on. We would invariably have to provide a whole lamb on a spit, hips of rare roasted beef and dozens of other dishes, salads and cold meats, in the middle of the night!

At the drop of a hat, the whole kitchen would be turned inside out to accommodate his wishes. Parties would be held for all the women, his friends, staff, general entourage and all the rest of the groupies who managed to gatecrash the events.

On one particular occasion, while I was grilling meat on the barbecue, an English woman came over to get some steak and say hello. She stood talking to me for a while and explained that she was one of the sheik's guests staying on the top floor. She confided that she was being paid $2,000 a day for the twelve days she was there, and as he wanted all the women to always look their best, they were also given an additional sum to go and buy clothes. What's more, this was her fourth year as a guest of the sheik in the Bahamas and she had still to be formally introduced to the big man himself. Now there was a good deal, I thought.

At another of the sheik's beach parties, I saw a young boy around 14 years old, selling T-shirts. The top man himself came over to speak to the boy.

"How many shirts do you have?" he asked.

The boy, looking very surprised, told him of his 'forty pieces of fine, top quality, hand-painted, light and cool, Bahamian cotton shirts'.

"How much do you normally sell these for?" asked the sheik.

The boy thought for a second about how much he could ask for and get away with, without spoiling the prospect of a sale, and said, "Usually around twenty dollars each."

The sheik glanced at him for a second, smirked and reached for his money pouch. He announced, "I will take them all for thirty dollars each, if you agree to go around and deliver them to all my friends on the beach."

The boy, who would normally be happy with the sale of perhaps two or three T-shirts for no more than ten dollars, was now getting ready to party, and the look on his face said it all. He could not believe his luck, and was running around the beach trying to fulfil his end of the deal so that he could get his hands on the loot and run home to tell his parents as soon as he possibly could.

At least this brash show of wealth had done something positive and the young boy would no doubt go to bed happy that night, even if no one else on the beach appreciated their T-shirt or gave a thought about what it represented.

I recall another one of life's less happy occasions working as a chef in the Caribbean. It had been a very busy day and we had just finished serving a huge dinner for around 1,200 people in the garden. The band was in full swing and as our part of the culinary festivities was just about finished, I went and sat with the chef in his office to quietly reflect on what had been achieved that day. Just then we heard a commotion going on outside in the kitchen area. We came out of the office to find two young female staff members in full swing.

I later learned that the two women shared a common secret with the rest of the hotel, namely that they had both fallen in love with the same man – albeit at different times – and both bore his child. Every week, on payday, a drama would ensue over who should get what of his salary. Sometimes, if he did not want to share his money with either, he would hide, telling his friends to answer the phone in his absence and to say that he was not there.

One of the women was 'lucky enough' – depending on how you look at it – to still have the man concerned in her life. The other, possibly jealous, and certainly put out by this, would start to squabble over him and sometimes it would get a little out of hand, as it was starting to on this particular day. The chef had explained to me that we had to keep an eye on them. He had tried to get one of them transferred earlier but the union would not allow it, as neither wanted to give in and lose face.

The two protagonists were now starting to push each other. According to the chef, this was a usual occurrence though, and there was nothing to worry about. Despite this assurance, one of the women lost control and picked up an empty glass and threw it across the kitchen at her rival. The glass smashed on the metal table, inches from the other woman, and the shattered glass sprayed her arm with splinters, leaving a nasty gash on her arm. She shouted with pain and shock as blood started to pour down her hand onto the floor.

"Is this also normal?" I asked sarcastically, scared to death at what I had just witnessed and wondering what was going to happen next.

I held my arms in the air, to try and broker a peace, and asked them both to calm down and back off from each other. Even that was too late, as they again went at one another, pulling hair and trying to scratch each other's eyes out.

With each swing, the blood from the already-cut arm sprayed everywhere, all over the nearby walls, onto the floor, and even splashing the ceiling. The girls were thumping each other so hard, I felt every punch as if I were receiving them. It was now totally out of hand. Both were crying and there was blood everywhere.

The chef at last entered the fray, shouting at them to stop and trying to intervene physically. At this point, one of the women reached into the sink where all the unwashed utensils were and grabbed a large metal mixing bowl, still dirty from the night's action. In the general melee, she swung her arm and caught the chef square on the nose with the mixing bowl, with such force I swear I heard his nose crack.

The dirty leftover contents of the mixing bowl sprayed across my face, but my immediate thought was that I, at least, could wash this off, unlike the chef who I wagered was going to find it difficult to even wipe his face tonight. The chef fell to the floor like a ton of building bricks dumped out of the back of a truck. He was out like a turned-off light and completely motionless. But even this did not have the desired effect of stopping the free-for-all wrestling bout.

Fortunately though, the combatants were getting tired, and in their weary state one of them slipped in the puddle of gathered blood, dragging the other over with her. The first woman landed heavily on the tiled floor, banging her head and covering her hair with blood. The other fell on top of the first, and they both squirmed around on the floor like two crazy people in a bath of blood.

At that point, mister lover boy, who had heard about the fight through the hotel's 'news network', came running to try and pull his little harem apart. The two women were now totally exhausted and seemingly had nothing left to offer this unofficial championship bout. The man stood between them and told them not to move. Standing opposite each other, gasping for much needed air, one of the women leant forward with both hands on her knees, trying to fill her lungs with oxygen.

I was just thankful and relieved that it was all over, when suddenly the woman bending over straightened up her body and, in doing so, while the other woman was not looking, sucker-punched her. It was a punch any title contender would have been proud of. It struck her opponent square on the chin with such force it knocked her head back, banging it against the wall and completely turning out her lights. Her knees just buckled as she fell to the floor, back propped against the wall, eyes closed, fast asleep. The contest was very definitely over now.

Typically, the security guards arrived when the show was all over, and took the two women away. Both would later go to hospital for treatment.

As the hitherto unconscious chef stirred to life, I helped lift him to his feet and immediately realised that he, too, was not in good shape. So we sent him over to the same hospital. I also knew that sadly, and likely as not, both women would be fired the next day, and that we would now be short of two valuable staff members.

To my shock and great surprise, both were there at work the next morning, laughing together as if nothing had happened. Apparently, they did not want to press charges against each other and had kissed and made up. The union and the hotel had then made some kind of deal to save them their jobs. Lover boy's name was never mentioned again, and so the whole story was brushed under the carpet. That night, the two women left work together in the same car, and it was as if the incident was a mere figment of my imagination.

We used to get multi-national corporations bringing incentive groups from the US to the Bahamas, and since they would spend a substantial amount of money, it made them very important customers to the hotel. We once had a very well-known computer company come for Christmas, bringing their top staff with their families to our tropical island resort for the festivities. They had a huge, very extravagant Christmas Eve buffet, catering for 800 people, with no expense spared.

The decorations on the buffet tables alone took us all day to arrange. We had butter sculptures, vegetable and fruit carvings, as well as local artefacts and traditional decorations. There was a huge fruit display for the dessert and many other Christmas goodies scattered all over the tables making it a buffet to remember. Onlookers were popping in and out of the ballroom all day to check on the developing masterpiece at its various stages of construction.

Finally, it was time to start to lay out the food. Typically, this is around an hour or so before the arrival of the guests. First came the dozens of cold platters of everything one could possibly imagine, then the array of mouth-watering desserts and finally an endless procession of kitchen staff, rather like a chain of ants, carrying out the hot food.

We managed to finish before the arrival of the first guests and just had enough time to walk around and do the last-minute checks and to reflect on what could be done better or differently next time. Such was the display that some of the staff took photos to be used for their resumes or, indeed, just as a keepsake.

We were all still standing by the buffet, admiring our work with a real feeling of pride and satisfaction, considering our mammoth all-day effort to prepare it and get it ready, when suddenly out came a cook from the kitchen area, shouting and screaming. We all looked at him and laughed, thinking the excitement must have really got to him. Not wanting to cause a scene in the ballroom, and since he was new to the job and not very well known, everyone just ignored him, thinking he would soon go back into the kitchen. Gradually, we filtered back into the kitchen to get ourselves ready for the evening's onslaught, when this time the banqueting manager came running in, shouting and waving his hands.

"It's ruined, all ruined," he cried, pointing to the ballroom.

"What's he talking about?" I asked the chef, as everything was as perfect as it could be only moments before. When we went out to the ballroom to see for ourselves, we knew instantly that we had a huge problem. There was a very strong smell of bug spray pervading everywhere – the kind you use to kill cockroaches and other delightful creepy crawlies. The unknown cook had evidently run around and sprayed the entire buffet with the stuff, rendering it totally inedible, before disappearing and leaving us in the lurch just as the guests were starting to arrive for their pre-dinner cocktails.

We had barely thirty minutes to do the impossible, and try to salvage the function which had taken us the best part of the day to prepare. The only course of action, after quickly calculating our options, was one of damage control. So we ran around collecting all the spoilt food, taking it back through the kitchen and dumping it into the now overflowing rubbish bins. We cleared away all the lovely table decorations, changed all the tablecloths and made a new buffet with the back-up food we had intended to use for refilling the original buffet.

Miraculously, we somehow did all of this in the time it took the guests to have their pre-dinner cocktails, but the price to be paid was a sparsely decorated, poor-looking buffet, with a measly selection of food. What a stark difference it was from the earlier spread and an absolute heartbreaker when we saw the looks on the guests' faces as they entered the ballroom. Instead of expressions of admiration for our culinary skills, they had looks of deflation and disappointment, if not disgust. We later found out that the new cook who had caused this upset had had a nervous breakdown and that he had been taken to the local mental hospital for treatment and rest.

Some days after this catastrophe, the executive chef sent me over to the hotel next door to ask the boss there if we could borrow some equipment, as we had another large group coming in and our gear might not be sufficient for us to cope. Hotels often help each other out by borrowing cutlery, tableware and even foodstuffs, as needs or emergencies arise. The problem with this system is that after a while all the various hotel equipment gets mixed up, and if you sit down at a banquet, you could have a knife from one hotel, a fork from another, and a spoon from a different establishment yet again.

I entered the next-door hotel's kitchen via the back door and saw one of the biggest women I had ever seen in my life, standing in the middle of the kitchen. She stood there with her hands on her hips, looking totally unamused at my untimely arrival. She looked like a huge bronze sculpture. Her forearms were wider than the thickest parts of my thighs, and I am not even going to get into how big her thighs were, save to say that the Fijian rugby players at the Hong Kong Sevens paled in comparison to the natural size of this woman.

She looked hard into my eyes and asked me the daunting question, "And what can I do for you, young man?"

Now, I had been caught a few times with that question in my younger room-service days, so I felt I had to choose my words carefully in reply.

"Actually, I just wanted to speak to the executive chef, madam. Is he around?" I proffered.

"Are you trying to be funny, my little friend, because if you are, I would strongly advise you to be careful. Otherwise, I may have to personally introduce your face to the kitchen floor," she responded.

Feeling more than a little put-out by her less than helpful response, I replied somewhat gruffly, "Listen here, I'm very busy. Is the chef here or not? Can you call him for me as I need to borrow some equipment."

"Is this equipment important to you, boy?" she countered.

"Yes, it is, and I would be pleased if you didn't call me 'boy'," I said. "Anyway, why do you ask?"

This incredible ebony hulk raised her arms in the air and roared like a lioness at the top of her voice, "Because I am the executive chef. What the hell do you want?"

Her voice was so loud and powerful, its sheer force took my breath away. I stood bolted to the floor and, after my pathetic attempts to apologise for my thought-less assumptions, I explained what kind of equipment we needed to borrow and when we would give it back. We had helped them out before, so the feeling between the two hotels had been friendly. I only hoped that after my undiplomatic encounter that the relationship was still good. Fortunately, for me, it was still intact. I grabbed the gear, placed it in the car and went back to the kitchen to say goodbye.

Perhaps to rub in my predicament, or maybe just to be friendly, the executive chef asked me if I was new to the Bahamas. When I said that I was, she asked me if I had been given the customary welcome hug.

"Welcome hug?" I repeated. I looked across at her giggling staff, and before I knew what was happening it was too late. She grabbed me and gave me the biggest, breathtaking, bone-crunching hug I have ever had. It seemed to last forever. When she finally let go of me, I gasped for air as if I had just come to the surface after escaping from a sunken ship.

As I made towards the door, to make my quick and greatly embarrassed exit, she shouted after me: "By the way, whitey, I gotta tell you man, you got the smallest arse I ever did see!"

This, I concluded, was my just desserts for my earlier thoughts about her size, and for my dreadful faux pas in not recognising her as the executive chef. Fair-do's, I thought.

One fine payday, I was so pleased to receive my own cheque that I handed out the pay cheques to all the other staff as soon as I received them. The cooks all looked so surprised and happy that it made me wonder what I had done different from usual. After a few seconds, I remembered the chef telling me never to give the staff their pay cheques before the banks close. He had explained that if you gave them their cheques while the banks were still open, they would invariably go during work time to get their money and, likely as not, some would not return until the following day, and then usually the worse for wear after a drink, or two, or three …

Vainly, I asked them to give me their pay cheques back but it was already too late. Before I could say 'I am in the shit', they were down the street on their way to 'the house of big money'. I waited for a while until the banks closed to see if they would return, and then had to go around the beach in front of the hotel searching for the missing staff. Eventually, I found them getting ready to party under a coconut tree, and knew that this was going to cost me big time.

There was no way that I could manage the hotel functions that were planned that night on my own, so I knew the 'inducement' for them to return to work was going to have to be substantial. In the end, I had to go to the hotel storeroom and take out four cases of beer to get these guys to agree to come back to work.

A further part of the price paid was that when I went along to the storeroom with the requisition to get the beer, the storeman took one look at it and said very matter-of-factly, "Don't tell me, you gave them their pay cheques too early! You clowns will never learn," he chuckled. Then he started to look at the floor around me with a puzzled expression.

"What's wrong? What are you looking for?" I asked him.

Quick as a flash, he replied, "I thought maybe your arse had dropped on the floor, but I don't see it anywhere. Do you know you ain't got no arse?"

I shrugged my shoulders and said, "Can I have the bloody beer or not?"

"Hey!" he continued, to his own great amusement. "There's no point getting angry with me, man. It ain't my fault you ain't got no arse."

If there is one thing I learnt about the Bahamian sense of humour, it is that they are very proud of their full, round and curvy bottoms, and that they would take every possible opportunity to let me know how small mine was.

We did an outside catering contract for a wealthy local company, and while they had a pretty normal dinner buffet, they had a very unusual 'open bar'. This meant that the guests at the event could order whatever liquid refreshment they wanted during the evening and the company would settle the bill at the end of the function. The company would have to trust whatever the hotel calculated as the drinks consumption for the evening, as there was no other way to work out the costs.

The hotel decided that the best way to control this situation was to set up a mobile bar, loading up a small truck with every kind of alcoholic beverage imaginable. The company's organiser would witness its loading, and on its arrival back at the hotel, the returned bottles would again be counted in the presence of the company's organiser, and the used alcohol charged accordingly. We knew that at the site of the function, the staff on duty would probably, and illicitly, drink some beer, and a little of the harder stuff too, but we thought this would not be too difficult to control. The organiser accepted a little leeway in the stocktaking and on this basis we had a clear understanding on how we would proceed.

Off we went to the party, placing solid trust in the guy we had put in charge of the bar, and we were very pleasantly surprised when he refused to give the other staff at the party anything to drink at all! At last, we thought, someone trustworthy. It was nice to see. We felt comfortable with what was going on with the bar, so were able to go about our business on the cuisine side with added assurance.

At the finish of the function, we set off to go back to the hotel, but somewhere along the way managed to get split up from the booze truck. We drove around for a while in the hope that we could rejoin it but could not find it anywhere.

Arriving back at the hotel, we asked if the truck had already arrived and were told that it had not been seen at all. So we decided to go to the house of the person whom we had put in charge of the bar and entrusted with the truck, to see if he was okay. When we arrived at his house, the scene was like something out of a comic Hollywood movie.

The same guy, whom we felt was so trustworthy, had the back of the truck open, and was shouting at the top of his voice to the people rapidly gathering around.

"Whisky, ten dollars. Gin, ten dollars. Vodka, ten dollars. Brandy, ten dollars. Any drink you want, ten dollars."

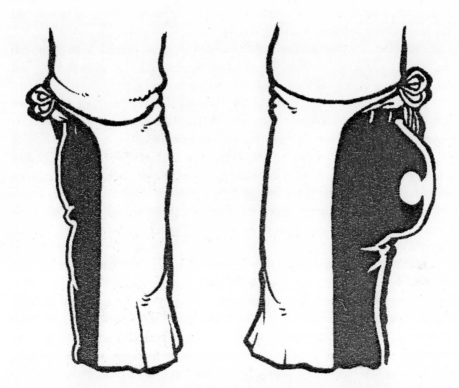

On receiving the due ten-dollar payment from a grateful customer, he would literally throw the bottle of booze through the air to the waiting arms of the would-be party animal who immediately slipped away into the nearby shadows.

We watched the goings-on from a safe distance and tried to think what we should do. There was obviously no way we could get the booze back, and the money he was selling it for was certainly not going to settle the bill. This guy had dug himself into a deep hole, so we resolved to let him settle it on his own. We quietly drove away and went back to the hotel, announcing that he was nowhere to be seen and left the others to await his return.

When he did eventually show up, as he was opening the truck to allow the stocktaking to be done, I could hear an imaginary drum roll in my head. Just wait until they open this thing and see that almost all of the bottles were gone, I thought. This is going to be memorable!

As the back of the truck went up, all the assembled staff looked at one another in shock. On observing a near-depleted truck, which at its outset had been stocked full of every conceivable liquor, the bar supervisor immediately turned to the booking company's representative and said, "I'm so sorry, there seems to be some kind of mistake here."

The company representative's response, however, was one of reason and good grace. "Oh, I don't know, there were a lot of people out there. I mean, how would you know how much they drank?"

After the counting was done, the company's organiser agreed to settle the bill and the deal was done. The hotel's good name and reputation had been saved by the reasonableness of this one individual, or so we all thought.

On the way home that night, in the shadows of a large casuarina tree, I am sure I saw our infamous barman sharing his stash of loot with the all-too-reasonable company's representative. Or was it just my imagination?

We were in the kitchen one night, when the wife of one of the waiters called by to see her husband. The other waiters had been giving him a hard time for months about his being henpecked and bullied by his new wife, and I could see he was getting fed up with it all and desperately wanted to prove himself to his chauvinist tormentors. He looked very surprised to see her, but rather than being happy, his face changed to one of rage.

His wife was a very pretty, tall and elegant woman who, probably on account of being newly married, I imagined, might simply have wanted to tell her husband how much she loved him. Since the waiters worked such long hours, it was not rare for loved ones to show their face, to say 'hi' and to ask their partner when they expected to finish work. However, on this occasion, the waiter was very angry indeed, and I guess in some way felt embarrassed that his wife had come to work to fetch him, in front of his so-called friends, the very ones who gave him such a hard time for being 'henpecked'.

Anyway, he walked up to his wife, in quick step, presumably wanting to save face, and started to shout at her at the top of his voice.

"You see this," he said, reaching down and grabbing his 'wedding gear' with his right hand. "This is a dick. I got the dick, you got the pussy. That means I'm the boss of the house. Now you go home, clean the house, cook the dinner, put on something sexy, and I will be home when I am ready."

His poor wife was speechless and totally humiliated. She turned round and left in tears. The kitchen was so deafeningly quiet you could hear a pin drop. Though as soon as she stepped out of the room and the door closed behind her, all his macho friends broke into rapturous cheers. There were numerous high-fives and lots of backslapping.

"And you all say that I don't have a way with women," he boasted. I was disgusted with the whole show. It actually made me sick to be a man. I could not help but think, you'd better enjoy this brief moment, my friend, because you still have to go home and face the real music, and that is going to last a lot longer that the five minutes of glory you think you have now. She may have let him have his moment, but goodness me, I thought, I would not like to be him come closing time.

We had a European chef, Karl, arrive to join us at the hotel and the executive chef asked me to take care of him. Karl came with the reputation of being something of a 'hard case', so they assigned him to take care of the toughest kitchen in the hotel. I showed him round for the first few days until he settled in, and since we got along reasonably well, I tried to explain to him that some of the staff were themselves quite battle hardened and that he should take care a little.

"They may be tough, my friend, but I am tougher," was his adamant response.

Famous last words, I thought, but only time would tell.

A few days into Karl's appointment, the executive chef asked me what I thought, and I told him that everything looked to be going okay. A week or so later, I passed by to check on our newcomer, and he looked a little uptight to me. He had a way of standing in the kitchen with his hands behind his back, like an army general, watching every move of his staff. It seemed that no one had told him that this kind of intimidating management style had thankfully died a long and painful death, many years ago.

Not surprisingly, Karl was soon given the nickname by the staff of 'Rottweiler' on account of his aggressive approach. A further indication of what the staff thought about him was that they would sometimes shout, "Aye, whitey, where did you find this clown?" Or else they would simply point at him, shake their heads and laugh.

A couple of weeks went by and being consumed by work, I had not seen or heard from Karl until one morning when I was driving to work. I was about five minutes from the hotel, when I saw someone come running down the street, with a suitcase in each hand. I quickly realised it was our newcomer fleeing from the scene, as if the island had been hit by a newly erupted volcano.

"Hey there, big guy," I shouted after him, "where's the fire?"

Seeing me, he responded, "You guys are all nuts to stay here. You can kiss my arse goodbye. I'm going home."

As we at last drew level with each other, I still in the car and he walking, or rather running, I explained to him that it was a twenty-mile run to the airport and that in this heat, even without the suitcases, it would be difficult. With the full suitcases, he could just forget it!

He literally begged me to take him to the airport, to the extent that I knew I was looking at a seriously desperate man. So I took him. I did not see the point in trying to persuade him to stay if he was so desperately unhappy.

For the remainder of the day, I acted as if I knew nothing about Karl's departure and stayed mute on his whereabouts. Until, that is, the chef informed me that he had received a phone call from Karl who was at the airport and about to leave the Bahamas. I, of course, quickly pleaded ignorance to the whole thing.

"Did you know he had left, Saxon?" asked the chef.

"No, chef, I would have told you if I had known," I pleaded.

"That's funny," the chef said. "Because he told me to thank you from the bottom of his heart for the ride to the airport. Funny thing that …" And off he went.

I could not believe it. A seemingly good act on my part had turned bad on me. I had to keep a low profile after that, until the chef finally realised that what I did had actually been intended as an honourable gesture on my part. Even so, the temperature only cooled when he managed to find a suitable replacement for the poor departed soul.

———— ◦•◦•◦ ————

We were preparing a seafood extravaganza in our restaurant and needed to find an eye-catching way to promote it. I racked my brains on how to sell this to the locals and tourists alike, but could not come up with anything imaginative. The next day I went down to the local seafood market to see if there were any good photo shots we could use, but there was nothing much doing at all.

Still desperate for an idea, that night, as I sat in my apartment, as luck would have it, I browsed through a fishing magazine I had borrowed from another chef. In it I saw a photo of the biggest tuna fish I had ever seen. There was a guy standing next to this monster specimen, holding his fishing rod, presumably signifying that he had caught this beast single-handedly with his very ordinary-looking rod. A flash of inspiration came to me straightaway.

The next day, I took the magazine along to show our art department and our in-house computer wizard to ask them if they could somehow replace the real fisherman's face with mine. They said they could, and the game was on. We recreated a photo of me with this huge tuna and sent it to the local media, subtly implying that I had caught it in the harbour on a boring Sunday afternoon. We went on to say that it was a great way to make sure that our seafood was the freshest it could be, while also keeping costs down, and that if people came to the hotel for our seafood extravaganza they could taste this beautifully fresh tuna for themselves.

The newspapers picked up on it and gave the item full coverage. We fielded calls all day asking about the huge catch. I was a local hero, for a short while at least, though in reality more for my imagination than anything else. The evening the story broke, I was driving along the harbour near my home. I saw dozens of fishermen out with their rods trying, I presume, to catch their own big tuna. I must admit that I laughed all the way home, but consumed by guilt, called the executive chef that same evening and explained that we had taken the story as far we should. So we decided that we would hold a press conference to announce, or rather renounce, our hoax.

Fortunately for me, and for the hotel, everyone took it in a humorous and light-hearted way and the promotion was a roaring success. Even months after the incident, and despite my coming clean, I would be walking in the street and people would shout out, "Hey, there's the tuna guy. But look, he ain't got no arse!"

Perhaps I viewed the Bahamas through rose-coloured sunglasses but life there was by far the best I had ever experienced up to then. It really is a true tropical paradise, with pristine beaches and clear water teeming with colourful corals and an abundance of marine life. With its near-700 islands, some of which remain totally uninhabited, the only way to reach the more outlying islands is by a small seaplane, which enables you to hop from one island to another.

This is a land where even the regular taxis are often stretch limousines, where houses are painted pink or other glorious pastel colours and never seem to discolour due to the lack of pollution in the atmosphere. This is the land of the conch shell, where a glance out to sea might reveal dolphins jumping around in their natural habitat. This is also the land where most of the general population love reggae music and worship Bob Marley as a huge cult figure, and, as if to prove this, drive around in their cars with Bob Marley's 'Buffalo Soldier' blaring out at a deafening level.

There is a KFC outlet in Nassau, the capital city, which boasts of selling more chicken per capita than anywhere else in the world. This is also a land where a hungry man is an angry man, and a horny man is worse still.

Having sex and boasting about how good they perform is something of a national pastime. 'Grinding', as the rudiments are called, is a term frequently used in common parlance. For instance, 'I am going home to give my woman a good grind' would be a fairly typical way amongst some Bahamian men of saying, 'See you tomorrow'.

Bottoms and their relative size are the real national obsession in these parts. People talk about each other's bottoms with a lot of admiration, fondly calling them 'bungies' – except for my bottom, of course, which was so small it didn't count!

Almost every day I had off from work I would spend at the beach, as it felt as close to being in paradise as one could get. I would take long walks that would find me on stretches of white sandy beaches without a single soul in sight. The notion of having your own private beach is not too difficult to find in the Bahamas. When I found what I regarded as mine, I would often sit there for hours just looking out at the sea, trying to imagine that I was on a desert island – it was that easy.

One day, I decided to take another of my long solitary walks. Having already walked a good way, I climbed over some rocks and jumped down to the other side, landing at a lovely secluded beach cove. I stood there admiring the view, with the waves crashing onto the rocks, sending a delightful cooling spray over my face, when suddenly I heard a friendly voice from behind me.

"Hi, what's your name?" the voice called.

As I turned round to say hello, I saw sitting there in a secluded spot on the beach four of the most gorgeous women ... all of them stark naked. Not a single stitch of clothing between them, and it took me by total surprise, I can say. They even invited me to come over and sit with them for a while, which I did. We chatted for a few minutes – which believe me, was no easy feat, as I had real difficulty in looking straight at them. I was so embarrassed I didn't know where to look.

No doubt, sensing my bumbling predicament, one of them asked if I was shy, and that if I was, I shouldn't be, as they were used to men staring. They explained that *Playboy* magazine had flown them to the Bahamas so that they could get nice all-over suntans for the photo shoot they were going to be doing. Tan lines were not only out of the question but would very likely get them kicked off the shoot. So here I was, getting a somewhat reluctant eyeful of what other men were going to pay good money for, and having good conversation as well. For them, it was nothing out of the ordinary, and they added that as long as men treated them with respect and did not become cheeky, they were quite happy for them to look, but not to touch.

During the day, the beach was a beautiful place, but at night if you strayed too far from the protection of the hotel, you could step into some funky goings-on. From ladies of the night, drug dealers and robbers, to young lovers with nowhere to go, these were just some of the hazards one could encounter on a night-time stroll. Some of the hotels even went as far as to advise guests not to leave the hotel grounds at all after dark.

A group of us decided one New Year's Eve to have a midnight barbecue on the beach by our house. It all started out fine, and everyone was in good spirits and well behaved. A few of the staff had been there a lot longer than the rest of us and had by now seen it all. There were also two couples among the group, where for some reason the wives had not taken a liking to each other.

With the festivities over, but the night far from finished, one thing led to another and a few of the old-timers decided that it was time for them to go skinny-dipping, and show us newer ones how to have a good time. This got me more than a little worried as there were some big fish in these waters and these party animals were already pretty drunk, so I sat on the beach and watched the clothes for fear of them being stolen, or in case anything happened to those in the water – well, that's my story, and I still stick by it.

They were all in the water, making a lot of noise, splashing and carrying on, when suddenly one of the men started to struggle. He had obviously drunk too much, so the others decided to bring him in. Back on the shore he found a spot to lie down and, unsurprisingly, quickly fell asleep. Another of the couples started to argue and went back to their room. By now the evening was starting to unravel and in danger of fizzling out, so we decided to call it a night.

The drunken swimmer's wife, who just happened to be the mortal enemy of the wife of the couple who had gone off bickering with each other, decided to go back to her room and leave her husband to sleep it off on the sand. However, the wife of the other couple, not knowing the party was over, came back to find only the drunken guy fast asleep. But as the drunken guy woke up and went back into the water once again, she worried about his welfare, or so she claimed, and decided to jump in and make sure he was alright.

Once in the water, his drunken state soon dissipated, and he grabbed the woman and started to get naughty. Just when he had both hands on her breasts, his wife, feeling guilty that she had left him to sleep on the sand, returned to take her husband to bed. As she arrived at the beach, all she could see was her husband in the process of 'getting it on' with 'the enemy'.

Seething with rage, she waited for them to return to the beach, at which point World War Three broke out. Another crazy fight erupted, with much shouting and screaming, not to mention the scratching and pulling of hair. The altercation was so loud that everyone else came running out of their rooms to see what was happening. The two protagonists were eventually pulled apart, and once things had calmed down, we all went our separate ways, finally calling it a night – or so we thought.

We were rudely awakened, however, at around three-thirty in the morning, when we heard a blood-curdling scream coming from the apartment of the guy who had fallen asleep and then got lecherous. In the dash to get to their apartment, we really feared that he had maybe hit his wife, or worse.

When we reached the apartment, we found her alive but soaking wet. The crazy guy, it seems, had gone and got a big bucket and filled it full of ice cubes and sea water. When his wife was finally fast asleep, he had thrown the contents of the bucket all over her. Unlike the previously mentioned scrapping kitchen staff this duelling duo did not forgive each other. Instead, this wife took the first flight out in the morning, rounding off a very eventful and not so enjoyable welcome to the New Year.

Making friends when you move from location to location and working such long hours is not easy in this industry, but I managed to make some good friends while in the Bahamas, most of whom worked in the hotel's casino. Included amongst my friends were some of the women from the cabaret show at the casino. It was a million-dollar production and could be compared favourably to any show offered in Las Vegas.

One day, my dancer friends asked me if I would like to go to a pool barbecue at their house, and they could introduce me to their friends; perhaps I might meet someone I liked. They asked me to go to their house at around ten o'clock, by which time the party would be up and running. I thought all day about what I should wear, and could not decide if I should wear jeans or shorts. I desperately wanted to fit in and maybe meet a nice girl whom I could hook up with, so getting my dress right for the party felt like an important decision.

I arrived at the party a little late and it was already in full swing, with everyone actually in the pool. Despite agonising about what to wear, I had not thought to bring a swimsuit. I was just contemplating what to do when some of my friends saw me and started to shout, "Come on in, it's great."

There were around forty people in this huge, partially lit swimming pool when I feebly announced to the crowd that I had not brought my swimsuit, to which they all laughed.

"You don't need a suit," someone responded. "We don't have one either!"

This time I looked into the pool below the water line, and suddenly realised that they were all naked. I couldn't believe my eyes.

By this time everyone was cheering and shouting, "Off, off, off!"

Now if you have ever been to one of these parties, I would imagine it would be easier to get naked when everyone is doing it at about the same time, then no one pays much attention to what anyone else is doing. The problem was the whole crew was now watching and waiting to see what I had to offer.

I had a dilemma and, in my fear, my imagination ran wild. If I had a huge pecker, I imagined I would be the envy of the party. On the other hand, however, if I was not so well endowed, they might all laugh. I thought about it, weighing up the choices for what seemed like an eternity, but was probably in reality only a few seconds, and made the best decision I could at such short notice. I went home.

The next day, everyone was calling me 'the small boy' for my lack of guts, or whatever else they wanted to insinuate. But I did not care. I knew I had a nice arse.

After realising that no girl was going to want to come anywhere near me after the famous pool party, I took up fishing instead and had some great fun. Dennis, one of the croupiers from the casino, had a boat and he asked me if I wanted to go out fishing with him. It sounded like a good idea, so off we went. We went quite a way out to sea, so far in fact that I started to get nervous, as it was beginning to get very choppy.

We went out to a place they called 'the tongue of the ocean'. We aimed a very powerful spotlight down into the water and the flickering light seemed to go down forever before it finally disappeared in the very deep waters. Starting to trawl, it was not long before we had what seemed like a very big bite. The boat was at this point already rocking as a storm was coming in. I asked Dennis what sort of fish he thought he had on the line, and he said, "You'll soon see."

Dennis must have pulled and tugged for at least twenty minutes, strapped into this wooden-backed, stand-up chair, with a leather harness. During the struggle, I happened to look over the side of the boat, only to encounter one of the scariest sights I have ever witnessed. There was a huge shark coming up alongside the boat.

I shouted to Dennis, "It's a shark, and a bloody big one as well."

He looked confused. "What are you talking about? Our fish is still way out there. It's nowhere near the boat."

I looked over the side again to see another, and another. The water was teeming with these things and some of them were very, very big. The struggle had attracted the schools looking for an easy dinner. The storm was getting worse, the boat was swaying back and forth, and I was scared to death. So I shouted to Dennis to let it go and let us go home.

"Are you crazy?" he said. "This is a monster. I have never had such a fish on the line," showing his obvious delight with a "Yee ha!"

Was this guy nuts or what? These sharks were big enough to eat us, and we were playing with goodness knows what he had on the line.

Dennis pulled his would-be catch alongside the boat, just enough for us to see what it was.

"Oh shit," he yelled at the top of his voice. "It's Uncle Tom!" I looked over to see a huge hammerhead shark, and it was looking really pissed off, I can tell you.

So here we were, the storm was now getting very bad, making the boat rock back and forth, with the possibility of our falling into the water and becoming dinner for these huge fish all too real. I was already feeling seasick, sunburnt and very scared, when Dennis suddenly pulled the shark to the side of the boat and shouted, "Quick, lean over, grab it and pull it in."

My reply was swift, calculated and straight to the point, especially since the other sharks had obviously smelt blood and sensed the death of one of their fellow species. I somehow managed to find the nerve and the strength to hold the fishing rod in place while my adventurous friend brazenly pulled in the catch. There in the bottom of the boat lay 'Uncle Tom', wriggling around like a crazed animal, and I immediately felt remorse and sorrow for this wonderful creature. It was around five feet long, and I wondered how many years it had taken for it to reach such a growth.

"Look at this wonderful fish," I said. "Look at how helpless it is out of the water, lying on the bottom of this boat."

It was gasping for air and finding nothing but breathlessness. I asked Dennis to return it to the sea. He joked about how many wallets he could make from it and how nice he thought the jaws would look hanging on his bedroom wall, and then stopped laughing when he looked at me and could sense my seriousness.

I was his guest, he said, so the choice was mine. Together we picked the shark up and threw it back to its natural environment, and watched it quickly swim away. Almost instantly, the rest of the sharks disappeared, realising either that their meal had escaped them or that their captured friend had been released.

It was now time to go home, so we turned round, aimed the boat for the island and headed towards the distant lights. As we neared the shores, it was a great feeling to be able to see the bottom of the sea once again. Every small colourful fish was now easily visible from the side of the boat, and so we decided to drop anchor and have a cold drink, reflecting on the experience we just had.

As if to cap the evening, or maybe in my relief at having made it home in one piece, I was clowning around. I grabbed hold of the anchor and jumped overboard with it. I thought that because the water was not deep, and the anchor not that heavy, it would be a fun thing to do after our experience out in the deep. Unfortunately, the water was around twenty feet deep instead of the seven or eight feet which I had expected, and the weight of the anchor quickly dragged me to the bottom. The shock of going down so far made me swallow about half a gallon of salt water, which made me throw up for the next half an hour. My just desserts, I reasoned, and probably how the shark must have felt when it lay on the bottom of our boat.

We sometimes used to go down to the harbour, and sit there listening to music with a picnic basket and fish all night; talking and laughing as we fished until the sun came up the next morning. We knew that there were some funky things going on in the harbour and some scary characters passing through, but felt safe in numbers.

One night we heard a boat chugging slowly up the harbour, as if it was just passing through on its way out to the other side. All of a sudden, the passing boat shone a very large beam of light at us, completely blinding us, and I sensed that we had unfortunately become people who were in the wrong place at the wrong time.

We heard one man shout, "It's alright, it's just some clowns fishing. Leave them alone." They continued to pass by slowly, with the engine almost silent, clearly keeping their whereabouts secret to the harbour patrol. As they passed us they dimmed the light, and I saw two men looking at us, each holding some kind of large automatic weapon.

This was the first time it felt like a pleasure to be called 'a clown'. In fact, I wanted to say to him, 'Thank you, sir'. We later learned of gunrunners, pirates and drug smugglers who sometimes slid through the harbour at night, making it quite a busy and dangerous thoroughfare.

Paradise or not, like anywhere else, there were some less desirable things going on in the Bahamas, and one time we heard that there had been a very serious crime committed against some tourists and the news was already filtering out, scaring people. With tourism the biggest foreign revenue earner, the islands could ill afford any bad publicity, especially concerning the safety of American citizens – their largest group of visitors numerically and financially.

On catching the culprit of this particularly serious crime, the police who had already beaten him black and blue, paraded him across the island and even strolled him right through the packed hotel casino during its peak hours. This show was evidently to tell other would-be criminals that crimes against tourists would not be tolerated, as well as to let the tourists know that the authorities were coming down hard on offenders who threatened their safety.

I was watching one guy losing so much money at the casino one night, and knew he was having a very bad run. But I had no idea just how bad it was. At the end of the evening he called over the casino boss and asked if they operated any house rules to provide assistance to someone who had lost a serious amount of money, to enable them to settle their hotel bill and catch a ride to the airport to get home.

The casino boss promptly asked, "How much have you lost, sir?"

"Four hundred and fifty," came the reply.

"No, sir, for $450 I can do nothing, I'm afraid," said the casino boss, with something of a smirk.

"Actually, I mean $450,000!" said the gambler.

The casino boss instantly dropped the smirk. "Right this way, sir," he beckoned. I later learnt that all the gambler's hotel bills were waived, that he was sent to the airport in a stretch limousine and, of course, put on VIP status for the next time he arrived. The funny thing in all this was that the gambler did not look particularly upset. His expression was more that of someone who had experienced an inconvenience.

For a part of my time in the Bahamas, I rented a large white house with a lovely garden. As beautiful as the house was, it was not uncommon for the lights across the whole island to go out for hours at a time. Not surprisingly, opportunist criminals would use this time to the fullest, to do their thing. The hotel had emergency generators, so they did not have to worry unduly about this, but at home it was different, and it was pitch black.

One night when the lights went out, I was at home on my own. I lit some candles and waited for the lights to come back on. Sometimes they were out for an hour or so, sometimes longer. But this night they stayed off altogether. As I was sitting there, looking at the candles shimmering, I was startled to hear someone moving about in the garden. I quickly blew out the candles, and ran round the house making sure all the doors and windows were locked.

I contented myself that I had by luck rented a house with bars on all windows and doors, so I knew there was no way in for whoever it was outside. Unfortunately for me, these particular uninvited visitors were either very persistent or none too bright, as they smashed every window in the house, one by one, trying to find a way in.

I thought about letting them know I was there, wondering if it would scare them off, or would it have the opposite effect, and prompt them to stay there all night, making threats to me to open the door? It was a very long night, I can tell you, until they finally got fed up and left in the early hours of the morning. The owner of the property was none too happy either, so I just told him that I had been out and found all the windows broken when I got home!

The bridge that separates Nassau from Paradise Island is a long, two-lane toll bridge that humps way up in the air to allow boats to pass under. Walking over the bridge to work before I bought a car was quite a hike but very good exercise – although I did not always think that way while doing it.

One day while walking to work, I arrived at the foot of the bridge and saw a long line of cars clearly going nowhere fast. Many of the drivers were evidently ticked off, as they were continuously and very angrily blowing their horns in frustrated protest. I started the steady walk up the bridge towards the top where the toll booth was located, and the scene there was even worse. People were out of their cars, shouting and pushing each other. It was not only a bad scene, it was also a dangerous one, as the drop from the top of the bridge to the water below was a long one, and these were very deep waters besides.

As I stood there, watching the drama, I began to understand what the whole thing was about. It appeared that one driver had the regular habit of driving to the top of the bridge and, on getting to the toll booth, would feign that he had forgotten his money. The attendant would have no choice but to allow him through. Today, however, she lost her patience. He had pulled this trick once too often, and the result was mayhem.

The driver had gambled that the attendant would always want to avoid the mess which was ensuing, but this time it seemed she wanted to teach him a lesson, and would not let him through until he paid. Dozens of drivers were now out of their cars, gesticulating and shouting; a few were even offering to pay the guy's toll themselves. But the attendant stood fast and refused, saying it had to be his money and no one else's. I stood there, watching the incident unfold, and could not help laughing to myself, as it was such a comic mess. Even the police did not want to get involved with this now very angry attendant. The deadlock was only inadvertently broken when the attendant saw me standing there with what must have been an inane grin on my face, which I was desperately trying to wipe off.

"Hey there, no arse. How's it hanging?" she called after me.

"Oh, not bad," I said. "But you seem to have a situation here today. How are you going to settle this one?"

Quick as a flash, she replied, "Well, I'll tell you what. If you agree to bring your sweet self here tonight and take me out to dinner, I may feel the goodwill to let all these clowns off the hook and allow them to cross the bridge."

"Why not," I answered. "I finish around ten o'clock tonight. I'll see you then."

And as I started to walk down the other side of the bridge, making my way to work after the morning's entertainment, some of the drivers were cheering and whistling to me as they drove by, presumably thanking me for my valiant Horatio-like effort to 'free the bridge'. It appeared that I had given her a way out of the situation, saving her face at the same time. She could now act as if she was still tough, and that she had settled the problem merely because she had a date. By the by, the dinner and the company were both great.

Near my house there was a small chicken farm, and apparently every day some of the chicken blood would leak into the nearby coastal waters. Local people repeatedly warned me that I should never swim in, or near, this stretch of water. It was held that a couple of large sharks could occasionally be seen lurking around these waters, trying to figure out where the blood was coming from.

One day, I was feeling a little bored so, somewhat mischievously, I called one of the other chefs and asked him if he wanted to go fishing near to the chicken farm just for fun. He explained that since his spear-fishing accident he never went near the water … ever.

"What spear-fishing accident?" I asked.

"I don't really like to talk about it, but since you are intent on going fishing for those monsters, I'll let you in on a little secret … Keep well away from those things!" He went on to explain that he had gone out one day to do some spear fishing and had speared a lovely large grouper. Using the old-fashioned spear system, where the spear was not tied to a rope, it meant that he had to go into the water and retrieve the fish himself. So he jumped overboard and dived the short distance to the bottom to pick up his dinner for the night, whereupon he got the shock of his life.

As he was retrieving his fish, he saw a huge shark coming his way, presumably having smelt the blood from afar. He immediately dropped the fish and started to swim like hell back to his boat. After finishing the appetiser, the shark wanted to have its main course and came after the chef.

Reaching the surface, he was horrified to find that he was further away from the boat than he expected and he started to swim, literally, for his life. As he was swimming, his poor wife, who was waiting in the boat, was desperately screaming for him to swim faster, as the huge shark's fin had surfaced a little further away. The gap between him and the shark was narrowing, and his wife was frantically crying and shouting for help.

Just as he was pulling himself up onto the side of the boat, assisted by his wife, the shark reached its prey, opened wide and went for his legs. The shark's jaws grazed his left leg, catching the flipper he was wearing, tearing it off and leaving a deep gash in his leg. He lay at the bottom of the boat, gasping for air, as his wife cried uncontrollably. His dice with death could not have been closer.

I listened intently to the story but didn't know whether to believe him or not, until, that is, he pulled up his trouser leg to show me his eight-inch-long scar trophy. Madness, I know, but despite this gory tale, I still went fishing next to the chicken farm anyway – albeit on my own. Indeed, because I was alone, I have no proof of the following story, but I swear it happened as I am about to explain.

Perched on the bank of the shore near to the chicken farm, I placed a large piece of squid on my hook and threw it into the water, then sat down and opened a cold beer. I had the radio playing softly and was enjoying my solitude. Suddenly, I noticed my fishing rod moving – I had placed it on the ground with the tip hanging over the edge of the water – and just as I went to pick it up, thinking it must be a bite, it started to be dragged along the ground.

I chased after it, scurrying along the bank, and finally managed to pounce on it and get a good hold. I pulled the rod to me and realised that I had a very big fish on the line, and since it was moving quite slowly, wondered whether it was maybe a large snapper or grouper. Even holding the rod in my hands was hard work as the fish was very strong and heavy. After about ten minutes or so of struggling with whatever it was, I managed to bring it closer to the side of the bank where I was standing. I looked at it and, sure enough, it was an absolute beauty – a lovely red snapper. I was just about to lower my net to pick it up, when this huge shark came from nowhere at an incredible speed and grabbed my dinner.

As the shark opened its mouth, it made a loud, terrifying noise and was splashing around as it grabbed my fish and took off with it. What the heck was I going to do now, I thought, as my reel was spinning out of control with the run of the shark? I quickly stopped the reel, hoping that the line would break and that I could at least save my rod. Unfortunately, the line did not break, and I, being stubborn, held onto my fishing rod as if my life depended on it.

I pulled, and the shark pulled. Back and forth we went. It must have looked quite funny, with me standing there talking to myself, trying to save my rod.

"Oh no, you're not going to take my rod today, my friend," I shouted. "This bloody thing cost me a bomb, and by the way, how does my dinner taste, you son of a gun?"

After a long and painful fight in which I was getting absolutely nowhere, the line finally broke with such force it sent me reeling back onto my bottom. I sat there for a while, feeling somewhat proud of myself that I had not lost my fishing gear, but also silently making a pledge that the chicken farm was very definitely out of bounds for me from now on.

One of the most endearing stories for me happened towards the end of my great stay in the Bahamas and helped me leave on a high and happy note.

One afternoon after I had officially completed my last working day at the hotel and was enjoying my remaining free time, I decided to make a visit to the casino. Unbeknown to me, an elderly couple had walked in with a few dollars to gamble and not having any expectations, or even knowing how to throw the dice or the general rules of the game, they asked the croupier how to play. He explained the basic rules to the beginners, and the elderly gentleman started to throw.

I was sitting a few tables away, and when he started there was only himself and his wife at the table. About a half an hour later, a crowd had started to gather and people were beginning to cheer. I stood up and walked over to see what the commotion was all about and saw the elderly gentleman's wife crying. She was telling him to stop now and that they should go home and keep the money they had already won. The husband, however, wanted to throw a few more times and kept on shouting, "All or nothing." He kept on throwing the dice and just kept on winning. Soon there were dozens of people shouting and cheering as the husband announced that this was the last throw. "All or nothing," he said, for the umpteenth time, and he blew on the dice, shook them in his hand, and threw.

"Craps," said the croupier, disbelievingly.

I could not believe my eyes. He hugged his wife and they were both weeping tears of joy. Everybody was cheering and screaming at the top of their lungs. Even the casino boss, who had already taken the opportunity to grab the publicity by taking plenty of pictures, congratulated the lucky couple.

This lovely golden-years couple had come to the casino with just a few dollars and no real gamblers' knowledge, and had beaten the odds hands down, walking out with almost $350,000 and a security escort to boot. It was a heart-warming end to a great and fun-packed year of my life that I will never forget.

Towards the end of my contract in the Bahamas, I was offered a job in Lagos in Nigeria. I had to have various inoculations within a short period of time – yellow fever, cholera, typhoid, tetanus, and goodness knows what else – which made me feel very ill, and taking the malaria pills made me feel constantly drowsy. I also started to hear terrible stories about life in Nigeria that unsettled me somewhat, and I had plenty of second thoughts. Literally, on my last day in the Bahamas, just as I was getting ready to leave for Lagos, I received a strange phone call, quite out of the blue.

It was someone unknown to me asking if it was true that I might be looking for a job. I said maybe, and they asked me if I would like to come to Hong Kong. They wanted to know when I could start, as the position was currently available. I had never felt so lucky, and so blessed as at that moment. I immediately accepted the offer and cancelled my plans to go to Nigeria, booking instead to go east to Hong Kong.

As chance would have it, I subsequently heard that the chef who had filled the void that I had left in Nigeria was hospitalised for some seven months and almost died with a severe case of dengue fever!

On my last night in the Bahamas, my work permit had expired, which meant that I was no longer officially a Bahamian resident. As a tourist I could now legally gamble, so I decided to go for broke and went down to the blackjack tables with my $100. I sat down at the table like a high roller. Inspired by the elderly couple I had seen win so much earlier, I played a few games, and in less than ten minutes, had lost it all.

V

IT'S ALL IN THE GAME

ARRIVING IN FAST-PACED Hong Kong after working in the sleepy Bahamas, I had a severe dose of culture shock. Hong Kong is Chinese for 'fragrant harbour' – well, I can tell you there is nothing fragrant about it any more.

Hong Kong is by far the fastest environment I have ever experienced. Everyone who is anyone has a mobile phone and a pager – often as a status symbol – even if they are not actually subscribed to a telecom company! The need to feel rich and a big shot, and thereby having 'face', is of paramount importance and everything, bar nothing, pales in comparison to this need.

I was employed as the executive chef of a soon-to-be-finished very large hotel. When completed and opened, it was to be the largest hotel in Hong Kong. Now this was going to be a major professional challenge, as I had to set up and establish the restaurants and the whole catering side of the hotel, totally from scratch.

When I arrived at the hotel, or rather, construction site, I was surprised to see what I would describe as a mere shell of a building, seemingly years away from anything even remotely resembling an operational hotel. Since this was a live-in position, I had to stay at another hotel as our hotel had no rooms even close to being in a liveable condition.

Every day for months on end, we would have meetings in order to plan the restaurant concepts, the kitchen designs, the purchase of equipment, staffing, budgets, recruitment, training and the myriad other things that were needed. We would also regularly visit the hotel site to check on the construction, making sure the right things were in the right place and everything was up to the specifications imposed by the hotel operator.

We had a food and beverage manager, Phil, who was a little squeamish, to say the least, about rodents. If we went to the site too early, that is before the construction workers arrived, we would sometimes see huge rats running across what would one day be our pristine new Italian marble lobby floor. Whereas, if we timed it properly and the workers were there first, they would be the ones to give our furry friends their early morning wake-up call.

Some months into its construction, Phil and I decided that since we were going to be living in the hotel, we should go upstairs to see the layout of our rooms and how much progress was being made. He was very reluctant at first, especially as the electricity was not yet installed, but since it was still light, I managed to convince him to come with me.

As we climbed the stairs beyond the lower floor, we started to see graffiti on the walls of the stairwell, presumably written by the local construction guys. 'Gweilos go home' and 'Gweilos kiss my arse' were just two of the more welcoming signs we came across – 'gweilo' being the slang name for white foreigners, which roughly translated into English means 'ghost man'.

"Do you think they like us?" Phil asked dryly.

We went into a couple of the upstairs rooms and thought they were alright size-wise and that the work looked to be coming on nicely. I went along the corridor and into another room, and just happened to peep round the door into an adjacent room. There, in the middle of the floor, was a huge pile of human excrement which, no doubt, some construction worker had kindly deposited. I looked at the mound and started to laugh as a wicked thought came to mind. I knew it was not nice, and I knew it was not fair, but I just couldn't resist it.

"Hey, big guy. Come over here. I want to show you something," I called out to Phil. "I think this is your room."

I could not control myself and was already on the verge of bursting into hysterical laughter before the joke was finished.

"How do you know it's mine?" Phil asked.

"They must have already allocated the rooms because your name is written on the floor of this one! Go and have a look," I said mischievously.

He was so happy to pull open the door to look and see his name, but the look of horror that registered on his face actually made me feel bad that I had played the trick ... well, for a second anyway. I laughed on and off for ages, and every time I saw Phil, I would start all over again.

Phil later told me that for months after that day, when he was sleeping in his then ready room, he would occasionally wake up in a cold sweat, imagining that he was being chased down the street by a runaway farm cart full of warm, steaming dung! He would also find himself wanting to mop the floor of his room to make sure it was clean before he could more restfully go back to sleep.

As the hotel was not yet open, and I was effectively working office hours

– something of a treat for a chef, given the more usual long hours of our industry – I decided to try and get to know some of the other chefs around town. I found one would-be friend, Bruce, with whom I thought I could relate, and started to socialise with him. Since he had been in Hong Kong for some time, he showed me a few places of interest and pointed out the good and bad spots. He was a great guy until he was under the influence, and then he would go a little crazy, throwing beer bottles and wanting to fight, so before long I began looking for someone else to hook up with.

I eventually got friendly with another cook, this time a famous celebrity chef – I shall call him 'Shane' to save any embarrassment – who had become a long-serving member of the restaurant community in Hong Kong. He was so well known and his status was such that he would regularly have some journalist or local dignitary visiting him in his office, and he would invariably get fed up with the constant stream of uninvited guests.

Being the character that he was, one day Shane decided to hammer a few small tacks up into the seat of the chair in his office, so that the points of the tacks would just be protruding through but not enough for them to be seen. His intention was that whenever people sat down in the chair, they would feel sufficiently uncomfortable, and he surmised that not wanting to offend, they would quickly make an excuse and leave.

I remember a particular occasion when Shane and I had arranged to meet in a bar in Wanchai late one evening after work. I did not know the place but fortunately found it easily enough. As I entered, I went down two flights of carpeted stairs to a basement club. The place was packed. It had great rhythm and blues music playing, and there were women dressed in swimsuits dancing on the tables. What kind of funky place was this, I thought, and why did these women have numbers on the bottom of their very skimpy outfits?

I stood there not knowing what to do, or what the form was, until an older woman came to my rescue and asked if I wanted a drink. Before I could properly mutter yes, she led me to the bar, sat me down and gave me a beer. The women who were dancing had now started to wink and smile at me as if I knew them. Shortly after, another woman sat down next to me and asked me to buy her a drink. I said alright, and she ordered. By now I knew exactly what kind of place this was, and wondered where my friend had got to.

Realising that there was no action to be had with me, my uninvited drinking partner eventually left, so I went to stand by the door to wait for Shane and watch the scene from a safe distance. Suddenly, I heard the entrance door at the top of the stairs bang shut, followed by someone laughing, and then the sound of 'bump-thud, bump-thud, bump-thud'. Still standing at the bottom of the stairs, I looked down at my feet and saw that my celebrity chef friend had careered fully down two flights of stairs. He was so drunk he had not even registered that there were stairs to be negotiated, and he proceeded to stand up as if nothing had happened.

Shane looked at me and smiled. "Saxon," he bellowed, "why are you so late? I've been here ages."

Given his rather dramatic entrance and the state he was in, there seemed little point in trying to set the record straight. Anyway, after a few pleasantries and a drink or two, I decided to leave. He, though, clearly had other plans as regards the entertainment on offer at the establishment. On paying the bill, I noticed that the single drink I bought for the woman who came to my table was double the price of the one I drank, which itself was not cheap, making it an expensive two-minute talk.

Subsequently, during my stay in Hong Kong, I found a place where a lot of the expatriates hung out and was introduced to the DJ there. He was dating a woman at the time who worked for one of the well-known Asian airlines, and because we got on quite well, she decided to introduce me to one of her female friends. To cut a long story short, since her friend and I found that we also got along well together, we started dating.

She, Cleo, was from a small town in Malaysia, and was a flight attendant on the same airline as the woman who introduced us. Cleo would regale me with stories of her flying experiences, and some of them were startling, to say the least. For instance, how she and the other members of the crew would occasionally catch people – especially in the middle of the night, on long-haul flights – initiating each other into the 'mile-high club'. The amorous couples would either use the toilet cubicle or the more brazen would wait for everyone to go to sleep and get it on right there in their seats.

She told me of one occasion where a man suddenly appeared in the aisle stark naked and asked if she needed some help in serving the drinks. As he refused to sit down and put on his clothes, the captain had to handcuff the passenger to his first class seat until they arrived at their destination. The funny thing was, the next day when Cleo and the rest of the crew boarded the return flight, she was taken aback to see the same man sitting on the aeroplane, this time dressed in an expensive suit and behaving in an impeccable manner. Apparently, he was so relaxed and at ease, it was as if the previous day's events had been a figment of Cleo's imagination.

Another time when she was serving drinks, Cleo smelt something burning and heard a sizzling sound. On investigating to see what was going on, she found a guy in the aisle stir-frying his own lunch on a small gas canister stove!

On another occasion, Cleo recounted how they arrived back from a long flight only to find a bus waiting alongside the plane ready to take the crew straight off to another flight as the crew for that flight had been detained somewhere else. They were obviously already very tired, but still had to do this additional flight to somewhere else in Asia because of commercial necessity. I sometimes wonder how trusting we are as passengers to place ourselves in the hands of others, putting our lives at their mercy, when we do not really know in whose hands we are, or anything of the behind-the-scene circumstances.

On a more pleasant note, Cleo would sometimes come home with huge tins of Beluga caviar and the like, explaining that when a flight landed, its stock was automatically replenished as the airline would assume that its supplies had all been used up. Whereas, the reality was that any unused items, especially the quality stock, would normally be divided among the staff to take home.

As the Hong Kong hotel was still far from being ready to open, I took a few days off to spend with Cleo – who had by now become something more than just a close friend. She asked if I would like to go with her to her hometown in Malaysia, to meet and stay with her family. I was pleased to accept her invitation.

When we arrived at her home after our flight from Hong Kong, I was sufficiently naïve to be surprised to see that in the middle of a hotter-than-hell summer, her family's house had no air conditioning. Apparently some Asian people consider air conditioning unhealthy and prefer to leave their windows open instead, though as I would learn, this can lead to problems of a different nature, namely an assorted procession of creepy-crawlies taking refuge in the house. This was in many respects my first real exposure to life in the East. For years I had lived in hotels and evidently taken certain things for granted, so I clearly had a lot of learning to do.

Also, on a more personal note, I should have smelt something afoot with my relationship with Cleo, when the first question her mother asked when we met was, "How much money do you earn?"

I was taken aback by this but recovered sufficiently to tell her, "Don't worry, it is enough," which in retrospect, was probably the worst thing I could have said!

My lesson in Asian culture continued that night as I went to take a shower before going to bed. Looking back now, I can laugh, but it didn't seem so funny at the time. The 'shower' was a huge porcelain tank filled with tap water. The idea was that one stood naked next to the tank, dipping a small plastic bucket into it, filling it with water and pouring it over your head. You then shampooed yourself and washed your body with soap, before finishing once again by dipping the faithful old bucket into the tank and pouring the water over yourself to rinse.

A couple of things worth mentioning about this ritual are that, firstly, the water was cold and the yelps of surprise I let out brought the whole family running to the bathroom door to see if I was alright. Secondly, the huge spider which had its very scary lair at the corner of the tin roof above my head took my mind, and one eye, off the job at hand – until the cold water hit my head, and I was then definitely focused once again. The small gecko lizards running freely around the house and the huge cockroaches cruising about as if they owned the place were something else I was not yet used to, not to mention trying to fall asleep while sweating buckets all over the bed sheets.

Strangely, after my new Asian-style showering experience, I felt I now better understood what it must have been like as a visitor to Yorkshire from overseas. Imagine taking a cold shower or using an outside toilet in some small farmhouse in the Yorkshire Dales in the midst of winter, while trying bravely to appreciate the beauties of the English countryside.

As it happened, I still hadn't made one of the essential adjustments to living in Asia – this was yet to come. Enlightenment hit me when I went to use the toilet, to find what I can only describe as a hole in the floor, with no seat to balance myself on. I looked at it for a moment and tried to figure out how I was going to perform this particular task. Initially, I tried to squat down but kept losing my balance, falling back several times and banging my head on the pipes behind me.

I took off my trousers to hang them on the door as the toilet floor was soaking wet, but found no hanger. So I decided to drape them around my neck like some kind of tribal wedding gown. Then with both arms sticking out and grabbing onto anything I could find on the sides of the room, to help keep my balance, I slowly lowered myself down to the bottomless pit. Now I was ready. Or was I?

I couldn't help wondering how I was going to know if my backside was directly over the hole, or if I was going to disgrace myself by doing the unthinkable on the rim. There was no mirror for me to use, like some kinky kind of aiming device, so in the end I just closed my eyes and thought of England.

I felt a great sense of achievement in accomplishing this normally taken-for-granted everyday act. Anyway, that was that, I said to myself before looking around for the non-existent toilet paper. What now, I thought! Were they intent on throwing all these challenges at me to see if I was worthy – but worthy of what? I pondered.

I resolved that I was going to show whoever was testing me a thing or two. I recalled that I had read somewhere in the dim and distant past that in the small kampong villages, people would just use running water and their bare hands to wash their bottoms, as paper was considered dirty. So I looked around and there it was, a small hose pipe. I turned it on and aimed it at my bottom. Unfortunately, in the process, the water ran down my legs and into the back of my new shoes.

So there I was with a wet bum, my new shoes full of now smelly water, my trousers wrapped around my neck, my hands certainly not smelling of roses, and no soap in sight. As if to cap it all, I heard Cleo calling to me to hurry up as she needed to use the bathroom.

I hurriedly cleaned up using the natural resources at my disposal, and was almost ready to leave. Now, the last obstacle to be dealt with was the fact that the toilet did not have a flushing system. As I looked around, I saw a bucket of water and another small scoop inside. Was I supposed to pour water over myself again? I wondered in my haste. Surely not, I concluded. This must be to flush the toilet, so I filled the scoop with water, holding it high above the toilet hole, and poured it all in at once, pushing its contents down the back of the pipes.

I opened the door feeling very proud of myself and my girlfriend, now desperate, moved in quickly. As I was walking away, she cried out to me, "Mike, can you get some toilet paper for me, please. Someone must have forgotten to replace it after finishing the last piece. By the way, what did you use?"

"Oh yes, I'm sorry I just finished the last roll," I said meekly, while thinking what a fool I had been.

Cleo and I spent a lot of time together in-between her flights, and after two years of what I believed was bliss, we decided to tie the knot. We were married in a small private wedding at a registry office, vowing to have a more luxurious wedding later. I was never happier, and was totally in love.

It was my birthday eight months or so into our marriage, and Cleo organised a lovely dinner for us in our hotel room. I was wondering what kind of sexy gift she was going to give me, and just the thought of it made me excited. So when the dinner was finished, I expectantly awaited my birthday present.

"Mike, we have something to talk about," announced my wife.

"Yes, I know," I said. "My special birthday gift, right?"

"No," came the reply. "I am leaving you … I have found a new guy and he is so rich he has even promised to buy me my own cherry red sports car."

I had an instant flashback to when her mother asked me that first question about how much I earned, and I could not help feeling that this was in some way connected to what was now happening.

This woman, whom I thought was the love of my life, had hit me with a sledgehammer in the deepest pit of my stomach. My heart faltered, missing alternate beats. This was brutal for me, and for a few seconds I had no idea what was going on, or where I was. My whole life had just collapsed with a single sentence. I pinched myself to see if it was a nightmare or something, and I could only look on dumbfounded as she stood up to leave. I had been given no time at all to grasp the impending reality of this loss, and before I really knew what was happening she told me she would pick up her things later, and the door closed shut behind her.

I sat there and broke down in tears. I did not know what to do, or say. Was this really happening? I started thinking ridiculous thoughts such as, what will my parents think? Or, what about the friends we share? Lost in the midst of these ramblings there was a knock at the door. I looked through the peephole to see Cleo standing there. My mind was swaying back and forth and was running at a mile a minute. Had she changed her mind? Or better still, was she just playing some sort of practical joke on me? I thought for a second and decided that that's what it was, just a big prank.

I opened the door with a smile and said, "You are playing the fool, aren't you?"

"No, I just forgot to give you your birthday gift," she replied, as she pressed a bottle of cologne into my hand, before leaving for good.

I stood there thinking how nice it was of her to give me this expensive bottle of aftershave, given the circumstances, then remembered that it was an item on her airline's in-flight shopping list. I wondered if she got this gift in the same way she acquired the caviar.

I recalled the day we married and how I had bought a twenty-year-old bottle of malt whisky as a surprise for Cleo. We talked at the time about how we would open the bottle in celebration on our fiftieth wedding anniversary. I would never have guessed that I would be opening it and finishing it on my own before dust had even settled on it. Wallowing in self-pity, I did not date for fully two years after that evening, and swore never ever to marry again.

Since the hotel was not yet open, the owner asked me whether I would mind doing the catering for a special party he was holding at his house. His house was like a fortress, located in the hills of Hong Kong. It was a very large, beautiful property with observation cameras mounted on the sides of the house, a large gate with round-the-clock guards and a great many Dobermann guard dogs in evidence. I had never been so close to such scary-looking dogs before and resolved to keep it that way. As we entered the grounds, we had to wait for a guard to come and lead the drooling dogs away before we could step out of the van.

Unloading the produce and equipment we had brought with us, I picked up three trays of fresh eggs and went to enter the kitchen through the back door. As I rounded the corner, heading for the door, I passed a stairwell with a large metal mesh gate, and I did not notice anything untoward. Just as I did so, a huge Dobermann dog lunged at the gate as if it wanted to tear my throat out. I jumped back in shock, tossing the eggs two feet into the air and 'splat, splat, splat', they landed on the ground. The look on the dog's face was pure evil, and a smell of death hung in the air. My death, if the dog had its way.

At that moment, the owner stepped out of the back door and coolly remarked, "So you've met Spot."

Spot! I said, tight-lipped to myself. What kind of name is that for an ugly, fanged, carnivorous killing machine like this? And where on earth, I wonder, is the so-called spot? Though I knew that I for sure would not be giving a beast like that any kind of body search looking for its birthmark!

Despite my mishap with the eggs, the dinner went well, but I went home vowing not to return to the owner's house if I could possibly help it. Luckily for me, I was not asked again until after the hotel had opened, and then being too busy myself attending to matters at the hotel, I was able to delegate the assignment to one of my staff. My escape was complete when I learned the next day that the chef I sent in my place had not resigned.

As the hotel got closer to being ready, they fixed up a few showrooms for the media and travel industry representatives to view during the day, and for us to sleep in at night. Now that felt really strange, staying in a vast hotel that was totally dark at night. So dark in fact that if you wanted to leave your room after sunset, a flashlight was an absolute necessity. Although there were a few other staff members staying in the hotel, besides me, one still had a feeling of being the only soul in the whole place.

I interviewed all the staff for my area, made my choices and told them we would call them closer to the opening date. The principal assistant I had chosen, Tan, was a great guy, and he suggested that since it was now winter in Hong Kong, I might like to go with him to a game restaurant to explore possible menu ideas. Not really knowing what he was talking about, I went along anyway because I was keen to try as many new things as possible.

We arrived at the appointed restaurant, which was located down a back street, or more rather some dark alley, such that you would never be able to find it a second time even if you wanted to. The owner and chef came out to greet us, and told us that if we were willing he would like to play a little game with us. He would bring out the food, and as we finished each course, we would have to guess what we had just eaten. It sounded a little scary to me, given that this was Hong Kong, but as I wanted to try things, and was also keen to fit in, I went along with it.

The first thing we ate was a very strong smelling, yet clear, soup which the chef said was, "Good for the body". Which part? I wondered.

He asked us what we thought it was. There I was, an international chef, and I had no idea.

"Let me guess," I announced. Well, I surmised, it was a game restaurant, and it was a soup. "Pheasant!" I said.

"What? What the hell is pheasant?" came the reply.

I knew then that I was in trouble, and this was going to be a long, long night.

Our host went into the kitchen and brought out a large cage on a trolley with wheels, covered by a dirty white blanket. He did his trick of pulling away the blanket like a television magician, revealing a huge, slimy, long-tongued, uglier than anything I had seen … lizard. My stomach started to turn over straightaway and I thought I was going to throw up on my shoes and, for that matter, on everyone else's.

Then came the next course, a small bowl of some kind of stronger-smelling, heavy stew. I nibbled at it since my appetite was already suffering under the enormous strain. "Game restaurant," I whispered to myself, "I'll give them *game* restaurant."

Out came the dreaded cage, once again, and away went the blanket to reveal a beautiful snowy owl, its huge eyes looking deep into mine. That, my friends, was the last straw.

I didn't care any more if I was going to fit in or not. Dinner was over for me and, as the next course came out, I announced that I was out of the game. So as not to cause offence, I decided to ask for something safe instead, and with which I was familiar.

"Hey, how about just giving me some chicken chow mein?" I asked pleadingly.

The manager looked at me extremely confused. "Chicken chow what?" he said.

"Chow mein," I reiterated.

"Are you trying to be funny?" he responded angrily. "If you don't like the food, I understand, but there is no reason to be rude."

"What was he talking about?" I asked Tan, and he told me that he had been living in Hong Kong all his life and had never heard of this dish. What was worse, 'chow' translated from Cantonese to English is 'stink'! For the full four years I was in Hong Kong, I was unable to find a single restaurant that had heard of the famous 'chicken chow mein', much less had it on the menu.

My protestations of being full had still not spared me from the third course. This was another thick stew, which the owner chef told us, "Is made especially to keep the body warm during the winter," while pulling away the trolley curtain to reveal a somewhat scabby-looking dog.

This time I tried a different tack.

"I think I must have eaten something which did not agree with me at lunch earlier today," I mustered.

This at last seemed to do the trick. Though still trying to extend hospitality and feeling sorry for me being unable to eat the delights of the main meal, he brought out some steamed prawns and steamed fish, insisting that would make me feel a little better. And guess what, my appetite was indeed encouraged back to life! It showed me, though, that if you have the taste for something and the money to pay for it, you can find it and eat it in Hong Kong.

The next night, Tan introduced me to the famous Dai Pai Dong concept of eating. Generally, these places are about the atmosphere, and the food can be great too. Unfortunately, this was not to be on my initiation night, and I felt as if I had seen it all.

The so-called chef was woking the rice and noodles in the street, as they do, but in his case while smoking at the same time. As he threw the food in the air, the sudden jerk of his arm sent ash from his half-smoked butt into his fine cuisine of 'Wok-fried Hong Kong-style ashed noodles'.

There was no toilet in close proximity to this particular restaurant stall, and as the chef was drinking his fair share of the night's profits, he needed to go to the toilet to relieve himself. As I looked on in amazement, he finished one dish, then went behind a nearby bush for a leak, wiped his hands on his shorts, pulled up his zip and casually strolled back to his open-air kitchen.

The chef had a singlet T-shirt on, with his hairy and sweaty armpits showing in full view, a cigarette in his mouth, very short shorts such that his 'wedding gear' was virtually hanging out from one side, and was wearing no shoes. Can't be bad, I thought. Let's eat.

The hygiene at this place left a lot to be desired, and you really had to concentrate to be able to finish your food. The secret I found to Dai Pai Dong eating was to not look around while you were eating, and to totally block out what was going on until you were finished. Now, because I was new, I did not know about this golden rule, so I had to learn the hard way.

While I continued to ignore this rule, I saw there was one guy on a nearby table who had obviously had a little too much to drink, and as I looked around, I did so just in time to see him vomit a spray the distance of around two feet, much of which appeared to be the five bottles or so of San Miguel beer – the local favourite – he had downed earlier.

The net effect of this, and the assorted other sights I witnessed while breaking the golden rule, meant that I went home very hungry that night. Of course, after years of living there, you develop the necessary knack of blocking everything out, making yourself oblivious to virtually anything happening around you, and in doing so you can enjoy some of the best tasting 'stall' food in the world.

Honkies, as Hong Kong people are affectionately called, love to gamble. This is especially so at the racetrack where millions of dollars are wagered daily. Yet if the racetrack was closed, you would be seriously mistaken if you thought that it would mean a respite in the gambling.

There is a well-recognised and observed custom on being invited to dinner of showing up well ahead of the formally stated time, for what is effectively the main part of the event, the 'mah jong' or 'sam khoong' entertainment. Mah jong being the local version of dominoes, and sam khoong their version of blackjack. People will play for hours before dinner, then rush through the dinner and the moment dessert is served – invariably fresh cut fruit – most of the guests are out the door and down the street before you can say 'good evening'. It is stating the obvious to say that the gambling is really the social event and the dinner is just the filler. Sometimes, even during dinner, the gambling will continue between courses.

Hong Kong people are also very superstitious and will do anything to change a run of bad luck they may encounter. For example, among the more amusing rituals I have seen to break one's bad luck, apart from the more conventional one of changing the dealing from right to left or left to right, or dealing the cards with the numbers face down or face up, have included dipping their HK dollar bills in soya sauce before placing their bet! In short, people will do anything they can to win.

The die-hard gamblers will also bet on anything. I know because I have seen this at first hand. I recall two of my staff coming up to me and asking me to take out a ten dollar bill and to show it to them. The reason being, they had bet between themselves what the last digit would be on the serial number of the bill I produced. On another occasion, I was sitting in a hotel lobby with two guys when one bet the other on the gender of the next person to come out of the elevator. As chance would have it, when the door opened, the first person out was a small child, and they argued for the next two hours because they were not sure if it was a young boy or a young girl.

The hotel was at long last just about ready to open, so I and other members of the management team went to do our final checks in preparation for signing the acceptance of the finished hotel. On checking the kitchen area, I found the finishing to be good, though it felt funny to be in a large, well-equipped kitchen that had never been used. There was a huge walk-in chiller at the back of the kitchen which had just been connected. So new was it that it had not even been turned on and tried out yet. When I walked through the kitchen, it still had the smell of glue and paint.

At the back of the chiller was another door that led into the smaller freezer compartment. I opened the door to check this out and couldn't believe my eyes. The same guy, I guess, who had taken a dump in Phil's room had done the dirty deed here, too. Was nothing sacred to this twit? Fortunately, apart from this calling card, everything else was alright, so I signed off my acceptance, and the staff training was now able to get underway in preparation for the hotel's opening.

We tried out some of the high-class dishes that business people like to impress their clients with in Hong Kong circles. Shark's fin soup is, of course, a classic and so popular now that sharks are becoming an endangered species because of their culinary value. Suckling pig, Peking duck, abalone, black chicken, sea cucumber, lobsters, Shatin pigeon and jellyfish all had to be on the menu. Best of all was a famous, expensive dish called 'Buddha Jumped over the Wall'.

The history of this particular dish is quite fascinating. It was said that many years ago, all the buddhas who lived in the temple compounds were vegetarians and this form of diet was preached daily to all the young buddhas. However, some of the younger, more daring ones would try to jump over the compound wall to catch any wild prey they could lay their hands on to supplement their meagre diets. They would cook frogs, eels, snakes, birds and all kinds of things, layering them in a clay pot like a stew to cook. These days, you won't find such weird and wonderful contents in your 'Buddha' but you may get shark's fin, fish maw – the outside of the fishes' mouths – and black chicken.

My brigade also geared up for seasonal dishes such as the famous Hong Kong 'hairy crabs', 'moon cakes' and 'Yee Sang' – a selection of fresh vegetables and fish tossed together with special spices and condiments and only served during Chinese New Year for good luck and prosperity.

Our preparations would not have been complete, however, without universal mastery of that key piece of equipment – the wok. Since I was the only one not fully versed in this great art, the onus was on me to prove myself. The first time I had a go it was a monumental affair, if not to say a comedy of epic proportions.

Everyone was standing around in amazement that I had the gall to even give it a try. This is nothing like the tame affair that we call stir-frying in cosy kitchens at home in England. Oh no, Chinese wok cookery in an industrial-style kitchen is a much more dramatic event. The chef stands next to the wok stove and does not need to move an inch because everything has already been arranged around him. Any items he does not already have will be fetched by a poor underling, waiting at his right hand for orders, which are screamed out at the top of the chef's voice.

Next to the wok stove will be a very large, burnt-on black wok, a large ladle – somewhat ill-designed for its rather delicate task – and a bucket of chicken stock which is liberally doused over most dishes during preparation. There will also be a tray with a varied selection of condiments, sauces and seasonings. The ladle is, of course, far too large to scoop anything up with any accuracy, especially when you are under stress to deliver the food quickly.

When the gas for the high-powered stove is turned on, it flares up so fiercely that it sounds like a Formula One racing car revving up and turns into a powerful blue flame, which makes the wok white hot in about five seconds. The chef holds the large ladle in one hand, the wok handle in the other, and turns the gas on and off with his knee.

To watch a seasoned veteran of the wok stove can be magic in motion and is actually a real art that the experts make look all too easy. But was it easy enough for a greenish Yorkshire cook to have a go? There I was, ready to start, standing in front of the wok stove with the ladle in my right hand and the wok handle in my left, while everyone stood around, grinning and contemplating getting the fire extinguisher ready, just in case. My 'teacher' stood behind me, ready to shout clear and simple instructions (probably in Cantonese) to his newest wok pupil. As I lowered my right knee and struck the gas control handle, I banged my knee bone and saw stars. I set off hopping around the kitchen, slipped on some spilled oil and ended up flat out on the floor.

The entire kitchen was now in stitches and some runners dashed off to gather further troops from other kitchens to join in the fun. I got myself up, wiped my hands on what was by now a very oily apron, and got ready for a second go. I kneed the handle and the hot flame surged out with such force that the fire came up around the sides of the wok, singeing the little hair I had on my arms and sending a burning hair smell across the kitchen. This just made everyone laugh hysterically yet again. Sympathetic lot, chefs!

I started to wok the chicken fillet and seemed to be doing okay, so I risked a touch of ladle work and splashed in some chicken stock from the bucket. Next came the seasonings, but I was horrified by how much salt stuck to my ladle. I tried to shake some off, but it showered all over the wok and its contents, since the ladle was so big and clumsy.

Suddenly, there appeared to be smoke coming out from underneath my wok. When I looked down to investigate, I was horrified to see that it was my apron on fire. I tore it off and threw it onto the floor, stamping on it wildly and burning my hand in the process. Now with a serious lack of options, I plunged my singed digits into the handy bucket of chicken stock. Some smart Alec quipped, "Essence of *gweilo* goes on the menu next week!"

Since that day the well-seasoned wok chefs of the world receive my deepest respect, and I hereby take my tall white hat off to them all.

At last, the day had arrived and the hotel was finally open. The grand opening party was an elegant affair held in the just-finished lobby. There was a nice band playing to help the proceedings along and a huge cocktail finger food buffet. We also started serving dishes from the various restaurants' à la carte menus that evening to managers from the hotel, as a practice run to ensure that both the food and our kitchen systems were what they should be.

On opening the hotel's doors to the paying public, we very quickly started to attract some of the large tour group business, and more especially a strong Japanese clientele. In anticipation of this, the hotel had employed a Japanese sales manager to grow this segment of the business and to act as our unofficial translator. He was settling in well, doing a good job and seemed to be a very happy-go-lucky kind of guy. However, one morning, he did not attend the daily senior management briefing, for which there was the equivalent of a three-line-whip for us to attend. Nothing untoward was said because Ken worked very long hours, and as the next day was his day off, he was given a break. He had hung a 'Do Not Disturb' sign on his door, and by late afternoon the next day, it was still there. One of the housekeeping staff became a little suspicious about this and decided to take a closer look.

When she entered the room, what she found would probably affect her for many years to come. Ken had placed a pillow to his face and shot himself in the head, spraying his blood all over the bed and walls in an extremely graphic manner. The hotel paid for the housekeeping attendant to seek therapy, and the incident was handled very discreetly; nothing about it ever got out into the public domain. We later learned that Ken's private problems had, at least in his mind, just become too much for him to bear, and so he had decided to call it a day.

The hotel was very quickly in full swing, and typically this was when all the fun started. And what an absolute, complete and utter zoo it could sometimes be!

One night, I was sitting watching television, when a couple moved into the room next door to my own. There was a door separating our respective rooms, which meant it could be used as adjoining or inter-connecting rooms when parents, for instance, wanted a separate room for their children. Almost as soon as the couple entered the room, and very likely before the suitcases had hit the floor, they were at it. She was moaning and groaning, he was shouting, and the door separating our two rooms reverberated at regular intervals. I could only assume they were right against the door and did not realise, or stop to think, that there may be someone in the next room.

I called down to the front office to ask how long they were going to stay, and was told two weeks. As I put the phone down, they were already starting round two, so I decided to go downstairs to the bar and have a beer, giving them this not-so-private moment on their own. Two hours later, I was feeling sleepy, so I decided to call it a night and entered the lift to go back upstairs to my room. However, as soon as I exited the lift on my floor, I could hear the woman screaming all the way down the corridor, and believe me this was no short corridor.

As I turned the corner to walk down to my room, I was amazed to find a number of the other guests milling around in the corridor, wearing their sleeping attire and wondering what the hell was going on.

"Good evening, ladies and gentlemen," I announced. "This live audio show is part of the in-house complementary entertainment offered to our guests as an amenity on their arrival. Just you wait and see what we do for turn-down service."

Everyone burst out laughing, which at least helped to relax the otherwise tense situation, and I asked them all to go back to their rooms and said that I would take care of the situation. Instead of screams of pleasure, it really sounded like he could be torturing her, or something, so I called the hotel security for their help. As the security guards arrived, they, too, could hear the noise and decided to knock on the door.

The noise instantly fell to a deafening silence for the first time that night. A security guard asked them to keep it down a little, and I heard the man give his apologies before the security staff left. Everybody then went about their business and I, and no doubt everyone else, thought that was the end of it. Sadly we were wrong.

About half an hour later, they had now started to argue and shout at each other. I heard what I thought was the sound of a slap, followed by the woman weeping while the guy was screaming and shouting at the top of his voice. On hearing this, I again called the hotel's security, as I feared that things may have taken a turn for the worse.

Once again the security guards knocked on the door. This time they found the woman with a bloodied face, and she was taken away by a female security officer. They cleaned her up and spoke to her for a while, and at the same time pointed out to the guy that any more action like this and the hotel would be forced to call the police. This seemed to do the trick as the two of them were alright for the rest of the trip, though the guy subsequently told our staff that he had beaten his wife because he felt embarrassed that the hotel security were called to ask them to keep the noise down, blaming her for excessive groaning!

When I first heard that account, I initially felt guilty since it was me who had called security in the first place, but deep down I knew that I was only doing my duty as a manager and a concerned individual, and that it was not my fault. The husband would have to pay for his action, I resolved, with his own karma not mine.

Living in a five-star hotel may sound prestigious, but believe me that is not always the case, as privacy is hard to come by. I remember one night during my time in Hong Kong. It was around midnight, and as I lay in bed, trying to sleep, I heard a key in the lock of my door.

As the door opened and whoever it was entered my room, I sat bolt upright in bed, crossed my arms, and waited for them to walk into view and get the shock of their lives when they saw me in what they thought was their bed. They seemed to stop, however, before proceeding to the bedroom. So I got out of bed and looked out into the living room area to see a member of our concierge staff showing two Japanese guests around the room.

"Well, good evening, everybody. Please come in. The party is just about to get started," I shouted out angrily from the bedroom door.

The concierge looked at me with horror as he ran outside to take a second glance at the room number. As he did so, the poor Japanese guests were profusely bowing back and forth, expressing humblest apologies. Despite my predicament, I felt sorry for them, as the concierge came running back in.

"Sorry, chef," he declared, "wrong floor!"

"Yes, it would appear so, wouldn't it," I laughed.

"You are the executive chef?" asked one of the Japanese guests. "Does that mean you will spit into the French toast tomorrow when we come for breakfast?"

I looked at them, pleasantly surprised at their humour. "I don't know, let me sleep on it," I answered, and we all smiled.

The next morning when the same guest ordered breakfast, he looked at me and said, "I will take fried rice, please. I hear the French toast is lousy here!"

On another occasion, I was asleep in the early hours of the morning when the phone rang.

"Chef, is that you?" the caller asked.

"I think so, but then it is three o'clock in the morning," I replied.

"Yes, that's right," said the caller. "It's Janet from the front office. Can you tell me what time breakfast starts?"

"Oh, sure I can," I said, "I'll be down in a second to tell you."

I was furious, to say the least, to think that the staff thought I did not need sleep like everyone else, and that they could disturb me on some trifling petty matter at any hour of the night. So I got out of bed and went down to personally 'explain' to her what time breakfast started. I obviously succeeded in clearing everything up satisfactorily enough as she never called me again.

The last laugh, however, was not mine.

On returning to my still-warm bed, I was just settling down when this time there was a knock on my door. Opening the door, I saw a member of the housekeeping staff.

"Did you order a rollaway bed, chef?" he enquired.

"Why the hell would I need a rollaway bed? Who would that be for, at this time in the morning?" I asked.

I then realised that my friend from the front office, upset by our earlier altercation, had decided to pay me back and needle me even more, thus grabbing the last word. So I told the housekeeping attendant that I did not need the bed, giggled, and then rang Janet to call an immediate truce and halt to the ensuing hostilities.

One morning, the hotel's public relations manager came to see me and asked if I would like to be on *Good Morning Hong Kong* – a morning TV talk-show. They wanted me to talk a little about Cajun cuisine and maybe cook a couple of dishes. I agreed and when I arrived at the studio, I was feeling quite confident. For some reason, I never gave it a thought that it was to be a live interview and demonstration. So when they said, "We're going live in two minutes, Mike," I nearly fell over myself.

Trying desperately to calm down, all I could think of saying to myself was, 'It's show time' – words I had used a thousand times before when things got tough, which in the catering business is all too frequent.

The first two minutes of the interview just flew by, and everything I had planned to say had been said, so I had no alternative but to ad lib – or, some might say, bluff my way – through the rest of the interview. Can you imagine the pressure of having millions of people watching you, possibly making a fool of yourself, knowing that you could not take back, or do over, whatever you did or said that was not quite right? The total segment was only ten minutes, but it felt like forever. I will never know how, but in some way I managed to get through it, and would later go on to do various other television and radio shows.

One night in the early hours of the morning, there was an armed robbery in the cashier's area at the hotel's front desk. The masked gunmen made a real scary scene and left with all the loot they could get. As they were leaving, there was a newly arrived guest filling out the necessary check-in paperwork at reception. Running out of the front door, the robbers decided to help themselves to his luggage, shouting, "Thank you, sir, for your generous donation," before they quickly scurried off into the night. Sadly, in all the commotion, nobody in the hotel had realised that the guest's luggage had also been stolen.

Nobody likes negative publicity, and hotels are particularly guarded about their reputation. So when the local media heard about the thrilling encounter, they called our public relations manager to find out more. She, though, was quick off the mark, and explained that we were in fact allowing a movie crew to film their latest epic in the hotel. They were filming overnight, she said, because there were too many guests around during the day!

"That's funny," explained the journalist. "Because we have a gentleman here who claims that the robbers also took his luggage." Clang!

The hotel ended up somewhat rosy cheeked, and had to go and meet the guest concerned and compensate him in the correct manner. Then the whole thing was buried once again, as if it had never happened.

Still on the subject of the thefts and robberies, another five-star hotel down the street from us, one lovely and very busy Sunday afternoon, had two large removal trucks pull up to its entrance. A group of workers from the trucks then walked in and started to remove the furniture from the lobby, loading it onto the trucks.

Puzzled by this, the hotel's duty manager asked what was going on, and the would-be foreman told him that the hotel owner had called personally to instruct that the furniture needed to go immediately for general cleaning. His company, he explained, had been contracted to shampoo all the seat covers and bring them back to their natural glory.

The duty manager, too scared to challenge the instruction of the hotel owner, thought this must be alright and allowed the work to continue. On Monday morning, however, when the matter was brought up at the executive briefing, the general manager called the owner to check, only for him to announce that he had no idea what the general manager was talking about. Talk about daylight robbery, and how embarrassing and costly that mistake was.

We brought over an Italian chef from Europe to conduct an Italian food promotion in one of the hotel's restaurants. Since Rocco did not speak any English, I was asked to keep an eye on him, help him out, and stop him from getting into any kind of trouble. On Rocco's day off, he explained to one of our Italian guests that he was going out for the day and that he would be back later. With him being new to the city, I was starting to get worried when by eleven o'clock that evening he had still not returned to the hotel. The next day, however, when Rocco came down to work, I was much relieved and asked him where he had been so late. In explaining his ordeal, he started to shout and gesticulate at the guest translator, and the guest started to laugh with great merriment. When he had finished his story, the guest let me in on the joke, and I laughed for days.

It seemed that he had gone for a walk along the Hong Kong docks, and had got lost in the process. He then stumbled across a large cargo ship being unloaded of its boxes of frozen fish. In fact, the ship was laden with thousands of these boxes of frozen fish waiting to be unloaded. With idle curiosity, he had walked up to see what was going on and was just standing there looking on with his hands in his pockets, when the ship's captain, thinking that Rocco was one of his crew, lazing about, trying to get out of doing his work, grabbed him and threw him into the fray. Every time he tried to explain in his very poor, broken English, the captain would speak over him and just would not listen.

"I don't want to hear your bloody excuses, alright," barked the captain. "Just do your job." So to cut a long story short, he had been there all day, carrying these boxes of frozen fish on his shoulders up and down until the job was complete.

The Italian chef took off his shirt to show me how the skin had been grazed and scraped off his shoulders, doing this work. As he was speaking, trying to say heaven knew what, he put his right hand in his pocket and pulled out a wad of small notes. We deduced that the money was the casual worker payment he had received when the captain finally found out that he was not, in fact, one of his crew.

I closed my eyes for a moment, imagining the ship's crew, having a beer somewhere, laughing about the Italian guy they had 'press-ganged' into carrying the boxes of fish all day, and I cracked up even more.

After the Italian chef had returned home to Europe and the promotion figures revealed how successful it had been, we decided to hire a full-time Italian chef to keep the culinary theme going. The appointed chef, Mario, was a married man, whose wife unfortunately was not ready for such a big move across the continents while their children were still attending school. So she elected to stay behind in Italy with them, and vowed to join him later.

A few months into his stay in Hong Kong, Mario evidently started to get lonely and decided to find himself a girlfriend on the side. He did indeed find someone but apparently did not tell her he was married – hoping, no doubt, to have his cake at home, and nibble a piece on the side whenever he was hungry. I pleaded with Mario to be careful, but unfortunately he was not thinking with his brain, so I left it at that.

Mario took his 'girlfriend' to Phuket in Thailand, on a nice little weekend trip, and came back as happy as a lark. However, a few days later, he came to me in great panic, announcing that he was resigning and that he had to leave the next day. I eventually squeezed the story out of him, and he explained that while in Phuket he had some photos taken of himself and his girlfriend, with her wearing only a very skimpy swimsuit. Also, apparently, whilst he was sleeping, she had craftily taken a photocopy of the two airline tickets booked under the name of Mr and Mrs Mario … Now, his part-time darling was threatening to send the photos and other items to his wife, unless he gave her US$2,000 in cash. Mario had told her that he was married when the relationship became more serious; in his mind his girlfriend would be happy with it due to the fact that he thought she was enjoying herself being with him. A major mistake that many spouses having affairs make; unfortunately the girlfriend/boyfriend generally and inevitably decides they need and want it all.

He knew that there would, of course, be further demands, so he had decided instead to run for his life back home to Italy, where he would try to figure something out before it was too late. A few months later, he sent me a postcard from Trieste in Italy, saying that he had sold his house and moved through fear that he would never get any peace as a result of his indiscretion. For my part, I always wondered how he explained to his wife his reasons for wanting to sell the family home on the spur of the moment like that.

I heard another story about a new chef who was a real womaniser and thought he was the cat's whiskers. Others, more politely, described him as a walking time bomb. One night, he was having dinner in his hotel's twenty-four-hour restaurant and was staring at, and generally giving the 'come-on' to, a beautiful young woman sitting across the restaurant. He made a point out of saying out loud that he fancied her but was told very clearly by the hotel staff that she was out of bounds on account of her being the girlfriend of a well-known and very powerful local gangster. Nonetheless, since the gangster was on the elderly side, the younger chef must have thought he would take care of the business which he supposed the gangster was not able to take care of himself.

One day, the general manager of the hotel was in his office attending to some paperwork, when in walked the uninvited gangster with two of his bruisers. I could imagine the general manager's heart racing as he tried to work out what the heck was going on, maybe wondering what he had done himself.

"Do you have a young man working in this hotel by the name of Joe Blow?"

enquired the gangster.

"Yes, we do," responded the general manager. "He's the executive sous chef here."

"Well," declared the gangster, "he has twenty-four hours to leave Hong Kong. After that, I will no longer be able to guarantee his personal safety, or for that matter, yours. Have a good day."

It is said that before the persuasive visitor had even left the office, the general manager had already picked up the phone telling the front office to book Casanova a one-way airline ticket out of Hong Kong, and he was gone the very next day.

One quiet and rather dreary evening, we heard sirens getting louder and louder as they got closer to the hotel. They eventually stopped right outside our hotel entrance. It was the police, and they rushed in announcing that there were illegal gamblers congregating in our Presidential Suite. A quick check of the reservation computer found that the room had been booked by a single man. So we escorted the police upstairs to see what, if anything, was going on.

The police rang the doorbell and informed the guest of their arrival. On opening the door, however, we were shocked to find around twenty of whom we were told were Hong Kong's elite gamblers, getting together for their 'monthly gambling party'. It was astounding how much money was confiscated that night, and what with all the 'celebrities' being arrested, it made for a very interesting evening.

I made friends with a very nice chef, named Fred, who worked in a hotel close to mine. We used to go jogging most nights, stopping for a couple of beers afterwards – no doubt undoing our good work and putting back on any weight we may have lost in the process – but it was enjoyable. One night, while we were out jogging, Fred told me that he had met a very sweet girl and that he was going to rent an apartment for her. Due to his work schedule and he always being very busy, he allowed her to have friends stay over as she sometimes became lonely and felt scared to be alone.

One night we were at his hotel and just about to go and have a quick drink before heading home, when the phone rang.

"Are you Fred?" asked the person at the other end.

"Yes, who is asking, please?" said Fred.

"This is the Hong Kong police department. Are you residing at Number 16 Fong Road?" the voice enquired.

I looked over to see him swallow very deeply and asked him what was wrong.

"Actually, I don't live there but I rent that apartment for my girlfriend," he explained. "Is there anything wrong, officer?"

"I think you had better come downtown to the police station," suggested the caller.

Fred put the phone down, sat still for a second, then opened another beer and took a large swig: "I think there's something wrong, Saxon. Will you come downtown with me to the police station?"

"Sure, let's go," I said.

He quickly finished his beer and we left. As we walked into the police station, we were rocked to our knees to see his girlfriend, Mai, there with six other women, all looking very scared indeed. We had no idea what the heck was going on, and I started to get scared for Fred, and for myself.

"May we please go into another room, gentlemen," said the police sergeant. As we entered an adjacent room, it had a large two-way glass mirror and we could see his girlfriend and the other women starting to talk just as the door was closing.

Their accents prompted me to ask Fred whether his girlfriend was from Hong Kong.

"Well, I thought she was," said Fred, "but that's the funkiest Cantonese I've ever heard." At that point, the sergeant interjected that the women were in fact from the Philippines and the police had apparently spotted what looked to be a very young girl sitting in the street, on the kerb, vomiting. When they had tried to see if she needed any assistance, she said she was suffering from morning sickness and would be alright shortly. The police officers decided to take her for a quick check-up at the hospital, where she was confirmed as pregnant. When they asked her to provide identification she could not supply any, so the officers confined her to the hospital room while they made some checks about her identity and looked into her welfare.

When they returned to her room, they found that the window was wide open, with no one inside, but through the open window they spotted her running down the street in her hospital gown. Naturally they followed her, and the chase led them to Fred's apartment. When they gained entrance, they found not only Mai, but another six girls. They all turned out to be illegal aliens, without papers, and hanging out in Fred's place. Now the question was fired at Fred: "Are you harbouring illegal aliens in your apartment?"

It turned into a very long night, trying to convince the police that he was an innocent party, but eventually his story was accepted. Sadly, the young girl had her baby in a Hong Kong jail and as soon as it was born, the authorities took it away until her sentence was completed. All very emotional, to say the least. Finally, when she was released, she was taken straight to the airport and deported back to the Philippines – thankfully with her child restored to her.

———————◆◈◆———————

Shortly after the Hong Kong hotel's opening, I decided it was time for a nice holiday and someone suggested that it would be great to visit China before the country completely opened up to the outside world. So off I went to Beijing, checking into one of the better hotels in the city.

I arrived during winter, and it was absolutely freezing cold and snowing. There was a huge pile of ice in the hotel's drive. At the top of the ice pile, a short intermittent squirt of water sprayed out every few seconds, adding to the mini ice mountain and making it slightly larger with each squirt. I asked the hotel's general manager why there was a need for the fountain to be on in this weather, and he told me that for good feng shui the hotel had built a beautiful fountain outside its main entrance, as a symbol of wealth and prosperity. But the owner, either on account of spending a bomb on the fountain, or not wanting to buck the feng shui advice, refused to turn the water supply off in the winter. When it froze it made a huge pile of clear ice, creating an unwanted skating rink and ice sculpture. A novel way of greeting the guests!

After skating up the drive, I was shown to my room. And as I turned the door handle to open the door, I got an electric shock.

"What the heck was that?" I asked the general manager, who was showing me to my room.

"The air is so dry here," he explained, "as you walk, your shoes rub the carpet and when you touch the metal handle, you get a jolt of static electricity."

"Well, you could have told me first," I grumbled.

At that time you couldn't simply drive around wherever you wanted in Beijing, so I rented a car and driver for a day and an official tour guide, and off we set to explore. Despite the official entourage, once we were outside the centre of Beijing, we soon began to get lost, and the guide would have to stop for directions. Before long, we were in the middle of nowhere and totally lost, so we decided to stop for lunch.

China is a huge country of vast, open spaces, and on that day I got my first insight into its scale. We parked and the road stretched as far as the naked eye could see. There was nothing but the road in both directions, other than some parallel train tracks. I felt very far from home. An ancient-looking cargo train came slowly down the tracks until it finally reached our picnic spot. It was making the sort of noises that children imitating trains make. As it reached us, the noise became deafening, and the train took ages to pass. At one time, the carriages stretched as far in front as they did behind. You could no longer see the beginning, or end, of this beast. More importantly, it was full of pigs and the smell, even in winter, was literally breathtaking.

I looked into the distance and I saw a very small speck, still far away, but clearly heading in our direction. It was getting progressively colder and we were jumping around while eating our food, trying to keep warm. About twenty minutes later, the small speck had become large enough for us to make out that it was a guy riding a tricycle with a Styrofoam box perched on its back seat. About ten minutes after that, the vision finally reached us.

The rider was totally out of breath but managed to ring a small bell on his handlebars and smile at us. We asked the guide to find out where he was going in the middle of this icy wilderness, on his tricycle. The guide spoke to him for a while before declaring, "He is selling something and it's in the box. You can look if you wish."

We had driven for over two hours to get to where we were, and since leaving the outskirts of the city, had not passed anything much in the way of inhabited spots along the route. According to the guide, we had another two hours' drive ahead to find any town or village. This, of course, was two hours if travelling by car, so goodness knows how long it would have been by bicycle. I was therefore curious to know where this guy had come from. Actually, I was more interested in just trying to get the blood running back through my frostbitten toes, but I opened the box to find … you won't believe it, but … ice cream! Yes, that's right, ice cream, but only about six pieces at the most. It was hard to tell exactly how many or what variety, as they looked so old and solidly frozen together in a lump.

I was flabbergasted, and when I indicated that it was too cold to eat anything that even resembled chilled, never mind frozen, food the peddler became quite angry. So angry, in fact, that I quickly changed my mind and bought two pieces of unappetising and unwanted ice cream – which he hacked off the lump – just to calm him down. He took the money, gave me the ice-cream and pedalled away.

"Have a good day," I shouted after him, and the friendly ice cream man turned round and gave me that worldwide expression of disgruntlement – the index finger.

We reached civilisation a while later, stopping at a local village to see the 'wet market' where the locals sell whatever fresh produce they have in the way of meat, fish, fruit, vegetables, and so on. Knowing that anything of value, especially the better produce, would be sold overseas, we knew that we would not see much, but what we did find surprised even me.

The first thing I noticed was a man chewing on a long piece of sugar cane. He was chewing with so much passion one would assume he was sharpening his teeth with it. The villagers looked very surprised to see us and quickly gathered around, touching my hair and generally having a good laugh at this strange-looking foreigner. Apparently, they hadn't seen many Westerners at that time, and I was a novelty, to say the least. There were some roads I would like to have gone down to take a look, but there were large signs declaring 'Foreigners Not Allowed', or so my trusty translator informed me.

Most of those selling fruit and vegetables had produce which was not in good condition, to say the least. Some of it was half-rotten, even in these temperatures, which told me that it had been there for a while. People in the West would have been offended if a market stallholder tried to sell them produce like that, even at knockdown prices. One guy was sitting at a rickety wooden table, smiling to himself. On the top of the table was a large pile of raw, very bloody meat, covered with flies. Amazingly, he had a long queue of people lining up to buy this unappetising flesh. I asked the guide if there was going to be enough meat – regardless of its condition – to go round, and he asked the rather smug-looking butcher.

"Actually," the guide informed me, "they're not lining up to buy, but just to have a look. It's not everyday that they get to see fresh meat like that."

"Of course he's joking?" I challenged.

"He's not," said the guide, "this is actually very expensive meat."

My mind flew back to Texas, where steak restaurants sell 26 oz steaks on the promise that if you finished the whole steak, you wouldn't have to pay for it. It really threw into stark contrast the difference between the world's 'haves' and its 'have nots'. I decided to look closer, and I approached the table. The big-bellied, smug-looking guy sat up with obvious anticipation. With the guide's help I asked how much the meat was and, not surprisingly, it turned out to be peanuts in western terms. I decided to make a purchase.

The guide asked the butcher to give me around a kilogramme and asked what type of meat it was. The man with the meat looked at us if we were the craziest people on earth.

"Who cares? It's meat! What more do you want?" With that he pulled out a rusty old Chinese chopper from underneath his table. I thought for a moment that we had offended him and that our days, or minutes, were numbered. But he just lifted the chopper dramatically high in the air and brought it down with all his brute force, hacking off a wedge of flesh as thick as a doorstop. One look from the guide told me that on this occasion it was not advisable to ask the butcher to weigh it. I'd better just accept whatever I was given and be suitably grateful.

"Well, it sure looks like one kilo to me," I whispered. After another ferret around under the table for a piece of old sun-bleached newspaper, a swift wrap was made of the blood-dripping hunk of meat, and the goods were handed over. The sale was done.

I passed the package to the guide and told him it was a small token of appreciation for looking after me. Tears welled up in his eyes, and he bent and kissed my hand. This brief exchange over an unappetising piece of meat was one of the most moving moments I had encountered. I thought of all that is taken for granted in the West, and the enormous waste that occurs in big hotel kitchens. I felt very sad.

The next day I decided to visit the Great Wall of China and on the way stopped off at a few small temples. At one of the temples, the guide showed me some underground storerooms that actually looked more like buried caves. We looked through a letter-box-like peephole, to see thousands of stone slabs which monks had used to write their scriptures on centuries ago. These sacred rooms had never been reopened, but had been 'built-in' by the monks, using the rough forms of concrete and cement of the time.

As we reached the Great Wall, it was almost dusk and just starting to snow. At the bottom an old man was selling T-shirts, some with a slogan declaring, 'I visited the Great Wall'. I thought these would make great gifts for my staff and asked the old man for half a dozen.

"I'm sorry, sir," he said, "you have to climb to the highest part of the wall first, and only then will you deserve to wear such a treasured gift. When you reach the top, there will be another man there who will give you a coupon, and when you bring it back down I can then sell you what you want." So off I set on the hard, upward trek.

Each step was a hike in itself. The large slabs had moved so much over the years that negotiating the gaps and the risers involved taking very large steps. In some places there were ropes to help you pull yourself up. I found myself breathing heavily, and the ice-cold air was burning the back of my dry throat with every struggling gasp from this tough workout. How I wished I had put my spare time to more effective use in the hotel's well-equipped gym. But it was too late for that now.

At the top, there was a tower where the security guards on duty would have stood watch over the centuries, on their frosty lookouts. On this crisp evening, all was calm. No sign of any marauding invaders. Not a soul, in fact. I looked down to the bottom of the Wall, and although it was by now almost dark, I could still see the shadowed outline of the T-shirt man, now waving mockingly at me. Yes, I'd been done up like a kipper. He had thrown me a line and I'd swallowed it, hook, line and sinker! But that didn't really matter now, as I had the view of a lifetime.

Before me was a towering and vast landscape that seemed to stretch forever across snowy-green pastures and rolling hills. It was bitterly cold, snowing and now dark, but the snow-covered ground kept the land in front of me bright as day. It was absolutely silent, except for the wind blowing in my ears and the sound of the icy hard flakes of snow hitting the Wall close by.

I had read somewhere that this was the only man-made structure visible from outside the earth's atmosphere, and had found it difficult to believe. I had no trouble believing it now. Its sheer size was absolutely staggering. The Wall spanned as far as the eye could see and thousands of miles beyond. The guides like to tell you that while constructing it, one man died for every stone laid in the wall and millions of huge stones must have been used to fashion this masterpiece. Whether this was true or not, standing on the Great Wall of China was an awe-inspiring experience. I thought about how lucky I was to be there.

On the next day's agenda were the Forbidden City and the Summer Palace. Inevitably, the Forbidden City was something of an anticlimax after the Great Wall, but the huge compound was an amazing sight, nevertheless. I had a new driver today, and he demanded to be paid in imported cigarettes, so I gave him two packets before leaving the car to look at the Forbidden City. On my return a couple of hours later, the inside of the car was a dense smog of cigarette smoke. I opened the doors wide for a quick fumigation and when some of the smoke had dissipated, got back into the car. The driver promptly asked if I had any more cigarettes, as in the two hours waiting for me to return, he had smoked the first lot!

The last stop on that day's tour was Tiananmen Square – what a sight. This is one of the largest single open-air meeting places in the world, and can accommodate millions of people at once. Of course, I had no idea that only a few weeks later, Chinese Red Army tanks would be seen driving right through the Square in the infamous crackdown on the pro-democracy student movement. Things were indeed difficult in China during this period. My friend, Jonathon, who was working in China at that time, told me that whenever he was going on holiday, he would invariably be the first in the queue, eager to board the plane to get away. When it was time to return to work in China, however, he would become the most reluctant of passengers and almost always the last to embark.

Arriving back in Hong Kong – China's little brother – I brought back an unwelcome souvenir … the worst flu that I have ever had. It knocked me out for days, but it was a price worth paying for the memorable visit I had.

Hong Kong is a roaring economic lion, or some might say, a raging bull with a mind of its own. It cannot be controlled, or made to follow a prescribed line, and certainly not without anyone trying to do so being very disappointed with the financial consequences, which are likely to be quite the opposite of what they would be if Hong Kong was left to its own devices. The people of Hong Kong are a very hardworking and proud people, with incredible entrepreneurial spirit, the likes of which are impossible to diminish. In my opinion, left to run things by itself, Hong Kong can surely overcome any obstacles or challenges it will ever face.

I was in Hong Kong during the Tiananmen Square massacre. It was a very sad day for all concerned, but was felt all the more acutely by my staff, many of whom were walking around for days afterwards, wearing black armbands. Although Hong Kong was not at that time part of the People's Republic of China, many Hong Kong Chinese people still have relatives across the border in the 'land of big brother'. The ambiguity and complexity of this tiny but thrusting territory is that Hong Kong people are very proud of their Chinese heritage and, despite Tiananmen, many were happy to go back to Chinese rule.

I loved Hong Kong and still do, and I have total respect for all its citizens who together have built this money-making machine into what it is today. It is a city where people run up moving escalators and where traffic can grind to a gridlock, sometimes for hours. They still have English-style double-decker buses, cruising around everywhere, and the famous Star Ferry, which transports commuters between Hong Kong Island and Kowloon or Tsim Sha Tsui, respectively.

The waters surrounding Hong Kong are deep and cold, holding some of the biggest great white sharks in existence. I remember once seeing a huge beached great white washed up dead on one of the nearby island beaches, and thinking, did that really come out of this sea, and if it did … oh, my, God!

A friend of mine, named John, used to work for the Hong Kong coastguard, and he would regale me with his stories about illegal Chinese immigrants trying to escape to the smaller, yet more prosperous territory next door. John told me how some people were so desperate to escape to Hong Kong and the hope of better times, that they would use literally any floating object available to try to sail across.

Perhaps the most compelling story he told me took place during a routine border patrol around Hong Kong's coastal waters. John and his unit were flying in the helicopter that night when they received a call from the coastguard's launch. The launch had picked something up on its radar and called the helicopter to go and have a closer look. It was thought to be a sampan floating around aimlessly, and that there may be something wrong, or that the vessel's crew may be in need of assistance. But when John and his helicopter unit arrived at the reported location, they found nothing.

The conversation with the base control on the radio went back and forth.

"I can't see anything," John told them.

"That's impossible," came the reply. "We're looking at it on the radar as we speak. It looks like a sampan or something about the same size."

After what must have been a countless number of sweeps across the area, shining the helicopter's searchlights down onto the water, John suddenly saw two guys trying to smuggle themselves across the border aboard a couple of oil drums tied together.

They were waving frantically at the helicopter and both had looks of horror on their faces. As the helicopter hovered above, John shone the light slightly to one side to see a huge great white shark eating another man close by. Aware that they would probably be next to receive the shark's attention, pure panic had struck, and the race was on to get them out of the water in time.

The pilot lowered down a safety harness which unfortunately could only take one person. One can only imagine what it must have been like for the two men, both in mortal terror, having to decide in great haste who would be lifted to safety first. Luckily, they were both saved, but their friend was not so lucky, and many more have apparently suffered the same fate each year, trying to get to Hong Kong.

Hong Kong residents love to eat out. This usually makes for full restaurants, and underscores that it is a good business to be in. Similarly, real estate is another profitable business line. Even a very small apartment can cost millions of Hong Kong dollars. Kitchens in many apartments can be so small there is only room for a portable gas stove, which is good for a wok and cooking Chinese food, but not exactly conducive to other styles of cooking. People might own a Mercedes Benz car but would still prefer to take their business associates out to entertain them, rather than take them home and lose 'face'.

Hong Kong apartments are so notoriously small in size it would not be unusual for two non-cohabiting people to share one bed, with one having the bed while the other worked the overnight shift. The roles would then be reversed during the daytime, as the person who worked overnight would sleep during the day while the other worked the day shift, thus making the apartment – and more especially the bed – big enough for both.

One night as I passed through the restaurant of the hotel, I heard – and I'm sure everyone else did too – a man screaming at the top of his voice down the phone in the middle of the waiting area. I was told afterwards that he was entertaining some people and when he had gone to settle the bill, his credit card had been rejected. Of course, he had lost face big time in front of his potential clients, and he must have reasoned that his only way out of this predicament was to make a manly scene by shouting and carrying on at those at the other end of the line, namely the credit card company.

When the executive sous chef briefed me about what was going on, I remember saying to him, "Yes, it must be terrible to be embarrassed like that, but surely that's not the way to behave. How can he carry on like that and disturb everyone else in the restaurant?"

The executive sous chef, being Chinese himself, just looked at me in a shocked manner, and said, "If that was me, I would feel like killing someone. How dare they embarrass the poor guy like that, especially in front of everyone? You see, now he has to let everyone know that actually it is a mistake, and that they at the other end of the line are the ones who are foolish, not him."

So all the shouting was really for the benefit of the audience, to let everyone know that he did have money and that he was not broke! For the many people passing through and who may have witnessed the scene, the nuances of it were probably too deep and too complex to fathom, but as I would learn, if you stay in a place like Hong Kong long enough, you start to understand the rules of the game, and that is when you can say you have truly adapted to the lifestyle.

The construction of a building in Hong Kong involves lengths of bamboo being tied to the outside of the structure to form scaffolding. Pieces of thick bamboo are tied together, like some kind of crazy spider's web, sometimes going up as high as thirty floors and more. The building workers walk on the bamboo without shoes or safety netting. How they do not fall off I will never know, but one thing is for sure, I wouldn't be able to stomach walking up there myself.

Then there is the art of feng shui. For many Westerners like myself, this can be very difficult to understand. In short, it is the belief that if a chair in your room is not positioned in the right place or at the right angle, absolute havoc can result in your life. When things go wrong for you or your business, you can call in a recognised feng shui master to tell you what to do. He will come to your house or your business and move a few things around to ensure they are at the right angles to enhance your feng shui and, of course, will charge you a bomb in the process. The strange thing is that it will probably work, and from that day on you will suffer no more.

I remember when the Hong Kong hotel where I worked had just opened its showpiece restaurant on the thirtieth floor, and one of the staff said he had seen a ghost sitting at a table with his legs swinging back and forth. Naturally I went up to see the fellow myself and was utterly disappointed that he was hiding somewhere, seemingly not wanting to meet me. The next day, all of the staff refused to go upstairs until we had performed a small ceremony which involved prayers and the offering of a suckling pig. It would appear that the 'hungry ghost' went home with his tummy full and all my staff felt able to return to work.

I do not mean to make light of it or to make fun of such beliefs, as their belief systems are theirs and are to be respected, especially if you want to do business in this environment. I would come to learn that if you do not follow these basic procedures, your staff will not respect you and will not work in an environment that has not been sanctioned by a feng shui master.

Some failed businesses have been frowned on after people learned that the owners had saved money on the feng shui, and you would invariably hear the words 'Oh, no wonder!' There have been cases where office buildings have been unsuccessful, and when the feng shui master has added a few bricks or tiles to the outside of the building, or in some other way changed the architect's design, the building's fortunes have also changed to the positive.

Each and every Chinese kitchen, be it in a restaurant, hotel, or even a humble coffee shop, has a small temple for prayer, the lighting of joss sticks and for leaving daily offerings. This, it is believed, will bring the staff good health and prosperity, as well as good business to the restaurant. It does not matter what anyone thinks of this, or whether it is a hygiene concern or not, there is no way that the staff will work if you do not have one.

The hotel's managing director was prone to paying us surprise visits. On one occasion I had a telephone call at about two o'clock in the morning, when all normal souls would be fast asleep.

"Is that you, chef?" came a voice at the other end of the line.

"Yes," I said sleepily, "how can I help you?"

"It's me, Mr Gregory." I caught my senses as I recognised his voice and quickly sat up, trying to imagine what the heck the big boss wanted so late at night.

"I need you to give me some face, chef. Tonight. Right now … I have some friends downstairs in the restaurant and they want some of your famous soufflés … chocolate ones," he pleaded.

Those of you who make soufflés will appreciate how I felt. They're not the easiest of items at the best time of day, much less when you're half asleep and it's two in the morning.

"Alright, Mr Gregory, don't worry," I said. "I'll come down right away." I ran around the room, pulling on my jeans and a T-shirt. I paused to give a wake-up call to Lim, my pastry chef.

"Hey there, Lim, we've got a problem. Mr Gregory is downstairs and he wants some soufflés, right now. I need your help on this one," I told him.

"You must be out of your mind," came the helpful, but understandable response.

But I didn't have time for any nonsense, so my reply was swift and to the point.

"Hey, if you don't get your backside downstairs right now, I'm going to …"

Five minutes later, we were running around the kitchen trying to organise the desired miracle.

First we needed to get the oven hot, which took about fifteen minutes. While this was happening we started to make the soufflés, quickly greasing the moulds and whipping up all the rich ingredients that make a chocolate soufflé so 'moreish'. Into the oven they went. I stepped outside to find Mr Gregory to let him know everything was in hand. There he was with four or five top brass embassy officials and their spouses. He and most of the party looked well plastered. No wonder, I thought, he had probably boasted after too many drinks how good our soufflés were and someone had challenged him to prove it. Now, just because he couldn't keep his mouth shut, we were out of our beds and running around the kitchen in the middle of the night like blue-arsed flies.

"Good evening, everybody," I declared, "your soufflés are on the way, but if you don't mind, be patient for just a little longer because as the saying goes, 'even kings' have to wait for a soufflé, a soufflé waits for no one."

With that, I went back into the kitchen and asked the maestro how much longer they would be, and he told me another ten minutes at least. At that point, I suddenly realised that he was standing there in only his underwear – Y-fronts, with his beer-belly bloated and protruding over the top – then I remembered that he had been out late that night drinking and was probably still hung over. He'd just forgotten to get dressed in the rush.

Eventually, our masterpieces were ready and I asked Lim if he wanted to go out to serve them himself, seeing that he'd done most of the work, only to remember that his attire was not exactly reputation enhancing! So I got myself ready to serve them. As I stepped out with the first of the three beautifully presented soufflés, I jokingly announced, "Ladies and Gentlemen, your much-awaited masterpieces are now served!" I emerged through the entrance of the restaurant and looked up ... to see that they had all gone home.

●━━●━○●━●━━●

The competition between hotels for the discerning diner is so great, executive chefs and food and beverage directors will do almost anything to come up with new and creative ideas in order to separate themselves from every other hotel in town. Sneaking around at night in the cover of darkness while 'checking out the competition' is not uncommon, but getting caught doing it usually is. The market in Hong Kong is very tough and you had to fight increasingly hard for your market share, so stooping low was the order of the day to steal as much business as you could possibly get your hands on. After visiting the local store selling party favours, I stuck on my wig, thick-rimmed glasses, false nose and an extra large moustache, and trotted out on the road to see what I could find out about the hotel down the street. The food and beverage director at our competitor hotel was an extremely arrogant chap who looked down on everyone else in the business, hence the made-up mug to enable me to dodge his barrage of insults if he found me snooping around.

After sitting down at my table, I very gingerly took out my pen and paper, ready to take spy notes for my report to be submitted the next day. I was coolly glancing around, studying the environment and trying to be as inconspicuous as possible, when I suddenly heard someone say, "Hey, Saxon, how are you doing?" As I turned round to see who the party pooper was, there was the executive chef himself.

"Hi, Peter, how are you?" I answered, with a gasp and a moan. "How did you know it was me?" I asked in a surprised manner. After he had insulted me by explaining that I was the only guy foolish enough to sneak around dressed like that on any night other than Halloween, he became very excited while sharing with me his compelling new idea that was going to corner the Hong Kong food and beverage market.

I was also very excited and had to cover my mouth to avoid screaming at every turn in the tale he was about to tell. It's great fun sharing ideas with the enemy and even better fun if you can get inside information about a great idea they have and implement it first, therefore making everyone believe that you created it.

I checked my pen for ink and was ready to scribble down notes, as he started to fire out his idea without even once gasping for air. "You know when we make our Club Sandwich here," he started out, "we place the roast turkey on the top layer and the fried egg and bacon on the bottom layer?" he asked me, with hopes of anticipation hanging in the air.

"Yes," I replied with hesitation.

"Well, I am thinking to place the fried egg and bacon on the top layer and the roast turkey on the bottom," he said, rather dead pan. As I waited for the idea to come to a grand finale, I realised I was going to have to squeeze it out of him.

"Then what are you going to do?" I asked rather kindly.

"What do you mean? That's it," he announced and looked at me, waiting for the comments of praise.

"That's your big, innovative entrepreneurial idea."

"Yes, that's it, what do you think?"

My first thought was to realise that the ink in my pen was certainly going to be enough, even if it was empty! I leant back in my dining chair, took off my party face and wig and tried to conjure up the best response that I could muster. "Well, it's like this, big guy, if you go on the internet and look up the website named 'lousy and rotten ideas.com', I think I saw this idea of yours featured on the front page. A European chef first thought it up back in 1922 and after being pelted with tomatoes and mouldy lettuce, I think they had him hung, drawn and quartered. Also, by the way, if you look up the word 'twit' in the dictionary it has your picture there to explain the meaning of the word in a more definitive manner."

I thought that was enough to make my feelings quite clear, but was astounded when he came back with:

"So what are you saying, you don't like my idea?"

I was just about to give him my no-beating-around-the-bush response when I heard: "Here to learn something are we, Saxon?" As I turned round yet again to see who else had decided to join the party and wondering why my table was fast becoming the busiest in town, I saw the food and beverage director standing there with his usual air of arrogance. I could not help but be reminded of Laurel and Hardy, the chef being short and stout, and the food and beverage director, tall, slim and silly looking, with a bow tie. Now I knew that this was going to get ugly unless I came up with a calculated response to bring him down to size, otherwise he was going to pull my leg all evening.

"Well, you know," I hesitated for a second to gather my thoughts, "as my root canal treatment was cancelled and I could not find anything else better to do … here I am, yours truly, suffering while choking on your delicate cuisine and listening to your chef blow me away with an idea that will shudder the pillars of the culinary world. I did come here to steal some of your ideas, but unfortunately, the only new idea you have is shifting the turkey around between the dough, and, trust me, that ain't gonna hack it. By the way, don't you have a wedding function tonight, maybe a company dinner perhaps, something to keep you busy so that you can earn your salary for once, or does everyone have a dentist appointment?"

It was no surprise to me that the third person to call my name was the security guard who was to escort me to the front door. We had a good laugh walking down the corridor.

"I have never seen him so angry," lamented the guard. "He was spitting hot fat when he asked me to see you out."

Writing my report the next day was not going to be easy. In fact, it was going to be the shortest report of all time. The only new idea I could write about was the turning upside down of our club sandwich, which was not going to go down well with my boss. I guess we would have to come up with our own idea that would have creativity and ingenuity to make us a leader in the market and not a follower. As my teacher once told me: "There are different people in the hotel industry; some will wait for it to happen, some will watch it happen and some will even help it happen, but leaders will always make it happen."

———— •◦•••◦•• ————

Most foreigners who get invited for a steamboat dinner in Hong Kong usually find it a remarkable dining experience. The experience sometimes offers the privilege of bragging about it for many years to come. One such occasion, that I will clearly remember to the day I die, was no less unforgettable. It was explained to me that the steamboat concept was conceived to gather all family members together to enjoy a lovely communal meal. In Hong Kong and China, steamboat dinners are usually enjoyed during the colder months when the warmth from the boiling pot would be comforting.

I was excited at my invite to the steamboat dinner of my friend's family, and I was looking forward to enjoying the experience of dining at a roadside, smoke-filled *dai pai dong* blasting Cantonese pop music. To be able to pack in as much food as possible without exploding so as to impress the family of my close friend Fung, I had skipped lunch.

By 7pm, when I was famished and feeling dizzy, Fung announced as we were making our way to the open-air eatery: "Saxon, we are going out to the New Territories in Shatin, the steamboat restaurant there is extremely famous and well worth the longer journey." The word 'longer' seemed to echo in my mind as we hit the highway to goodness-knows-where at a cruising speed of 120 km per hour.

I heard Fung ask the driver if there was a problem with the engine as there were strange noises, but the driver explained to him that it was impossible as the car had just been sent for servicing. I did not want to tell them that it was in fact my stomach rumbling so loudly that it outblasted the radio that was grinding out the latest heavy metal songs.

When we arrived forty-five minutes later in the middle of nowhere, I was on the verge of starvation so I was extremely happy to sit down and look at the soon-to-be-lit stove at the table. "Hey, Saxon, do you want to try *tom yam*, plain chicken broth or a Chinese herb stock?" asked Fung. At that point, I was so hungry I would have eaten the dirty, rotten fish of the stinking Sha Tin River. We quickly decided to go with the *tom yam* option. Fung was talking in Cantonese to the waiter, and I was hoping that he wasn't talking about how cold it was sitting in this corrugated-iron-covered shack and was instead ordering the chicken, beef, fish, lamb and prawns that my growling tummy was crying out for.

After a while, the first platter of raw food arrived and the first question that came to my head was, what the heck was that? "Fung," I started out, "what are these delicacies?" I asked politely.

"Well, this is a sea cucumber and …" explained Fung. Before he could carry on I decided to butt in a little and try to get to the bottom of the menu choices he had made.

"I know what a cucumber looks like. That, however, has no resemblance to a cucumber at all!" I remarked at the sausage-like thing.

"It's funny you should say that," rebounded Fung. "Here in Hong Kong we call it sea dick." He giggled. How appropriate, I thought to myself. I could not help but try to imagine what it was going to taste like.

"And here we have brains," said Fung, as his finger descended from dish to dish as he rounded the platter.

"Excuse me? What kind of brains?" I asked, perplexed.

"Pig's brains – they are a speciality and they taste like … let me think …" replied Fung as he went into deep thought. I, however, did not need to spend any time imagining what it tasted like – I knew I was going to have problems swallowing it anyway! To distract myself from the upcoming Fear Factor challenge, I asked where the thinly sliced beef was.

"Have you ever had sushi lately, Saxon?" asked Fung. I could not help but wish that I was eating sushi that night. "It sort of tastes like sea urchin, with that kind of creamy texture," Fung went on, describing the brain texture, oblivious to my squirming. "Now this here is my favourite," said Fung whilst making a slurping sound. "Fatt Choi!"

"What the heck are you talking about? If it's not a juicy, fat sausage, I am not interested."

"No, it's a kind of moss," he replied.

"You mean the kind that grows on slimy river stones?" I asked.

"Of course not! Sea moss, and it looks like black hair." Now, the thought of putting a rather large glob of tangled hair in my mouth – no matter what colour it was – was very much a turn-off. "While we are waiting for the stock to boil, I have ordered some side dishes for us to nibble on. Oh, here comes the first dish now!" announced the comedian. As I turned round to get a sneak preview of the latest horror show, I saw a rather large tray of small deep-fried things covered in a light black bean sauce.

"What do we have here, buddy? Chicken neck?"

"Actually, they are duck tongues, very tasty and delicious." As I placed the tongue in my mouth, the initial taste was actually quite pleasant, but the feeling did not last that long as I chewed it and found the thing to be eighty per cent bones, having very little meat.

"The next dish is here," says Fung whilst rubbing his hands together with glee. "These are fish lips."

"Fish what?" I asked rather gingerly.

"It's basically the fish mouth, teeth and all."

"Oh goody, that sounds yummy! I had been hoping that was going to be next," I exclaimed, causing Fung to have his beer spray out through his nose.

"Now, Saxon, you just pop one of these suckers in your mouth, chew and suck all the juice out of them and then spit the left-over stuff right onto the table."

"So let me get this straight, Fung," I said. "Somewhere, there is a farmyard full of ducks that can't say much, fish that are not smiling a whole lot these days and one pig that, as we speak, has a problem remembering anything, including where its sty is. I must say I am very impressed so far, tell me, Doctor Dolittle, what's next?"

"Doctor who? Well, it's funny you should ask because here comes the chicken feet!"

"Are you aware that chicken walk around the farmyard on their feet, and the last time I saw them their toilet manners weren't so good – they walk with their bare feet on their droppings and you are now telling me that we are going to eat them?!" I gasped.

"They boil them first. Don't worry," assured Fung.

"What with? Dettol?!"

This was turning into a great night – a real cultural experience. As I sat there, really not eating anything of substance, Fung remarked: "If I would have known you were not really hungry tonight, Saxon, I would not have ordered so much."

I was happy that he was enjoying the evening by amusing himself on my expense. However, I had eaten as little as I could of everything and I was starving. I was thrilled with the arrival of the mushrooms, vegetables and the bean curd – these were thrown into the boiling witches' cauldron, which, by now, resembled a dark sinister potion.

Before the rest could have their pick of the food, I had taken all the good stuff out of the pot as soon as it was al dente. The food had barely been introduced to the stock before they were at the bottom of my bowl. The noodles that came at the end were a very pleasant sight, and I wolfed them down as if I had not eaten for a week.

Most steamboat restaurants generally offer a wide range of dishes that are suitable for first timers and fussy diners. However, the roadside eateries that cater mainly to locals sometimes only offer items that may not be agreeable for everyone's palate, so be aware!

The steamboat dinner is the best concept that I have come across which offers a dining experience that will allow you to get to know your fellow guests better. Of course, a few mugs of beer may help to loosen up a few tongues, as well as help you overlook the fact that you are dining on the tongue of some poor duck. Your ability to dine on such exotic foods and willingness to try anything placed in your bowl will certainly endear you to the hearts of your hosts.

As my contract came to its end in Hong Kong, I was getting itchy feet. I had been told a lot about how great life was in the Philippines, and when a job came up for me in Manila, I jumped at the chance.

VI

MABUHAI MANILA

ARRIVING TO START my new challenge at my next hotel assignment in Manila, the capital of the Philippines, my experience at the international airport should have been a forewarning of what I was in for. What was to transpire during my time there, however, was like nothing I had experienced before.

I have spoken to many people who have lived, or spent time, in Manila about their views on the city, and the answers are usually the same; they either love it or loathe it. There is precious little in-between. It's a place which always provokes clear-cut reactions, never grey; always black or white. For example, Manila airport is the funkiest airport I have ever managed to scrape through in one piece. It gives an excellent impression, to put it bluntly, of sheer disorganised chaos. Even finding one's luggage, that time-honoured chore one is obliged to observe at all airports, presents a challenge of epic proportions. Not always the best welcome, or '*mabuhai*', to this challenging destination. What's more, as a tourist, or new visitor, you are sadly susceptible to being ripped off in Manila from the second you land at the airport until the moment you board the plane to leave.

I had a piece of hand luggage that I left for safe-keeping at the supposedly secure left-luggage centre at Manila International Airport. I handed in the bag and they gave me a ticket to collect it later. I had attached a leather baggage tag, commemorating the inaugural run of the Far East based Eastern and Oriental train, which had been given to me the month before, to my hand luggage. It was a lovely souvenir that I was particularly happy to receive, but on picking up my luggage I was surprised to see it was missing. After a few minutes deliberating with the left-luggage attendant and trying to point out that the tag had, in fact, been attached to the bag when I left it with them, I could see that I was getting nowhere, so I grudgingly gave it up as a lost cause and left.

Jumping into an airport taxi was no less of a rude awakening to the reality of the Philippines. The first taxi I got into had seat covers with huge holes in them, with the foam padding cascading out everywhere. What's more, as I leaned forward to tell the driver where I wanted to go, I noticed that the steering wheel was literally tied onto the steering column and held together with a makeshift piece of rusty wire. Not willing to offend so early, I told the driver the name of my hotel, said a quiet prayer, and off we went.

On asking the driver to put on the meter as I had limited local currency, without so much as turning his head, he laughed out loud.

"Meter!" he bellowed. "You're dreaming, my friend. Does this car look like it has a meter? I'm just glad it's moving!"

A little later, he turned round to talk to me and almost collided with the car in front. As he did so, I shouted to him to look out. At which point he turned and looked forward once again, just in time to pull the steering wheel hard to the left, narrowly missing a slower moving car by a couple of hairs' widths. Unfortunately, the feeling of sheer relief at narrowly avoiding a collision lasted only a few brief seconds, because at that instant the steering wheel came off in his hands. So here we were, making my inaugural taxi ride in my new country, and doing some 40 mph down the highway with my driver frantically trying to shove his steering wheel back into the vacant slot beneath the dashboard!

Eventually he succeeded, and managed to slip the loose steering wheel back into its slot. I breathed a sigh of relief. Presumably noticing through his rear-view mirror the look of horror etched onto my face, the driver casually sought to put me at ease once more.

"Don't worry there, sir, this is pretty normal, and after all the practice runs I've had, it's no problem at all. What were we talking about before that little distraction?" he asked almost nonchalantly.

"The meter," I told him in a quivering voice.

"Ah yes, the meter. Well, I don't have one, so let's just negotiate the price."

And that, if you want to put a positive slant on it, was when I discovered the art of Philippine-style negotiating, or when I first learnt how to put up with being shafted, if you are a tad more cynical. It eventually took about an hour to reach my hotel, and yet a few days later when I returned to the airport to pick up a friend, it took a mere fifteen minutes. Being driven all around town when you actually only want to go just a couple of blocks is not uncommon, so knowing my own way around soon became an imperative.

On my first day in my new job as executive chef at the first class downtown hotel which had engaged me, I decided to walk the course and see what the facilities were like. I also wanted to check out the restaurants because I was not altogether familiar with the national cuisine. In fact, the food of the Philippines is a delicious blend of many cuisines, including Chinese and Thai, but it is predominantly Spanish and Portuguese in heritage. Famous Philippine dishes include 'mechado' which is beef braised in soya sauce with garlic and shallots; 'chicken adobo', a stew with pepper and vinegar; 'lechon kawali', crispy pork with liver sauce; and 'sinangag', a garlic-flavoured fried rice. A particular local trick, I subsequently discovered, is to add a few cubes of hard milk chocolate to the breakfast rice to give it more flavour and get you going in the mornings.

I also learnt to cook 'pochero', a dish made from diced ham and Spanish sausages, and 'pancit molo', which is very similar to the famous wonton soups of Hong Kong. Then there are the many desserts that are to be found within almost all Asian cuisines. The brilliantly named 'halo-halo' is a concoction of tropical fruit topped with shaved ice. 'Leche flan' is a Philippine custard speciality, and 'bibingka' combines sweet coconut, rice flour and brown sugar to make a fine pudding. Inventive local chefs also have a good line in home-made wines to complement their unique cuisine, brewed from coconut, rice or even fermented sugarcane.

As I familiarised myself with the hotel, I found the front of house facilities – those areas which the customers see – to be very nice, while at the back of the house, the scene was totally different, especially in the kitchen area. The facilities were old and rather decrepit. Most of the equipment either did not work or was ancient or even obsolete.

The hotel's general manager had pointed out that he particularly wanted me to improve the desserts in the hotel's restaurant outlets, as he felt the quality of what was presently provided was poor and the subject of endless complaints. After talking to the pastry chef about this, I realised that his job was made all the more difficult, if not impossible, because most of his key equipment was almost permanently out of action. It was all too often being fixed by engineers-cum-handymen who probably did not know what they were doing in the first place. In particular, his most important machine, a large, heavy-duty, industrial-size food mixer, which was used to make doughs, cake mixes and pastry items, was totally useless.

I went to see the general manager about the state of affairs and he told me, very politely, to go and take a running jump. There was no money, he said, to spend on anything, even for the guests' comfort, let alone for the benefit of the staff's working environment. After a few days of futile effort, battling this back and forth, I decided to take matters into my own hands and to tell the boss exactly what I thought about the equipment issue, and everything else I had been dissatisfied with since my arrival. I told him that the hotel's cuisine, especially the desserts, would not get any better if I was not given the proper tools to do the job.

The very next day we took delivery of a huge and very heavy-duty, industrial pastry mixer. It took four engineering staff struggling in unison to deliver this beast to the kitchen, and was a real drama. There was a lot of shouting going on, and something resembling a tug-of-war, before it was finally placed in the chosen spot and the supplier's agent was able to properly install the machine, which needed a dedicated power source and special cabling.

The pastry chef and his staff, who had suffered for years without the proper tools, now considered me something of a hero and told me so. When the machine was ready to use we were given a demonstration by the supplier's agent, to show that it really was in good working order. They handed me the five-year warranty and I signed the delivery documents. We were now in business, I thought happily.

You can imagine my surprise when we went to work the next day to find that the brand new mixer, the same one that I had fought so hard to get, had 'gone for a walk'. It was missing and reported stolen. Talk about an inside job. This thing weighed about twelve tons and took a phalanx of guys to move it around. How on earth could a thief slip into the hotel, pick up the mixer and carry it out without any of the overnight staff seeing them? I was surprised and disgusted at my staff who, I felt, must have been involved.

What I subsequently learnt from my time in the Philippines is that any newish equipment is worth a small fortune when compared to local salaries. The money you could get from selling a single item would be enough to make a big difference to the livelihoods of a whole lot of people. In fact, probably everyone in the hotel who was on duty that night was in on the deal. It was a learning experience in more ways than one. It was also instrumental in my deciding to stay on at the hotel for at least a year, despite my inauspicious introduction to the country and my new post, to help the general manager cope with what was obviously a very difficult situation.

Things gradually got better for me on a personal level as I met a number of very nice local people, mainly through the hotel and its guests. Families especially seemed to befriend me, possibly feeling sorry for me, alone in their country. One particular family invited me to their house for Sunday lunch. They were apparently very well off, with a successful animal feed factory on the edge of town. Driving through downtown Manila was, for me, never an altogether pleasant experience and for some crazy reason, for the journey to their house, I decided to try out the 'Jeepney', the local shared taxi service. I stood at the roadside waiting for one to stop, and was still patiently waiting a good while later. Unfortunately, all the Jeepneys which appeared just kept passing me by. After some time a guy came up to me and asked if I was waiting for a ride. I explained that I was trying to flag a Jeepney down to go to my friend's house but was not having any luck.

"That last one that passed could have taken you," said the stranger.

"Yes, maybe it could," I said, "but it never stopped."

"They don't stop," he laughed. "You just have to jump on and off while they're moving, but they don't go that fast so you don't need to worry."

No doubt seeing the panic on my face about this, my good Samaritan friend took the trouble to show me how to get on, and at last I was on my way. A ride in a Jeepney is like travelling in the back of a pick-up truck, only it's usually very crowded and this one was no exception. Besides the jumping on and off while it's still moving and the overcrowding in the heat, one also has to contend with the thick black belching smoke that the vehicles emit, coupled with the general pollution of Manila – which is so bad it must be off all the charts. All told, it makes for a fun ride. I decided all I could do was sit back and think of England!

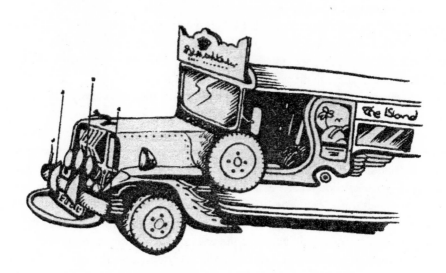

As we got closer to my friend's house, the Jeepney passed through what was evidently a very poor neighbourhood, much like a shanty town. There were people sitting in the streets and beggars everywhere. Women holding small babies came up to the sides of the Jeepney, tapping to get the attention and charitable offerings of those inside. The vehicle was now travelling very slowly as there were all kinds of things in the middle of the road, including cows and goats. And then came a big surprise.

We suddenly reached what I can only describe as some kind of compound. I say compound because it was surrounded by a large stone wall, high enough to stop those outside from looking in and, I couldn't help thinking, high enough to prevent the insiders from being forced to look at those outside. There was a guard on duty at the gate holding, quite openly, a heavy-looking machine gun. The driver was forced to stop at the gate to show identification before we were allowed to drive through. Driving through the gates was all the more amazing because it was like passing into a different world. The contrast was like night into day. There were dozens of huge, sprawling houses, with sprinklers watering the immaculately cut lawns. People were swimming in private pools, or having family games of badminton on their private patch.

I could not believe the difference between these two existences. How could some people be living like lords and others, only a few feet away, be suffering in such terrible poverty? I expressed my wonderment to the Jeepney driver, who told me that most of the people living outside the compound were the off-duty staff of those living inside it.

"You know, the drivers, maids, cooks, the 'help'," he said matter-of-factly.

When we eventually reached my friend's house, I saw that there were at least five or six staff working there – which brought home the words of the driver and made me realise how huge the differences were between the classes. I had not yet, however, seen the whole picture. This was only revealed a little later in my visit. During the meal, one of the staff, a really pretty young woman, entered the room and I smiled at her, and she returned it with a lovely warm smile of her own before leaving. When she had left the room, I joked with Angelina, the lady of the house.

"You know, I've not found a nice girl yet while I've been here in the Philippines, maybe you could introduce me to the young lady that was just in here a moment ago?"

Well, that was it. She stood up and told me that if I ever said anything like that again, indeed if I ever even thought anything like that again, she would immediately terminate our friendship. With that she stormed out of the room, leaving me totally taken aback and speechless. At which point, her husband, Roberto, leant across and whispered to me, "Michael, let's go for a walk, shall we?"

Not wanting to cause any further offence, and hoping that I might better under-stand what piece of etiquette I had transgressed, I nodded my agreement.

As we stepped out into the beautifully manicured grounds of the compound, I noticed Roberto was holding a small drinks carton in his hand, the sort that is pack-aged with a straw stuck to the outside of a small box. While we strolled through the grounds, a man followed about twenty paces or so behind us. I looked back nerv-ously, wondering if this guy was his bodyguard or something. All of a sudden, in mid-speech, Roberto raised his arm holding the box aloft to the follower, and sum-moned him with the minimum of words: "Box! Open, now!" The guy who had been walking behind us came running forward, pulled away the straw from the side of the box, removed the outside cellophane wrapper, stuck the straw through the small hole, piercing the foil, and passed it back to his boss.

For a second time in just a few minutes, I was stunned. Was it too difficult or too taxing a job to do for himself? Apparently so.

Then the lecture started.

"You see, Michael, here in the Philippines, you have to understand the culture. It is not accepted for people of our stature to ever, let's say, 'mix around' too closely with the help. So to 'date them' is completely unthinkable, and would be the easiest way to lose your standing in the community, and with it your self-respect. These people are not like us. You can see for yourself that they are different."

I decided at that point to interrupt and offer an opinion of my own.

"They may not be as rich as you," I countered, trying to be as diplomatic as I could, "and maybe not as educated, but they are human beings and they are also your own people, from your own country."

He started again, "It has nothing to do with them being our people or not educated; they live, and love, to serve us. We have had some of those people working for us for ten years or more, and they love us very much," he went on.

That was it for me. Time to leave! But before I did, I just had to get my final two-pennyworth in.

"Well, I can tell you now, if you give them all your money then ask them again if they are still happy to serve you, what do you think they would say?" I added for good measure, "Would you like me to give you my idea of their response?" Without waiting for his reply, I just made a run for the gate and went home.

Needless to say, they never came to the hotel again during my time there, but who needs that kind of business anyway?

I received a call from the local post office one day, informing me that they had received a parcel in my name and asking could I come to collect it whenever it was convenient. My birthday was fast approaching and even though I had left home some years ago, my mother kept a tradition of sending me two pairs of socks for my birthday every year. Bless her! So off I went to the post office to collect my parcel, and queued up for half an hour before finally reaching the counter.

"Good afternoon, sir, I have come to pick up a small package," I announced. I told the attendant my name and address and off he went to find my new, latest 'Marks and Sparks' cotton socks. My mother always bought me cotton because, to be blunt, she knew that, being a chef and working in a hot kitchen all day, my feet were always sweating and stinky!

The fun and games started when the attendant came back carrying my parcel under his arm.

"That will be twenty dollars, sir," he said coolly.

"Twenty dollars for what?" I blurted out.

"For the socks, my friend, for the socks," sounded the attendant, with his arms now folded as if to imply he was already bored by my protestations.

"But they belong to me," I argued. "Why must I pay you money to collect what is mine?" I didn't even register that he knew the contents of the parcel before I had even had the chance to open it.

"Because at this moment they actually belong to me," he said pointedly. "And if you would like them to belong to you, the price for these wonderful, brand new socks is twenty dollars."

I looked at him with glaring eyes. These were *my* socks, sent all the way to me from England by my loving mother who had made all the effort to go out and buy them, wrap them up nicely and send them off to her son, the international chef, in her now time-honoured way. Now, here was I, being charged a ransom to retrieve them. I thought about it for a while and then started my negotiating strategy.

"Listen here, top man, the socks probably did not even cost twenty dollars, and the package has got all its postage stamps on it. Can we be a little bit more reasonable here and talk about this?" I said, standing firm and trying out the 'disgruntled Englishman abroad' stance. Then I probably went a little too far, adding, "I'm not going to pay twenty dollars for them, so what do you think about that?"

At that point he nonchalantly leant back in his chair, tossed my mother's package into the waste-paper bin which sat in the corner of the room, smiled, and said, "That's what I think about that. Have a nice day, sir."

A security guard then came and asked me to move on as by now the other people behind me were getting impatient. I was so upset and frustrated by how this mundane and relatively trivial exchange had turned into a confrontation of mammoth proportions, I was shaking. Another lesson learned about my new home, was all I could say to console myself.

A few weeks later, while I was talking to my mother on the telephone, she asked me if I had received the socks. Praying that she did not ask about the colour and not wanting to upset her, I told her that as usual they were just what I wanted!

There are many powerful people in the Philippines' armed forces and keeping a wide berth of them, if you can, is usually a good idea. Unfortunately, that is not always possible as I found out to my cost on one occasion. Walking through the hotel lobby one evening, I was dressed in my chef's whites, on my way to meet an arriving guest. As I made my way through the lobby, I heard a man's voice shouting to me.

"Hey, you there! Come over here and serve me!"

I turned round to see who was raising his voice in that manner, only to see a very important-looking army official of some kind, waving at me to come over. I walked as slowly as I could towards him, asking myself as I did, who the hell does this guy think he is – Field Marshall Rommel?

As I reached him, I asked very politely in the circumstances, "Good evening, sir, how can I be of assistance to you?"

"Well," he said, "you can go and get me another drink this instant. After that I will see what else I need and let you know soon enough." I looked at him and noticed that his chest was decorated with every type and range of coloured medals and ribbons you could possibly imagine. He clearly wanted everyone to be dazzled by his prestige. I could not help but think to myself, all those medals yet he still has no class.

Instead, what came out of my mouth was more along the lines of, "I shall go and get a waiter for you right this minute, sir. You see I am the executive chef here and I cook things. The waiter serves them."

His smile instantly disappeared. At that time I had no idea how powerful this man really was, and it turned out later that I would be mightily grateful I kept my other, less complimentary, thoughts to myself.

"You don't seem to understand who I am," he explained. "I am telling you now, very clearly, that I want *you* to serve me and not anyone else."

I was just about to get myself thrown in jail, or at least lose my job, when Joel, the food and beverage manager and a Philippine national, came to my rescue.

"Colonel, how can I be of assistance?" he butted in. "This guy has just arrived and is completely stupid. Don't even waste your time with him. May I offer you a complementary cognac for your trouble here?" said Joel, trying to smooth things over and no doubt saving my bacon.

As time went by during my spell in the Philippines, I learned that there were few more powerful than the top brass in the military service, and doing as they ask, within reason, was always the best policy to avoid untold trouble.

For instance, one of my staff came to work late one morning and I was told how he had overtaken a car on his way to work, not realising that it was a top armed forces commander in his civilian vehicle. The military bigwig had then overtaken my guy, forcing him to stop his vehicle at the side of the road. Right there and then the affronted 'military brass' took out his revolver and shot at my staff member's car tyres. He then coolly returned to his car without batting an eyelid and drove off. All of this occurred during daylight hours, amid hardly deserted streets. He was probably just angry that this man had the audacity to overtake him and felt the need to teach him a lesson.

Believe me, the lesson was well and truly grasped and not just by the person to whom it happened, but by everyone else who subsequently heard the story.

In the Manila hotel we had a huge, though rather old and rundown, casino. Despite its need for an overhaul, it did good business as there were not many others in town to play at. In the casino the number-one-selling snack that people ate while playing the slot machines was fried chicken wings. We sold hundreds of portions of these crispy morsels each day, and with the various hotel restaurants also offering a range of chicken dishes, as well as the staff canteen, it added up to a ton of fresh chicken being consumed every week.

Somehow or other I found out that the supplier who was selling us our chicken was overcharging us, and I decided to get quotations from other suppliers to try to get a better deal. It was not long before another, more reasonably-priced, supplier was found, and I calculated that changing suppliers was going to save the hotel a bomb. The day after I changed suppliers I was sitting in my office doing some paperwork when in walked a stranger without an appointment.

"Can I help you?" I enquired, puzzled as to who this was.

"I am the guy whose legs you just cut off," he started. "Obviously you don't know how things work around here, so I came to explain to you in simple, easy to understand English."

"Is that right?" I said, leaning back in my chair, trying to get a handle on what was going on here.

"You see, here in the Philippines," he started off again, "we give you a price list of our products based on an additional five per cent that is paid to you at the end of every month. This ensures that everyone is kept happy. The last guy was very happy with this arrangement, but I can see that you are going to be a hard nut to crack, so I am willing to give you a starting bonus."

With that, he reached into his inside jacket pocket and pulled out a small envelope which landed with a thud on the table in front of me.

Curious, I opened the envelope to see a stash of $100 bills, with an elastic band around them. As I looked up, I could see members of my staff peering through the window, giving me the thumbs-up signal.

"Obviously," I began, now realising what was at issue here, "we have a serious misunderstanding here because I don't take, nor will ever take, bribes to do my work, my friend. If you want to do business with me, all you have to do is give me good quality at a good price. And since you've been our supplier for years, I'm willing to give you back the contract, if you can match the new supplier's deal."

As I pushed the envelope gently back to his side of the table, he did not look at all happy.

"You've just turned down $3,000 in hard cash. Are you crazy?" he asked, before adding, "I will see you again tomorrow." He then left as quietly as he had arrived.

That same night, I had a friend coming to visit me from Singapore. I went to the airport to pick her up, and as it was late, we decided to go straight back to the hotel by taxi. We hailed one and climbed into the back seat. I was very surprised as the driver looked at us and then turned on his meter without my saying a word. At last, I thought to myself in amazement, an honest taxi driver who was willing to give an honest ride for an honest price! I was even thinking about telling him how impressed I was, but thought differently about pushing my luck. I was watching him as we drove along. He kept peeping at us through his rear view mirror, until finally he asked Sandra, my guest, something in Tagalog, the language of the Philippines.

"Oh, I'm very sorry, I can't speak any Tagalog," Sandra said politely to the driver, "I'm from Singapore."

All of a sudden, the driver hit the brakes as if his life depended on it and skidded to an abrupt stop at the side of the road.

"What the heck is going on?" I shouted. "Did you hit something?"

"No, not at all," he replied, while clapping his hands together with glee. "I just realised that she is not a Filipina and this means we have to negotiate the fare since you are tourists. So how much do you want to pay?" he asked while snapping off the meter.

"No," I growled. "Wait a bloody minute, here. I'm not a tourist. I'm working here full-time. You know, living here and paying taxes here?" I remonstrated.

"That may be so, my friend, but you are not from here, which makes you a foreigner, and there is no meter service for foreigners, which means you have to negotiate."

I was getting really angry now, but what could I do?

"I ask you again, sir, how much do you want to pay?"

"Well, since you ask like that, I want to pay nothing. That's right. I want the ride for free."

The driver looked at me with a puzzled expression, as if to say, is this guy nuts? And then turned off the air conditioning in the car. Getting cheekier and angrier by the minute, I quickly responded by saying, "If you are going to turn off the air conditioning, I want some sort of discount, and since I am getting this ride for free, that means you should now be paying me money."

Just as I finished saying this, the driver stepped out of the car, opened the passenger door and asked us to leave his taxi. As we did so, frightened half to death at what was taking place and with our mouths wide open, he drove off, leaving us stranded – but alive – at the roadside. It took us an hour, standing in the street, waving our arms around, to get another taxi, but at least we got back to the hotel in one piece.

The next day, my supplier friend came back to my office, at much the same time of the day as on his previous visit, and equally uninvited. This time he threw another envelope onto my table.

"That, my friend, is $4,000. You are now testing my patience to the limit. Do not push your fucking luck!" he declared.

I slowly pushed the envelope back to him and said, "Have a nice day, sir. I will expect your quotation on my desk tomorrow morning."

Fortunately, he left my office, kicking the things off my desk and the chairs as he passed by, but not me. This made me more than a little uncomfortable, wondering how far his irritation and bad temper would push him.

Who should reappear in my office the next day but my new friend, the 'negotiator'?

"This is my final offer," he declared, and threw down the, by now, anticipated package with the familiar dull thud onto my desk. "That," he said, "is $5,000 in cash, and I will not give you a single cent more!"

He then stormed out of the office, leaving the cash still sitting on my desk. I quickly asked my secretary to go after him and to tell him he had left his envelope behind on my desk. When she returned without him, she told me he was very angry and had told her to let me know that it was not over yet, not by a long chalk. What I did not understand or know at the time was the depth of the problem I was up against, but I was soon to find out.

Many of the other cooks on the hotel's staff were already, and had been for a long time, on the payroll of the supplier. Over the following days, a person, or persons unknown, threw soil, small stones and other such 'delectable' condiments into the chicken prepared for the staff canteen. As the complaints grew, the union got in on the act, citing problems with the chicken product provided by the new supplier and demanded that we go back to the old supplier at once. Even the general manager came to see me and told me to revert back to the old supplier instantly, as the staff were threatening to go on strike.

That was it. I felt I had been pushed too far. I looked at the boss and told him that we had to make a stand on this matter now, or forever hold our peace. It was imperative, I told him, that if he had any desire to clean up the hotel, we did not give in to the corrupt tactics and demands we were now facing.

To my great relief, the general manager agreed, but added he could only give me a couple more days to sort the problem out and restore normality to the hotel.

That night, at about three o'clock in the morning, the phone rang in my hotel bedroom.

"Hello, who is this?" I enquired, barely awake as I answered.

"I'm going to kill you, my friend," came the reply. "You are dead, do you hear? You are dead. And as for your sweet little girlfriend there, I'm not going to tell you what I am going to do to her. It will spoil the surprise."

"Who is this?" I shouted down the phone, now fully wakened by what I had heard.

"Who do you think it is, Santa Claus? You have ruined my life and now you will pay!"

I quickly replaced the handset and lay down on my bed, trying to gather my thoughts and thinking about what to do. I then realised that the phone call had had to come through the hotel operator, and I wondered why they would put through such a crazed call to my room in the middle of the night. I decided to go down and have a word with the operator. I quickly got dressed and went downstairs.

As I walked into the operator's room there were two young women sitting there, reading local magazines. I asked them which one of them had just put a call through to my room.

"You must be mistaken, chef. There was no phone call to your room at all tonight."

I realised at once that they were also somehow involved, probably having been paid to turn a deaf ear and say nothing. Was nobody to be trusted? I bemoaned to myself. Was the whole hotel a giant conspiracy?

I went back upstairs to my room, still feeling disgruntled by what was going on and lost for words or for ideas about what to do for the best. Back in my room, Sandra, still visiting from Singapore, was sitting in an armchair, sobbing quietly to herself.

"What's wrong? What's happened?" I asked, but having a pretty good idea of what it must have been.

"After you'd left the room, the phone rang and thinking that it was probably you calling back to tell me something, I picked it up and there was a horrible, crazy man on the other end. He said terrible things to me and made disgusting threats. What kind of place is this, Michael?"

I hardly knew what to say to her, except to urge her to calm down and go back to sleep. It was just a horrible prank call, I assured her.

142

Later that morning, I told the general manager that I was there to cook and to manage the food operation, and that playing the hardball part of Rambo was not in my nature nor, for that matter, in my job description! I explained what had happened during the night and in the days before, and we decided to call back the former chicken supplier and resume the old contract, as the trouble we were having was just not worth it at all.

Believe it or not, it later turned out that the supplier in question was the brother of the army colonel who had shouted at me across the lobby to come and serve him. A few days later, the supplier came into the hotel kitchen, handing out $100 bills to all my staff, while smiling at me through the glass window of my office, and I could do absolutely nothing about it.

As a result of this unpleasant experience, I started to think that the task of helping this hotel become a quality operation was just too great, but somehow, although my spirits were flagging, I was not ready to give up quite yet.

I got a telephone call one day from an old friend who had just landed a job in a hotel down the street from mine. Charles wanted to know if I would meet him at the airport when he arrived and show him around a little. I agreed, and on the day of his arrival I was waiting in a café at the airport, having a coffee, when I saw him coming. I waved Charles over and offered him a drink, and he sat down next to me. As we talked, however, he seemed distant and his mind was somewhere else. He seemed to be focusing on something at one of the tables behind me.

"What's on your mind, big guy?" I asked.

"Hey, guess what?" he said, having barely set foot in the country, "there's a beautiful girl staring at me over there and I think she likes me."

I turned to see a whole table of 'working girls', just waiting for unsuspecting clients, like my naïve friend, to arrive at the airport.

We left in one of the VIP taxis and braved the bumpy ride back to his hotel. At his new abode, the concierge offered to whisk him up to his room to freshen up and inspect his new quarters. Charles asked me to come up for a drink. The concierge, for some reason, however, urged him to go up alone, but my friend was having none of it, insisting on my presence to keep him company over a can of beer.

He turned the key in the door and we walked into his room. We were surprised to see how large it was. Almost as soon as we entered, the phone rang and it was the hotel's general manager welcoming the new chef to Manila, and telling Charles to enjoy his welcome fruit and this larger suite for a couple of days. Then he hung up.

"I wonder what he's talking about?" mused Charles as I went through to his bathroom to use the toilet.

There didn't seem to be a single piece of fruit on show in the room. Perhaps they had forgotten to send it in, we remarked.

"That's not a very good starting point," he observed.

I walked into the bathroom to see, firstly, a huge jacuzzi, full of hot, bubbling water, and, secondly, a stunning woman, sitting in the bubbles, drinking what looked like champagne and wearing only a tattoo, saying 'made in the Philippines', on her elegant arm.

I was caught off guard and told her that we must have the wrong room and would leave instantly.

"No," announced the vision, "I am your welcome fruit."

Back in the bedroom Charles was hanging up his jacket in the wardrobe. "You know at the airport when you said there was a girl staring at you?" I said teasingly.

"Yes, so what?"

"Well, there's another one in the bathroom, waiting to stare at you right now!"

I never found out if he enjoyed his fruit or not – being too much of a gentleman to enquire. However, I remembered what my boss had given to me for my arrival present and turned green with envy, deciding just maybe I would take him up on it at a later date …

The next day I was off work and decided to watch some movies in my room and have a generally lazy day for once. While I was in there, one of the housekeeping staff who cleaned my room made small talk as she went about her work. She asked me if I was married or attached to anyone. I told her that I was not – missing out the part that I had been married before but was not any longer. Her response was emphatic.

"Young men like you are not supposed to be alone without female company. It's not normal. We'll have to do something about it."

I replied that she was very kind but being alone right now was exactly what I did need, and asked her – politely – to leave it at that. When she finished cleaning my room she went away, singing 'love is in the air', softly to herself.

Strange lady, I thought, then promptly forgot about the exchange.

In the early afternoon, feeling bored, I decided to head off downtown to do some shopping. The concierge called a taxi for me and was quoted an obviously inflated price for the fare, but I thought, what the heck, let's live a little, and got into the taxi. As we set off, the driver was singing and looked a happy chap, but the door was rattling and I asked the driver to stop so I could close it properly.

"Don't worry, it's been like that for years. It won't come open, so just relax," he said jovially.

Who am I to argue? I thought.

About halfway to the downtown area, it started raining heavily. The rain quickly turned to sheets of water flooding down the hillside towards the road. This was a low-lying area of town and the traffic soon came to a complete stop. My driver just kept on whistling and singing as if he didn't have a care in the world. The torrential rain flowed but we remained stationary. The rain became heavier and heavier, and the water heading towards us became a small, raging river. The flood drains at the sides of the road had long been blocked and were overflowing with old leaves and garbage. I looked at the driver as if he might know of some quick miracle way out of the predicament, but he started to honk his horn and the soft tune he was singing had now turned into a somewhat worrying shriek.

"Is everything alright, my friend?" I asked, trying to sound cool.

"Does it look alright to you? Are you stupid?" came the reply.

I then turned my head to the window and saw the water level reaching almost the bottom of the car door. By now the driver was getting frantic, and began shouting out of his window, telling the drivers in front to get out of the way. I felt my feet starting to get wet, and I saw water seeping in through the sides of the ill-fitting doors. When the water reached about six inches deep inside the car, my trusty chauffeur demanded action.

"Get out!" he ordered.

I looked at him with amazement: "Excuse me?"

He looked hard into my eyes and demanded again, "Get the hell out!"

"And go where, may I ask? There's no way on earth that I'm going to get out of this taxi!" I sat firm.

Then, as if he had no more energy left for bawling, he shrugged, saying, "I hope you can swim, buddy!"

Some young guys came swimming by, wearing their underpants as swimsuits, and having a great time splashing around and acting as if they'd been waiting for this downpour for months. They jumped up on the taxi, climbed onto the roof, and began using it as a diving board. After a while they got tired and offered – for a fee, of course – to push us onto dry land up the hill. The taxi driver shouted and swore at them, but I jumped with relief, reckoning the small bit of cash they were after was well worth a lift to dry land. When we eventually opened the car door, the water rushed out just like in a movie where a car goes through a car wash and the driver forgets to roll up the windows first.

As I arrived, somewhat damp and bedraggled, back in my room, I was surprised to see a strange girl sitting in an armchair watching my television, as relaxed as if she had lived there for years. I sat down, said nothing and waited for her to announce herself. She never took her eyes off the television, and as I couldn't stand the suspense any longer, I decided to take the plunge.

"Good evening, how are you?"

"Oh, I'm fine, and how are you?"

"I'm also fine. Now would you mind letting me know what you are doing in my room, watching my TV?"

"I understand you were talking to my aunt when she was cleaning your room and you told her you had no company. My aunt feels sorry for you and she's sent me over to live with you. I can do cleaning, cooking, ironing, and well, you know what else."

I listened to the matter-of-fact offer with amazement and explained there had been a huge mistake and that she would have to leave.

My visitor looked at me with a sulky face and asked, "Does this mean that you don't like me?"

Well, this had been one hell of a day and when I finally placed her in a taxi to send her home, I could not have been more relieved and happy – other than, of course, how one feels after escaping from a sinking Manila taxi … That night I definitely slept like a log.

One day, the hotel's most intimate dining room was closed for a private function and I took a look at the reservations book to check out who was expected and what the menu was going to be. Would it be a set dinner or an à la carte, or whatever, I wondered? I was surprised to find a reservation for a single table, and just one person at that.

"What's this?" I demanded. "Is this some kind of joke, or what?"

"No, chef," said the restaurant manager, "the 'old lady' is coming."

"Oh yes," I acknowledged, as if I was fully in the know. "And what time will she be arriving?"

"Around seven o'clock, chef."

"Oh, that's good," I carried on, "and by the way, who the hell is the old lady?"

"You know, chef," said the restaurant manager with a wink, "Imelda!"

"What? Imelda Marcos coming here? Tonight?" I blurted out.

"Yes, that's right," he added. "Would you like to make a bet?"

"On what?" I replied, still reeling from what I had just learnt, but at the same time trying to think ahead to what needed to be done in preparation for our visitor.

"What's wrong with you tonight, chef? … The shoes! … The shoes! I say they will be red tonight."

"I don't bloody care what colour shoes she will be wearing. What she is going to eat is what concerns me."

Another madhouse, I thought to myself. People are so concerned about what colour shoes this famous guest would be wearing but no one cares about the content of her dinner, even though the hotel would, of course, charge her top dollar as the restaurant would be closed to other diners. I went back to my office, totally cheesed off with the attitude of the staff and sat there for a quiet moment, contemplating how I could impress on them the importance of getting things right, and also survive the day without having a nervous breakdown … I also took a moment to decide that she would be wearing blue shoes and eventually found time to place my bet!

When Imelda Marcos showed up, she was wearing black, so there you go. She came with two tables full of hangers-on and set the hotel abuzz with her presence, getting the staff very excited and wound-up. I, at least, managed to get through the evening without the threatened breakdown.

———————

Once in a while, there would be torrential rainfalls in Manila which would flood the streets and block the drains, as I had earlier discovered to my own damp satisfaction. The water would, however, also start backing up the drains on the lower floors of some buildings, including, unfortunately, our hotel. Naturally, the hotel's coffee shop was on the ground floor and from time to time I would have to issue the cooks with waterproof boots. The first time it happened I was shocked and called another executive chef at a nearby hotel to see how they were coping.

"Hey, chef," I said, "my kitchen is a foot deep in dirty rainwater! It's an absolute zoo!"

"Yes, so?" bounced back the unsympathetic response, adding before the phone was slammed down in my ear, "Welcome to Manila, my friend. At least your hotel is not near the sewer!"

At the end of service that night, we turned off the kitchen lights and went home, hoping that the water level would have subsided altogether by the time we returned to cook breakfast. Curiosity, as ever, was my downfall. As I lived in the hotel, I thought I might as well go down later that night to see how we were doing. When I did so, I snapped on the lights to see the kitchen full of rats, scurrying around looking for hiding places from the unexpected spotlight. I just turned off the lights, and acting as nonchalantly as I could as if I had seen nothing unusual, went quietly back upstairs to my room.

I woke from an uneasy sleep during the night and realised I'd been having a terrible nightmare. I'd dreamt my bed was full of rats. I was sweating and disorientated and frantically fumbling for the light switch so that I could check out what was under my sheets. Unable to get back to sleep, I sat up for the rest of the night watching television.

What was this thing that I had about rats that drove me so insane? No wonder that I decided, after many years of toying with the idea, to buy a cat. I went out and found myself a lovely, chocolate Persian, whom I called CoCo. She became great company and over the years we formed a lasting attachment, with her travelling with me to each new destination. CoCo is always loving and happy to see me when I finish work, making my otherwise anonymous hotel quarters seem much more like home.

We had a brand new smokehouse in the kitchen. This is a piece of equipment that you can use to smoke seafood and meat. It was a huge one that you could actually walk into with trolleys full of food and smoke all the items in one go. It must have cost a fortune, and yet I deduced that it had never once been used. Apparently, they had ordered it from Germany and even sent for a German engineer to install it, then the hotel's engineering department had 'serviced' it and it had never worked from that day.

I asked the hotel's engineer what was wrong with the smokehouse and he confessed that it had come with a smart card which you needed to punch instructions into the brain of the machine, much like a pre-paid card for a mobile phone. Apparently, one of the staff had dropped the card which was then trodden on, and that was its nervous system shot to pieces. Not having a spare, they had not bothered to order a new one, and therefore this coveted piece of machinery remained useless.

I asked the chief engineer to give me the contact number in Germany and I would call them myself to get a new card. But no, this was not possible, as the contact number was lost and no one had any idea how to track down the manufacturer. I looked on the side of the smokehouse and couldn't believe that there was no name or logo attached. Seemingly, no one in Manila could fix it and there was no one who even wanted to buy it for scrap metal as it was too heavy to lift out of the kitchen. Like other things I would encounter during my time in Manila, I eventually gave up on that job as it was just too much like an exercise in futility and I was patently getting nowhere.

A more interesting challenge showed up a few days later, when the public relations manager told me that she had come up with a brainwave!

"As you know," she began, "there are many girls in Manila working as cooks."

"The 'help' you mean?" I said sarcastically.

"Yes, chef, that's right, but many of them are amateur cooks, so I thought maybe you could go on the radio and give cooking tips for maids."

I looked at her for a second, thinking that actually it was not such a bad idea. After all, I would get some exposure, the hotel would get some good publicity and, who knows, maybe it would be a bit of fun and even help a few people to appreciate the art which occupied my daily life. I agreed to take part, and after a few days, she told me that a date was fixed for the first live radio Michael Saxon cooking class.

I went along to a studio on the due date and prepared myself to take part in one of those *Woman's Hour* kind of shows with a large following and a charming female presenter. It had been advertised that she would be hosting regular, ten-minute cooking-tip segments on the show and that listeners could call in and ask her guest chef any cooking questions they had.

All went well and after a few weeks of 'radio cooking' I started to get a few listener letters, asking some quite good questions. Then came the fatal mistake that would spoil it all. At the end of one of the shows, the presenter said something in Tagalog, and asked me to repeat it on air. I had no idea what I was saying, and because it was a live show, I had no time to ask the meaning. I repeated it as asked and she gave out a pleasant, harmless laugh. I asked my host afterwards what she had got me to say, and she said, "I love you all!"

I thought no more about it until the next show when a question came in and the host passed the caller to me.

"What are you doing tonight, chef?" said the caller, "And by the way, I love you too." Then she hung up.

Some days later, I was in the hotel's restaurant when the concierge came to tell me that there were two guests waiting to meet me outside. In the lobby two young girls introduced themselves as my biggest fans and asked if they could have lunch with me and get some cooking tips straight from the horse's mouth, so to speak. I was caught off-guard again, and somewhat flattered. As it was the first time I'd been approached like this, I agreed.

We had a pleasant lunch and a nice chat in the coffee shop and parted company. A few days later, however, during my on-air cooking segment, one of the girls called in to say that they were very grateful for the lunch date and the personal attention I had given them. She said what a thrill it was to have had lunch with an executive chef and was surprised that such a busy person had made time for her and her friend. I was happy that I'd made her feel good and left it at that.

Unfortunately, after that, I was barraged for months by every Tina, Dorothy and Harriet who came to the hotel in an endless procession, wanting their own, personal, free cooking tips and lunch. There was nothing for it but I had to stop the radio programmes and revert to a much lower profile. Another lesson learnt the hard way!

The approach and pace of life in Manila is totally different from the rest of the Philippines. Outside the city, people are wonderful and kind but in the cut and thrust of the capital, life is largely lived on the edge. Manila is such a large place with so many foreigners and business people passing through, not to mention the wide extremes of poverty and wealth, and corruption – often just to get the simplest of things done – was never too far away. The experiences with my parcel at the post office and with the chicken supplier were just two of many examples that bothered me. For me, the city was spoilt by this side and I never felt truly at home.

I heard that the Americans had made arrangements to move out of their Subic Bay base, which they had occupied for a very long time. The race was on to gain the shipping contract to get all the moveable goods back to the States. This would be the very last chance for local companies to cash in big time on the presence of the Americans, and an acquaintance of mine was involved in negotiating on behalf of his removal company. Luckily, his company tendered the winning bid and he was told that the contract was theirs.

He had to make the necessary arrangements and organise the packing for what was veritably a small town on the move. The contract was for such a huge amount of money that the other top-line shipping companies tried to steal the business away from the company which had won it fair and square. There was talk of bribery, much false finger pointing and accusations of criminal action, all aimed at sowing doubts about the integrity and efficiency of the company. One day, his office was raided by the armed forces with threats of closure, until they themselves resorted to bribing the leader of those ranged against them to leave them in peace and allow them to do the job they had won on fair terms.

Although the job was completed and eventually paid for by the US government, my friend later told me that he had faced such severe corruption and even death threats while trying to fulfil the contract that by the time he had finished, so much under-the-table cash had been paid out, despite its size, the contract had been hardly worth it.

A staff member came to work one day looking quite distraught. The night before his house had caught fire while he was asleep. Fortunately, he had woken up and called the fire brigade, but when they arrived they had demanded money before they would put out the fire. He begged them to help, saying he really had no money, but they were not buying that and stood by watching as his house rapidly burnt to the ground.

There are lots of other things that people take for granted in the Philippines but which I could never get used to. For instance, paying money in order to bypass other people standing patiently in a queue, or being able to pay the police after being pulled over for a traffic offence and as a result being able to drive away scot-free.

There is an ongoing campaign in the Philippines around the 'right to bear arms', which is very well supported. A lot of people carry concealed weapons. I once asked a regular supplier who came to my office at the hotel what was in his very attractive-looking briefcase that I had never seen him open. He immediately opened it, and I wished I had kept my mouth shut. Inside was a shiny new handgun with a supply of bullets arranged around it, each in its own tiny individual leather pouch. I was staggered that this guy felt the need to carry a gun and ammunition – and he was only selling herbs and spices!

That sense of having to think twice about personal safety was everywhere and in everything. One very famous Manila hotel had a huge plastic arched metal detector at the entrance to its lobby. Every guest who wanted to enter the hotel had to walk through the detector and be frisked by the hotel's security, who waved a large plastic baton around your body, in anticipation of loud screeching sounds. It felt like being at the boarding gates of at an international airport, but far less secure.

Certain parts of the Philippines are prone to more than their fair share of natural disasters, making life there sometimes all the more difficult and desperate for local people. There have been floods, famine, earthquakes, active volcanoes and typhoons, not to mention the man-made disasters like terrible pollution, crime and civil strife. But against these odds, the Philippines manages to keep up with the times and its people are so delightfully friendly. The country also exports thousands of its workers to other countries who then repatriate millions of dollars back to their families in the Philippines every year, taking some of the burden of financial support for the poorer communities away from the government.

As a foreigner, sheltered by an expatriate package of good wages and benefits, I often struggled with my own conscience. For example, I bought some nice wood carvings from a factory in Manila and was then shown to the back to see the work being done behind the scenes. I was saddened to see so many young people, sitting on the floor, carving the pieces from thick tree trunks, and apparently earning just a few cents for each work of art they completed. I told the factory boss that I wished I had not bought my pieces because it was not right that these young people were working so hard for so little. He replied, in a well-versed tone, that if I had not bought the carvings they would not even have the fifty cents each that they would receive from my purchases, and that, he suggested, was what I should think about.

I closed my eyes, confused and struggling to make sense of it all. Should I revise my standpoint from my negative to his positive? I still struggle today to find an answer to this question.

I found my thinking challenged on even the great festive occasions. New Year's Eve in Manila is a crazy time, particularly regarding the uncontrolled letting-off of fireworks. We set up a small bar on the top floor of the hotel so that we could toast the New Year while watching the firework displays below. They began from early evening, building up to a fever pitch by the stroke of midnight. Millions of dollars are spent on this annual pyrotechnics show while many people remain in poverty. Of course, this dichotomy is nothing new and happens in many countries to varying degrees, but the carnage caused during this one night was not something with which I was particularly familiar.

The television news on New Year's Day would show maimed and desperately burnt children, bringing even the strongest of us to tears. Children who had been discovered holding fireworks in their hands, not knowing what the consequences would be if they went off. Firecracker explosions inevitably blew off fingers, and some were blinded when others thought it funny to toss smouldering firecrackers at their faces.

Another enduring memory of the Philippines was the so-called 'brown out'. This was when the government-run utilities did not have enough electrical power to run things for a full twenty-four-hour service, so the power in various areas of town would be shut down for unspecified periods of time. One would never know when it would be likely to come back on, and when it did, you would in turn have no idea when it would go off again, as it all seemed to happen at random.

One night, I went out with some of the staff to another hotel to 'check' on their buffet. A little bit of surreptitious market research really. The journey there and back would usually take half an hour, even in Manila's snail's-pace traffic. As we were approaching the traffic lights in the busy rush hour, all of a sudden, it was brown out. Everyone crept forward from each of the four points of the intersection, all expecting the other to be the first to give way, but of course no one did, causing total gridlock. People began screaming and shouting at each other, all blaming other parties and using the argument that they had got there first. Others stepped out of their cars; some sat on top of their bonnets, laughing, as though it was an everyday thing and free entertainment.

I sat back and felt my heart drumming wildly. I was getting really stressed out and the whole situation seemed out of control. Where were the police? How could the authorities turn off the power to the traffic lights at the busiest time of day? Why was no one else asking these questions? Maybe it had been happening for so long that everyone now accepted it as the norm, and I was the odd one out.

Eventually, one heroic chap jumped out of his car and started a one-man United Nations peacekeeping routine to free the intersection, standing there shouting at the top of his voice.

"You move forward two inches. Alright, stop! … Now you move back a bit. Go on, move!" He beckoned and cajoled others to do as he commanded.

After a frustrating half-hour, this guy edged a few inches here and that guy edged a few inches there, until the intersection was cleared and everyone was moving again. I slumped back in my seat, mesmerised by the whole experience, and just could not help but wonder how the Philippines managed to compete in the modern business world.

Traffic congestion is not the only thing you have to contend with on the streets of Manila. In the downtown area you see it all, women coming to the car or bus windows with children to beg, people selling cigarettes by the single stick, lighting it for their customers and even putting it into their mouths. I had no real objection to the selling. After all, it meant that people were trying to use their entrepreneurial spirit to move up in the world. But one cheeky fellow selling newspapers told me about the trick he used to make more money.

As cars stopped at the traffic lights, he would time things very carefully so that he would be handing over the newspaper to a driver just as the light would be changing to green. He would act as if he was disorganised and begin fumbling around, looking for the change, until the driver would say, "Oh, never mind," and just drive off. He knew that drivers got scared and intimidated by the cars behind blowing their horns, and made a fair few 'tips' out of their hastily abandoned change.

As I prepared to leave Manila for my next international job, I had a last drink in the airport bar while I waited for my flight. I prepared myself for the always-daunting stroll through immigration. When I arrived at the exit desks, I found a long queue which looked like it was not moving at all. Nervous now about missing my flight, a big, burly-looking guy just coolly walked in front of me and edged his way into the line. Not wanting to make a fight the last memory I would have of Manila, I kept quiet. It was only one person, so what difference would that possibly make? That question was soon answered when his friends arrived a few minutes later, and the tough guy called them to join him in the queue, setting me back even further. Fortunately, the flight schedules were as elastic as my pride.

When I finally reached the immigration officer's desk, he asked me for the departure card which had already been taken by another officer earlier. I tried to explain that it was already collected by his colleague but he just snapped at me.

"Well, go and get it then!"

I retraced my steps, asked the first officer for the document, and he gave it to me. Back at the front of the queue, the officer was still waiting impatiently for me. He stamped my passport, placed it on a shelf under his desk and announced, "Next!"

I looked steadily at him while reaching into my wallet for the customary ten dollar bill, and handed it over, saying, "Would this ease the situation, officer?"

Instantly the passport was returned and the officer announced, "You have a very good day, sir, and a safe journey home."

At the eleventh hour, I had finally learnt the rules of the game …

VII

GOING BATS IN BATIK

I WAS HIRED by a major hotel group to help open a hotel which was still under construction on an Indonesian island near to Singapore. I was very happy to be moving on after all my adventures in Manila, and the prospect of doing another grand opening made me feel excited. I spoke to the hotel's general manager on the phone about the precise location of the island.

"Well, it's very close, just about forty-five minutes from Singapore by a speed ferry, more like a hovercraft actually. It's very fast indeed," he informed me.

That made me feel great as I could go to Singapore on my days off to go sightseeing or shopping. In fact, since the hotel was nowhere near ready, I was to be based in a Singapore hotel first, not least because there was nowhere else to stay on the island.

Though it should have sounded some kind of alarm bell in my mind, the implication of that very important hint did not properly sink in. I was so blind with excitement that I didn't catch on. Then, after a few days in the pre-opening office, saying hello to everyone and signing my two-year contract – thereby locking myself into the job – it was time to show me the island. I remember feeling a little uneasy when I saw the general manager smiling contentedly as he locked my newly signed contract in his safe almost before the ink was dry – but maybe that owes more to hindsight.

I was at last on my way to 'paradise' aboard a luxury ferry – after all, the general manager had spoken very highly of this 'beautiful resort' that was soon to be my new home. I started to think something was a little amiss when this brand new, just-launched ferry, built for 400 people, was completely empty except, of course, for our small party. I tried not to overreact and settled back to enjoy this luxury cruiser, effectively giving me a personal ride. On the Indonesian side of the Straits of Malacca, there was a carbon copy of the same ferry terminal that we had boarded from in Singapore. A construction-worker-like chap was waiting for us in a four-wheel-drive jeep, covered from roof to tyres in a thick, caked-on, orangey brown mud.

He greeted us with a cry of, "Hey, guys, where are your boots?"

Here we go again, I thought, as I looked down woefully at my brand new, gleaming white tennis shoes. It seemed to take forever to drive out to the construction site but it was probably only a good forty minutes via the fast four wheel drive. As we got closer to the hotel, the alarm bells finally sounded loud and clear. We had not passed a single house, other vehicle, traffic light, road sign, nor any other human beings or even animals during the entire journey. In fact, we had not come across anything that, if you were arriving from another planet, would have given you any idea that the human race existed at all. I kept looking around at the lush tropical jungle for anything that would ease my fears.

When we arrived at the site, I stepped out of the vehicle into five inches of orange mud, which squelched up over the bottom of my blue jeans and finished off my new sneakers. We walked around the property to try to get our bearings about where everything was going to be, especially the restaurants and kitchen working areas. I had only now started to ask the basic questions that I should have asked on the phone from Manila. The questions were numerous, flooding my head, and when I found I was alone with the boss for a second, I put the squeeze on him.

"By the way, boss, I just have a couple of silly questions that I would like to share with you. For instance, God forbid, but should anyone get sick out here, where is the nearest doctor, dentist or hospital? What if the hotel catches fire – how long does it take for the fire brigade to reach our property? You know, silly little questions like these?"

The general manager looked at me with a sheepish grin.

"I thought you might have a few queries, so I've already organised a meeting for when we return to Singapore."

Four hungry hours later we arrived back at the ferry terminal to travel back to Singapore. The ride across to the Indonesian side earlier in the day had been great, the water had looked like a sheet of polished glass and the boat flew over the surface, giving us a very smooth ride indeed. Unfortunately, during the afternoon, a storm had blown up and the ride home would prove to be an entirely different story.

Not to worry, the captain reassured us. Instead of the boasted forty-five minutes, it would now take just fifteen minutes extra. If only! With the journey less than a quarter complete, a floating plastic bag got caught up in the propeller and the engines automatically shut down. Now the boat started to sway side to side, up and down, like some kind of funfair ride. Looking out of the window, one minute you could see the sea level, the next land and the next, only sky.

The captain had to send one of his crew diving over the side to retrieve the bag from the motor, adding another forty minutes onto the already painful trip home.

My self-styled image as an intrepid traveller plummeted as I was as sick as a dog and had to spend most of the journey home vomiting in a tiny, claustrophobic toilet. The only diversion was that I was so worried about spending two years on my very own 'devil's island' that it took my mind off how sick I was feeling. It was like if you stamped on someone's toes hard enough they wouldn't think any more about the headache they had before you did it.

Eventually, back on solid ground in Singapore, the boss called the promised 'extraordinary' management meeting, so I went and sat down in the boardroom, eagerly awaiting the start. What a sight I must have presented. Sitting there with my brand new trainers caked in a thick coating of brown mud, topped off with a fresher coat of vomit! My apparel aside, I knew that this meeting was going to be an absolute dandy. The boss strolled in, sat down in front of the department heads and his opening line got my blood boiling instantly.

"Don't worry, everyone, I know there are some concerns, but remember it's only forty-five minutes away from Singapore by our very own speedy ferry."

I couldn't contain myself any longer: "Oh, is that right? When does the last ferry leave?" I asked pointedly.

"That's a good question, chef. Around five in the afternoon."

"And when does the first one arrive in the morning?" I retorted.

"That would be at ten o'clock, chef."

"Alright, so there is no way that anyone can get off the island at night, then. Would I be correct in saying that, boss? And what are the plans for any kind of emergency, such as one of us getting seriously ill?" I said, with the bit between my teeth.

The boss just smiled and assured everyone that all these things would be worked out in due course and that we should not worry about them.

It was easy for him to say, I thought, and I became even more upset about it, but as the meeting slowly chugged along, I kept quiet, not wanting to portray too negative an attitude so early on.

That evening, I went to have a drink with a friend I knew working in a hotel in Singapore, and he got all excited for me at the prospect of opening a hotel on a 'desert island'. I felt like telling him that he was welcome to swap; he could take my job and I would gladly stay in Singapore and fill in for him.

"By the way, though," he asked, "if there are no people on the island, where are your 600 trained hotel staff going to come from, and where are you going to buy all the foodstuffs for your five restaurants? What are you going to do for a doctor, dentist, haircut, getting money from the bank, entertainment, etcetera and, by the way, do they have malaria there?"

Angry with my own predicament, I snapped right back at him,

"Yes, yes, I understand what you are saying, and I don't bloody know, alright?"

I knew, however, that I was in for some sleepless nights until I knew the answers to at least some of these questions.

Through contacts, we eventually discovered that a small, bungalow-style hotel, with about thirty chalets, was due to open on another part of the same Indonesian island as our hotel, at about the same time that our start-up team would need accommodation in the months leading up to the grand opening. So we moved into our new home as very long-term guests, giving the place the hotelier's dream ticket of 100 per cent occupation from the start.

Our mission was to work all the hours we could to be ready in time. We would take just two consecutive days off each month, so that we could travel back to Singapore and take care of our housekeeping needs and catch up on some of the basic everyday things most people take for granted.

It was a strange feeling on our first night on the island after the last ferry had departed. It felt like we were some kind of latter-day pioneers, preparing ourselves for unknown hardships and setting out to go where no man had been before. Luckily, the food in our simple hotel was not bad, though it was not as if we could go and try somewhere else if we didn't like it. Talk about a captive audience! The nearest small 'town' was three hours inland, and that was only if you were travelling by a fast four-wheel-drive vehicle. Our rooms had no television, the beer was prohibitively expensive and there was absolutely nothing to do regarding entertainment – but if you were not working, the beach was nice. What a paradise!

Fortunately, a friend came to visit and kept me entertained with some good yarns about his work for one of the big shots in nearby Brunei. Peter had lots of great stories as he had been involved in organising entertainment and travel for his very wealthy and powerful boss. He told me that at one time when his boss had wanted to stay in one of the most prestigious hotels in London, he had asked my friend to book the entire top floor of rooms for a week. However, Peter discovered that it was fully booked and that unfortunately the hotel could not accommodate his request. The boss told him to make the booking for a period when there was space, and to go ahead and organise the trip.

When they arrived in London a few months later, however, his boss arranged to meet the hotel owners and purchased the hotel on the spot. It cost him tens of millions of pounds and when all the papers had been signed, he promptly fired all the staff, kicked the guests out, turned off the power and telephones, locked the doors with huge padlocks and left. His departing words were, "If I can't stay here, then no one can." Apparently, the hotel stayed empty in the heart of London, collecting dust, for months.

Similarly, an instruction Peter had to observe was to always have a large amount of very expensive Russian caviar in the house. The ludicrous thing was that it would usually be given to the staff to eat before it turned sour. They would then order another few kilos of fresh caviar just to be kept in case there was a need, only for it to also be eaten by the staff at a later date. Peter thought it might be a good idea to save money by ordering only a small supply, as visitors never ate that much anyway.

However, a few days after he initiated the new purchasing arrangement, his boss announced that a senior member of the British Royal Family was coming to visit and that he was so pleased he had a good supply of caviar on hand. So Peter immediately confessed that he had actually only ordered a small amount. This made his employer furious and he sent him running down the corridor shouting, "Get the jet ready! Get the jet ready!"

Peter's punishment for his unsanctioned budgeting was to accompany the flight team on a jumbo jet to Moscow, simply to pick up twenty kilos of Beluga caviar!

We swapped stories and shared more than a couple of 'cold ones', whether the tales were true, or embellished a touch, really did not matter; it was just great to have Peter's company. And I figured that visiting friends were going to be my salvation during this contract.

Back at the newly emerging hotel, there were no less than three professional, 18-hole 'designer' golf courses under construction and plans for hundreds of condominium resort homes to be built later. The first of the golf courses was to be named after the famous golfer who was involved in promoting the project – for a sizeable fee, of course. We had heard on the grapevine that the developers were trying to save money by mixing a cheaper soil for the greens. The soil for the greens, as we subsequently learnt, has to be of a very high standard compared to that of the fairways, which should also be top-notch but is not so vitally important. Apparently, the famous golfer's representatives had given very strict specifications for our guys to follow, but the owners had tried to skimp a little and had somehow got caught, and now he himself was coming for a spot-check.

Not surprisingly, the result of the inspection was that the famous name was unhappy with the quality of the soil used on the greens. He demanded that, in future, the hotel send a sample of every mix of soil to him in the United States for final approval before it could be used on any of the eighteen greens. As this was a multi-million dollar contract, the owners had to go along with his demands. So in the end, a few failed shortcuts to save money turned out to be a very expensive mistake indeed.

I made friends with some of the Australian contractors who had come over to construct the golf courses. They moved into our small bungalow hotel and we started a nightly tradition of cooking our own dinners on the beach. The barbeque grill was made from some makeshift metal bars which we welded together, and the fires were built on the beach using old bits of driftwood. The meals usually began sedately enough until the guys got a little drunk, and then it was skinny-dipping and generally playing the fool, trying to amuse – or, more likely, irritate – the wives or girlfriends who had accompanied some of these carefree characters.

The women would sit, complaining about their partners' Neanderthal activities, on a large, half-buried log next to the fire, which was our only light source at that time. Being sat close to the fire was also a good idea because it was our protection from any wild animals that might come cruising around at night, such as wild boar which were a very common sight on the edge of the bush. At least a couple of big snakes had also been spotted.

Of course, you also did not want to have too big a fire, in case you attracted the unwanted attention of the local pirates who sometimes cruised around these parts, looking primarily for vulnerable ships or small family boats. If you attracted them you were most definitely on your own. I mean, who were you going to call? The pirate police?

Sitting on the bus for our daily ride out to the site, I heard a crackle over the funky handheld radio – one of the few means of communication on the island.

"John. Come in, John. Come in. Over."

John was our driver extraordinaire, in whose hands we – not very happily – placed our lives on the daily drive to mudsville.

"Yes, John here. Come in."

It was the ex-Indonesian Army guy in charge of all the construction workers and he was trying to let us know that it was not safe to visit the site today as a huge riot had broken out. Workers of two different religions had decided to battle it out to settle some old scores that, for all we knew, may have started with their grandparents, or even further back than that. Since we couldn't go to the site, we prepared for another boring day at our 'base camp'. Hanging around the beach was becoming a real drag and it was to get even worse.

The next day, there was no sign of any struggle at the site. Indeed, the only hint of the earlier problem was the fact that some of the construction staff were missing, apparently – as we would learn – they were in the 'hospital' with some quite serious injuries. The injured had been transported in the back of the builders' dump trucks, along the very dusty and bumpy road for the three-hour ride to the one and only small town on the island. When we sent someone from the hotel to check on the injured workers, we learnt that the hospital had not been able to do much for them as it was ill-equipped to handle such cases. My worst nightmare was beginning to come true.

The local hospital had contacted another hospital in Jakarta, the Indonesian capital, to see if it could borrow the equipment it needed, but as it was going to take a couple of days for whatever it was to arrive, our hotel decided to charter a small plane to transport all the injured to a proper hospital. One of the staff had broken his leg during the fracas, and had to bear the excruciating pain of a broken bone sticking out of his leg throughout the whole transportation drama.

The newly appointed food and beverage manager was due to arrive the following day on the last ferry, and the boss asked me to go and meet him. He also told me that he was organising a recruitment tour of Indonesia which would enable us to conduct interviews and hire the hotel staff we needed. As the executive chef, I was to be involved in this and we would be leaving in a couple of days. The schedule included visits to Medan, Jakarta, Bali, Surabaya and Balikpappan, keeping us on the road for around three weeks, and the food and beverage manager and I would meet and interview around 2,000 candidates, sifting through the applications before making offers to the ones we wanted.

So I made my way to the ferry terminal to pick up Jeffery, our new colleague – and soon to become the next disillusioned victim – to welcome him to what I habitually called 'the zoo'! On the long drive back to the hotel, the first question he asked was, "Where is everybody?" I spent the rest of the evening with him in the bar of our bungalow hotel trying to get the poor guy to settle down and stay calm.

No doubt still reeling from the shock of the isolation of his new home, Jeffery kept muttering, to himself as much as to me: "I was never told this. All the boss said to me was, 'Don't worry, it's only forty-five minutes from Singapore.' He never said anything about needing your own private helicopter to get over the water in that time."

Two days later, as we were getting ready to leave for our Indonesian recruitment tour, I called by Jeffery's room to pick him up on the way to breakfast. His room was empty and a solitary white envelope leant against the telephone with my name written on it. I opened the envelope and read the note it contained, which showed signs of having been written in a rush.

'Sorry, Mike, the job is not what I was told and by the time you read this note, I will be halfway back to Singapore. I like the good things in life far too much to be able to hack it here – basically, everything that you don't have on the island. I know that I can't handle this, so please accept my deepest apologies and let me say good-bye to you. To the boss – can you please tell him that he can go and f**k himself, twice over!'

Well, that was that, and now I had to go and break the bad news to the boss, whose only response was, "Never mind, chef. Now you can interview the service staff as well."

So there I was, with my back firmly up against the wall yet again, trying to get myself mentally prepared to interview 2,000 people in three weeks. Not only would I be asking the same questions over and over again but, as most of the candidates would not be able to speak English, I had to take a crash-course in the national language – Bahasa Indonesia – so I could at least ask the questions.

On the first day of the interviews, the same questions kept popping up: "What is there for us to do in our spare time and where can we do our shopping?" So I called the boss, who was in Singapore just getting ready to go out for a nice dinner, and explained the problem.

He told me to tell them that every building of the staff dormitory housing would have its own television in the general rest areas, and that we would also be opening a small shop selling basic items in the housing compound. Assured by the boss, I used this information to entice the new recruits out to our 'desert island' and gave them my personal guarantee these items and facilities would be waiting for them on arrival.

Over the course of the recruitment tour, I selected some 350 staff on my own, briefing them about the property, the island and, of course, telling them all not to worry about its remoteness. In a few cases, mothers came to see me during the interviews and asked me to take special care of their much-loved teenagers. This did not make me feel any more comfortable.

A few weeks later, when the new recruits arrived at the hotel, they were greeted by their newly appointed department heads. The only person from the hotel the new recruits had seen before was me, and they were all excited and eager to say hello. They seemed very happy and all was going well, until they entered the staff quarters to find no television sets and no promised shop from which to buy their essentials.

Naturally, as I was the one who had given them my personal guarantee regarding these facilities, they came after me like a school of sharks which had just smelt blood. Mine! Off I went to see the boss, since it was he who had given me the assurance which I then relayed to them.

Fat lot of use he was. All he said was they were 'on the way', and over the next few months it became hotel culture for staff to reply, if asked where something was, "Oh, like the television, it's on the way."

On one of my visits to Singapore, I spoke to the managing director of the hotel group about the situation at the hotel, and he promised to come over for a visit to see for himself. The Balinese staff, hearing of this, made traditional kites to fly outside their housing area, and swore they would write pointed and uncomplimentary slogans on the kites for the big boss to see. I told the general manager what was being planned and urged him to organise the promised facilities in order to settle the problem, but as usual all he said to me was, "Don't worry, chef, I'm going to take the managing director to the housing area late at night when it's dark and he won't be able to see any kites." Clearly chuffed at his little plan, he added for good measure, "Sometimes I even surprise myself!"

I just had to bite my tongue since I spent most of my time at the hotel in the company of the general manager, and did not want to make my life any more miserable than it already was.

When we escorted the managing director around the site during his visit, the staff housing area was in darkness, just as the boss had planned. However, when I looked up, there right on cue were the staff's handmade kites, with their messages in bright yellow and orange luminous ink: 'Where are the television sets?' It was so dark the luminous messages stuck out like a sore thumb and were very easy to read.

Well, that was that. Very soon afterwards, the staff were given their promised television sets and a small shop duly opened on site. I, too, could work feeling a little less guilty about what had not happened after my much-publicised promises.

The next hiccup occurred when the owners wanted to open the hotel before the supply lines for our food stocks and perishable goods, which were due to come in from Singapore, were properly in place. I couldn't believe what I was hearing and the general manager, who knew I would be upset about this, looked at me nervously.

"I'm sure we can work something out, chef," he said. "Maybe we can get what we need from the small village across the island."

I looked at him for a moment and asked if he would like a cup of coffee. He said he would love one. We had only just received all the kitchen equipment, which had since been installed and was now in good working order, so I asked the general manager if he would not mind making it for himself, and as he did this I stood and watched.

He took a clean, never-been-used coffee cup and placed it under the nozzle of the coffee machine, and pushed the button. Out poured wonderful, sieved, clean-as-a-whistle boiling water. He looked at me, looked at the empty coffee bean container on top of the machine and then glanced at me again.

"Okay, chef, where's the coffee?" he asked in pained frustration.

"You tell me! Do you really need me to explain to the owners why we can't open the hotel?"

He gave me a filthy look but off he went to call the owners and tell them that it was impossible to open without our first shipment of supplies.

Fairly soon, the hotel was finished and the first major food delivery was finally received, so we opened for business. The lobby area was huge and open in design, with a very high pitched wooden roof that subsequently proved impossible to get to for cleaning, but looked wonderful, nonetheless. The whole place sparkled and it really was a credit to everyone involved.

For a short while, we seemed to bathe in the splendour of the new hotel and the efforts, not to mention sacrifices, we had made to get it operational. Then, steadily, this honeymoon period was worn thin by the series of design and operational problems which emerged.

One problem proved to be a real mystery. Every morning, when the front office staff came to work, they noticed that the lobby was covered in animal droppings. The overnight staff were told to watch and find out who, or what, the culprit was, but every night they somehow missed the action. Totally bored and starved of entertainment on what was still effectively a desert island, I decided to get involved and do my bit to solve this vital mystery.

After the last guests had retired, I went to my room, picked up a pillow and returned to get comfortable on one of the lobby sofas. I sat there for ages, became too comfortable and must have dropped asleep, falling into the same trap, no doubt, as the ever diligent overnight security guards. I was woken from my deep sleep by a funny sensation, as if I was being rained on. I turned over and, for a second, forgot where I was, thinking that I was dreaming. Then I realised that I was not dreaming at all, and wherever I was, I knew it was surely not outside, and that I shouldn't be getting wet.

I jerked up into a seated position, opening my eyes to find dozens, if not hundreds, of large bats swooping around my head and high up in the roof space. They swarmed around the lobby, occasionally diving down to get a better look at this clown who must have had too many drinks and forgotten where his room was. I stood up and looked at the roof, but there were so many bats that it was hard to see the wood in the ceiling.

The entire roof was a large black moving blanket. Then, all of a sudden, as if they were called back by their maker, they were gone, at least until tomorrow. Now this was a real problem, and it was only really cleared up when we sent for a pest control company from Jakarta, but that's a whole different story.

A few weeks later, we had our first tropical storm, a real howler with torrential rains which made the swimming pool overflow and flood the gardens. As the lobby was high and open, and the wind so strong, the rain blew in fiercely at the front entrance and passed all the way through the lobby and out of the back exit. Everything and everyone who was anywhere in the middle got a soaking, including the guests and our expensive furnishings imported from Europe.

Could the bright sparks who designed the hotel not have done any research into the weather patterns on an Indonesian island? Now we would have to send to Singapore for huge bamboo shutters, which would cost a fortune, to enable the guests to enjoy an evening cocktail without having to keep both hands on their glasses while wearing swimsuits!

The last restaurant to come on line at the hotel was a wonderful seafood spot, nestled down on the beach at sea level, with an awesome view of the sunset each evening. This was to be the trademark 'Sunset Restaurant', billed as the most elegant and romantic place on earth. There was only one small problem, however. The construction guys had left a mound of earth between the ocean and the seating area, and had planted a landscape of wonderful small tropical trees. When we tried out a mock dinner before going live, we sat there and just had to laugh. The trees totally obscured the view and nothing could be seen of the setting sun. Of course, the next day we had to bulldoze the area flat again, destroying all the beautiful landscaping work in the process.

I kept telling the boss that we needed some rubber kitchen matting to go on the floor besides the dishwashing machines, to prevent staff slipping on grease or spilt water. Unfortunately, these mats were very expensive, and as we needed about forty pieces, the idea was put on hold. The boss did not see the need to buy these expensive rubber mats until, that is, the day he was walking through the kitchen in a bit of a hurry and slipped with a cup of freshly brewed coffee in his hand. This went all over the newly purchased, tailor-made batik shirt he was wearing. Then, of course, the rubber mats were promptly ordered and another problem solved.

I ordered some good charcoal firelighters for the barbeque grills in the hotel as we wanted to get the grills lit and ready for cooking. I asked an assistant to get someone to light the grills and leave them to heat up for the afternoon, while I went for a short break. I had just arrived in my room when my assistant called, shouting down the telephone, "Chef! We have a fire in the kitchen. Come quickly!" I ran out of my room, taking a shortcut through the middle of the gardens, and into the large kitchen area.

The chief steward was lying on the floor with his eyes closed and someone had smeared his body with burn cream. On first observation, I must admit I was not overly worried because it didn't look too bad, but I could not be sure as the cream was on so thick. Concerned for his well-being, we sent him to the hospital – ill-equipped as it was – which was at the other end of the island, and I went to visit him later that evening.

I walked into the ward, half expecting to see him sitting up and sharing a joke about how he just wanted to get out of going to work for a few days or something. He was always such a light-hearted guy. But what I saw made my eyes well up with tears. He was terribly burnt and the nurse explained to me that it generally took time for the burns to show after an accident like this, and that the cream had slowed down the process. The top layer of skin had completely peeled off his chest which was red raw and shiny wet. His nipples were about ten times their normal size, and full of liquid. He had not been able to recognise anyone before he slipped into a coma.

The room was poorly lit and was very hot and humid. The staff had opened the window but this had allowed flies and mosquitoes to get in and these were now buzzing around his open wounds. I could not believe my eyes, as I knelt by his bed and whispered to him in a gentle tone, hoping that he could hear me. I felt terrible and I blamed myself for not being there to help him with the job. I demanded that the hospital move him to an air-conditioned ward immediately, which they did – I think just to shut me up – and later the hotel owners agreed to pay whatever extra monies were needed to give him the best treatment and facilities available.

I learned afterwards that he had wanted to start the fire the way he was used to at home, and had not bothered to use the firelighters I had sent for. Instead, he picked up some paraffin, filled a glass bottle he found in the rubbish bin, and had gone to light the grill with this lethal concoction. Apparently, the wind had changed suddenly and the flame ignited the paraffin in the neck of the bottle, the flame shot inside and the whole thing exploded, setting his clothing alight which then stuck to his body. The other staff had rolled him on the ground trying to extinguish the flames, but it had taken too long and the damage was done.

Some weeks later, when Sulaiman returned to the staff housing quarters, I organised a rousing welcome home with the other staff members, cheering and waving as his car pulled up. Any lighting aids other than the correct firelighters were outlawed in the hotel, and the purchasing department was banned from ordering anything else for this purpose. Amazingly, a few months later, I saw another staff member using the same lethal liquid Sulaiman had used, and when I asked him where he had got it from, he told me that he had bought it with his own money! He said it lit easier than the 'white bricks' we had bought for them to use. My jaw just gaped.

———————

We kitted out the waiters in one of the hotel's restaurants with traditional batik shirts so the guests could see the local clothing style. The only problem with that was that some of the senior-ranking people in Indonesia also wear batik shirts as a sign of authority, as well as for elegance. One day, some government officials came for a courtesy visit and lunch. We were desperate to get into good standing with the local authorities for obvious reasons, so this was a very important lunch indeed. The visit was going well, with the health department chaps giving us the thumbs-up, and then we guided them to the twenty-four-hour restaurant for their meal.

As we entered the restaurant, there was a bunch of foreign tourists sitting there, and seeing me in my chef's uniform and the others in their batik shirts, they must have thought that the guests we were hosting were members of the service staff. One of the diners had obviously drunk a little too much and shouted across the open-air restaurant, "Hey there! How about some service over here? We need some more beer. Bring more beer!"

We knew instantly that this fracas was going to cost us dearly. We had embarrassed our government guests, and what was worse, made them lose face, which in Asia, as I had discovered, is the worst thing that you can do to anyone. To avoid this ever happening again, we had to call the uniform designer and immediately order new sets of non-batik shirts for all the staff.

Another one of the problems we had to overcome was that of refuse collection. The local government promised to set up a collection agency as soon as they possibly could, but the hotel was open before they could get properly organised. So we were advised by the local authority to burn or bury all our kitchen refuse, and not to leave it out in the hot sun to rot, for obvious reasons.

Since it was going to take a few more weeks to set up the refuse collection system, I asked the stewarding department to bury our waste far away from the hotel. On the first couple of occasions, I went out to the outskirts of the grounds to help them dig the hole and show them how far to dig down. This system seemed to be working alright, except that I didn't notice that it was taking them less and less time to do the job. I never went to check as the system looked to be running smoothly. One day, however, I was looking out of my bedroom window and saw near to the edge of the jungle, one solitary bag of garbage. That's funny, I thought, so I decided to take a stroll and see why it was there.

I was staggered to find that the staff had been dumping all the refuse just behind the bushes instead of burying it as instructed, and some of it had spilled out from behind its hiding place. There were thousands of black bags full of wet, stinking, rotten garbage just sitting there. The effort of burying it had obviously become too much of a strain and they had taken to dumping it in the bushes to make life easy for themselves.

Millions of maggots were teeming over the ghastly pile and many were now heading in the direction of the hotel. I could not even have it burned now as it was in the dense bush and the whole area would catch fire. That night I hardly slept a wink, worrying how we were going to solve this one. Just sometimes though, problems can take care of themselves, or nature finds the way to solve it for you.

When I woke up and looked out of the window, I couldn't believe my eyes. There were hundreds and thousands of different kinds of birds flying around and swooping down on the great feast they had discovered. It lasted non-stop for a week, all day and every day, an absolute feeding frenzy. With most of the maggots gone, the guilty staff were ordered back out there to bury the leftovers. Remarkably there were hardly any maggots or flies left. Thank goodness for Mother Nature!

The boss called me with his next challenge and this one was a dandy. The hotel had bought a brand new 46-seater luxury coach to transport guests from the ferry terminal to the hotel. They would be served with a welcome drink and handed nice ice-cold towels to refresh themselves as they journeyed. The problem was that, for some unknown reason, all too regularly as the coach made its way back from the ferry terminal, its battery would go flat, stalling the bus and stranding the passengers.

The local mechanics could not solve the problem and the dealer who sold the bus said, on the phone from Singapore, that it was a German-made coach of international standards and it was therefore impossible that we could be suffering with this sort of problem so early on. Very helpful!

I asked where the coach was parked at night and they told me in the hotel car park, outside reception at the front. I set my alarm for three o'clock in the morning, forcing myself to get up and check on its whereabouts. I was surprised to see that the bus was not where it was supposed to be and that it had somehow disappeared into thin air. As I was already up, and now even further intrigued to know what was going on, I decided to make my own investigations, starting at the staff housing quarters. I took a steady drive over there.

As I neared the housing quarters, I started to hear a lot of noises and even some cheering. It was very late indeed and I surmised most people would be sleeping by now if they were going to be of even the slightest use at work the following day.

As I got closer, I couldn't believe my eyes. The parked coach was rocking and rolling, and the tape deck going full-blast with the latest sounds. The buggers had turned our hotel's bus into a mobile disco.

This was obviously a regular routine. Closer to dawn, they would apparently all help clean it up, and someone would drive it back, park it in the same place and leave it there as if nothing had happened. I realised that while they were running the electrics, nobody had thought about turning on the engine, hence the flat battery every other day.

I stood on the bottom step of the bus and shouted at the top of my voice, "May I join the party, please?" There was instant silence. This gave me the chance to explain that if the bus was driven back to the hotel straightaway and this never happened again, I would not have to tell the boss what had been going on.

The flat-battery problem evaporated overnight. The boss was none the wiser, and suddenly I was getting a lot more respect from the staff because I'd been willing to forget the whole mobile disco story.

Always looking for a different promotional angle, we started a new activity at the resort where a couple could pay 'an arm and a leg' for their own very private barbeque. We would organise the food, the grill, the serving equipment and so on, and sail it over to a very small and uninhabited island. The staff of the hotel would light the fire, prepare the food and then sail back to the hotel, leaving the guests alone for a very romantic dinner. The loving couple could sit around the fire and eat, while whispering sweet nothings into each other's ears. It was impossible to be seen on this island and they were promised total privacy. Although we charged a fair bit for this adventure, it proved to be very popular indeed, and as the whole idea was to take just one couple at a time, we sometimes had quite a waiting list.

One young newly wed couple made a booking, saying that the dinner sounded awfully exciting and they could not wait to be 'marooned' on a tropical desert island. They packed their video camera so they could make their own Robinson Crusoe movie to show their friends and family back home, and they were soon on their way over to the blue lagoon. We did the usual; dropped them off and set up the camp fire, lit the grill and then left them alone for the allotted time. The two guests said that they had a great time and that they would like to go again before they returned home.

The next day, they said they were keen to watch their home-made video, to relive their great island adventure, and asked to borrow a video player. They returned the video player a day or so later and that seemed to be that. A few days later, however, one of the staff said he wanted to show me something which everyone else had already been enjoying. I walked into the staff quarters and was rather shocked to see some of the staff watching what appeared to be a blue movie, when I suddenly realised that it was our amorous young newly-weds. They had filmed themselves frolicking around naked on the beach, and even making love on the sand.

The silly fools had forgotten to retrieve the tape from the machine and the staff, starved of entertainment, had been getting a free show. I gave the staff the appropriate telling-off and removed the tape (after it had finished, of course!), then called the guests to give them back their souvenir.

The wife was very red-faced and when she asked me if I had watched it, I said, "No, why would you ask that? Is it a good movie?"

"No, not at all," she said, "just some jungle stuff we saw when we went for our island barbeque, that's all," and off she went.

For the last few days of their holiday, they kept a very low profile. I think they knew that someone had seen it, and they must have been a little embarrassed, to say the least.

Although we had been open for a while – as they say in these parts, with a 'soft launch' – the day of the grand opening party had finally arrived, and two of the most important guys in the region were coming – the leaders of Indonesia and Singapore. They were going to conduct the opening honours in front of the assembled media of Indonesia and Singapore respectively. A lavish buffet was set out in the lobby. All the other restaurants were open and had prepared a sample of different foods from their particular repertoires.

Mr Goh Cheok Tong, the Prime Minister of Singapore, arrived with a modest entourage of just a couple of people, his advisor and a personal security guard. President Suharto of Indonesia, however, was a little different and the security checks for his arrival started months before.

I remember being called into the general manager's office and introduced to a very senior-looking army official who fired a barrage of personal questions at me. What religion did I observe? Did I belong to any political groups? Did I have any strange illnesses? And so on, and so on. I thought it was a little too much and felt offended to the point where I did not want to cook the food any more, and was quite willing to pass the baton to someone else who could be trusted more than me. I had no idea that this was just the tip of iceberg. Before the big day, I had to justify, introduce and excuse myself to countless agencies before actually being allowed to conduct the trade that I had spent twenty years learning.

The health department came to check on the cleanliness of our brand new kitchen, asking endless ridiculous questions that made me choke on my pride every time I answered them. Then came the police to interview me and ask me to fill out a couple of forms with much the same questions the army official had asked me. Then came the medical to prove that I was fit and healthy enough to cook the food. Next, I was told that the President's personal assistant would have to vet the menu I was going to prepare.

This was a drama in itself, as the menu went back and forth from one fax machine to another. Finally, he pronounced he was happy, so I was surprised when I had to go through exactly the same rigmarole when the President's 'personal chef' came knocking on my door.

Now the menu needed to be changed again, so I had to explain to him that it had been chosen by President Suharto's personal assistant. But the chef insisted that he held rank over the personal assistant and that it was he whom I should listen to. I called the personal assistant and he was upset by what I told him. He, in turn, informed me that he was, in fact, the number one authority and demanded I follow the menu he had finalised with me previously.

Now I was just about pissed off with the whole thing, and ready to go to the office to plead my impossible case to the boss when the ultimate happened. I walked into the kitchen and saw a guy standing there holding some kind of gadget which was blinking and making a continuous bleeping noise. Despite my bewilderment at what was going on, I asked him politely, "Excuse me, sir, can I help you at all?"

"No, I can help you. I am from the government health department and this thing here tells me if there is enough light in the room. I can tell you now, it's short, so can you please call your chief engineer here immediately."

Well, that was it. I had been pushed right over the edge with this bureaucratic nonsense. I went to see the boss and explained that I just could not go through with this any more. For the last two months I'd had to swallow my pride on a daily basis but I had now reached the limit of my patience. He begged me to just hang on for just a short while longer and asked me to go back down and humour the clown, which I did after I had calmed down sufficiently.

The next day, the entire staff of the hotel was asked to go to a makeshift office the authorities had established at the hotel where they would interview everyone, one by one, for one last time. I just could not believe it. They told me that if I did not go through this final interview, they would not be able to give me a security pass and I would not be allowed into the kitchen on the big day. I thought long and hard about that one, thinking it would be a welcome blessing if they did turn me away – I could maybe return to my room, have a couple of beers and watch a football game or something. But, of course, I lined up with all the rest.

On the day of the opening, when I was in the kitchen getting the food ready, in walked a besuited man with a large and expensive-looking briefcase. He matter-of-factly asked the banqueting manager to prepare him a table to use for 'testing' and then waited patiently for it to come. He pulled a chair up to the table, sat down, and started making preparations. When he opened his briefcase, there was a kind of chemistry set with test tubes and different coloured liquids in small bottles. Undeterred by our bemused stares, he then sat there without saying a word, and waited patiently for the dinner to start. His face remained absolutely expressionless, as if he could be amused or angered by nothing.

When the first course was ready to go out, he signalled to an assistant who then came over to speak to me.

"May we have a small piece for testing, please?"

I told him he could have as much as he wanted.

He then took a sample to the first man who stuffed it into a test tube, added this, then added that, until finally he must have obtained the colour he was looking for. He looked up at the assistant and gave a faint nod of approval, and his colleague motioned to me.

"You may go ahead and serve this course now," he declared.

This interchange went on for the whole meal, with me, and my staff, having to wait for a go-ahead nod at each course. The food was served almost cold. I was even wondering if they would complain afterwards about having a luxury hotel serve up lukewarm food. When the meal was finally over and everyone else had left, the man with the briefcase passed nearby and offered me his hand to shake.

"What is your name?" he asked, in a cold, toneless voice.

"Chef Michael Saxon, what's yours?" I answered in a pleased-to-be-alive tone.

He did not answer but simply said, "We shall remember the job you did today. Thank you." And then he left.

Despite the rigours of my desert island introduction to Indonesia, I grew to love it. It is a wonderful country, full of warm-hearted, kind and gentle people. I came to understand that many Indonesians have vast reserves of patience. They seem to have a fuse that lasts forever, but if and when it reaches its end, there is a huge bomb that is likely to go off, and you don't want to be anywhere near it when it does.

While I was working there, the average kitchen hand's salary was the equivalent of around ninety US dollars a month, and that was when the exchange rate was around a modest 3,000 Rupiah to the US dollar. People were poor, on the whole, and in some small villages even starving. Some, it was said, had even resorted to eating pounded bark from trees, mixed with water to make a kind of gruel, while others collected short, fat tree worms to eat in a stew, like something from a horror movie.

When the downturn came in the late 1990s, triggering off the Asian economic crisis and sending food prices spiralling out of control, the Rupiah hit an all-time low of nearly 20,000 Rupiah to the US dollar, making local salaries almost worthless. This was the last piece of straw that broke the camel's back, signalling the start of the well-publicised riots. The Indonesian people just could not take it anymore, and the view that it was the endemic corruption that had effectively brought the country to its knees especially contributed in bringing matters to a head.

Small bribes, known as 'tea money', were the norm when I was there, and each time I arrived at the island's ferry terminal after a break, the immigration or customs officer would say quietly, "Oleh, oleh." This meant that they wanted a small gift in return for allowing you entry into the country, a small bag of sweets, perhaps a plastic souvenir, or simply a few dollars to keep them 'sweet'. If you played this game, and remembered everyone, you would not be troubled, and could even call on their ready help if you had a problem. They rarely checked my baggage and let me pass through unhindered, sometimes with a salute of respect if they were in a good mood. You basically had to play the game, and it was the only game in town. If you were not prepared to play, you would get nowhere fast. It was just the nature of the beast.

Another convention was if you had been successful in business, you never boasted about it for fear of someone else wanting to take your business away from you. One guy I heard of, for example, started a small white water rafting business in Bali, and when it grew into a money-making enterprise, he started spending a lot of the profits and began boasting of his success. Standing out like a sore thumb, he eventually attracted the wrong sort of attention. One night, while playing pool, he had had too much to drink and began to opine, boorishly, on how backward he thought Indonesia and its people were. Pity for him that there were some high-ranking officials playing at the very next table. The next day, he was escorted to the airport and flown home, without being given the time to close, or sell, his very profitable company. The white water rafting business continued to boom and made a very large and substantial amount of money, though unfortunately, not for him.

I had my own problems to contend with. I had ordered a consignment of 'hairy crabs' from Hong Kong, which are famous for having a very short season within which they can be eaten. The consignment arrived late one Friday afternoon and I sent one of my staff to collect this very special delivery from customs. I had no idea the messenger would refuse to 'play ball' with the ferry terminal inspectors. As a result, he came back to the hotel empty-handed, so I rushed back myself, only to find the terminal closed.

On the following Monday, when I returned to the customs house to collect the crabs, they were sitting outside the terminal on the floor, exactly where they had been left on the Friday night. Two days packed in a wooden crate and dumped out in the sun. When I finally got them in my possession and opened the case, I wasn't surprised to find all of the crabs were dead and the consignment totally useless. From that moment on, I made an agreement with the top inspectors at the terminal to call me if there were any further hiccups with any of our goods, and I would come and take care of the business 'personally'. I had learnt that if you don't want to play ball, the necessary paperwork will never be in order. If you do play ball, it doesn't matter a jot if the paperwork is in order or not, or for that matter, if there is any paperwork at all, because you have made sure that everything will operate as smoothly as it should.

———————•◦•⬥•◦•———————

One day, I was invited to a *'nasi padang'* lunch out in a nearby village. I went along for the experience and to get away from the hotel, even if it was just for a short while. Our hotel group was put together at a large round table. Without any of us placing an order, the food arrived promptly.

"*Silahkan makan*," implored the waiter – a very polite invitation for one to start a meal, before which it would be impolite to start digging in – and we prepared to tackle the dozen dishes that were placed in the centre of the table. *Nasi padang* is a communal or family-style lunch where you pass the bowls of food around the table and everyone serves themselves. I managed to make good work of the wonderful spicy dishes.

Indonesian food is big on coconut milk, anchovies, candlenuts, cardamom, chillies, cinnamon, cloves, coriander, galangal, garlic, lemon grass and pandan leaves. These items are often ground together using a primitive granite pestle and mortar with painstaking effort to create very exciting and distinctive-tasting dishes.

'*Sambal*' is a key home-made sauce, used as a base for many dishes, and varying in recipe from one master chef to another. I particularly loved the '*gado-gado*', a strange name for an innocuous but delicious vegetable salad with peanut sauce, and '*otak-otak*', a fish mousse cooked in banana leaves. Pork is infrequently seen in this predominantly Muslim country, although Bali, with its majority Hindu population, does serve pork in hotels and public restaurants. A dish often prepared to delight the children is '*satay lilit*', minced meat wrapped around lemon grass stalks, then grilled and served with the ubiquitous peanut sauce. Of course, no meal is complete without a platter of '*pisang goreng*', or banana fritters, often served with ice cream. That day's *nasi padang* lunch offered a good rendition of all these tasty dishes.

When we received the final bill, we were surprised to see that we had only been charged for a small portion of the food that had actually appeared. Thinking rather chef-like, I was not impressed with their idea of food management, and the wasted food, not to mention poor billing, that this system seemed to create. I was obviously still naïve, despite my years of experience.

Leaning back in my chair, feeling very content, out of the corner of my eye I saw the owner of the restaurant clearing the tables. I was taken aback when he took the bowls of unfinished food which had been passed around our table at least a dozen times, with numerous sets of cutlery dipped in and out, and mixed them in with the leftovers from the other tables, obviously to be reheated later. Evidently the victuals are then served up to the next group of locals or tourists who come by in search of *nasi padang*.

I was told that this was totally normal practice, and it was taken for granted when you ate at one of these places that likely as not the food may have been 'recycled'. Who was I to argue? I asked myself. In fact, with people on the verge of starvation, it is probably the most appropriate thing to do. Though I'm not sure my stomach will be quite so stretched next time I go for *nasi padang*.

After feeling like Robinson Crusoe for too long, the constant sensation of sand in my shoes, in my eyes, in my bed, and on a bad day, what felt like in my brain began to turn to 'island fever'. However much I had come to love the pure air and the wonderful clean beaches of our Indonesian island, I still craved for some of the niceties of life that one takes for granted in more populous and developed environments. I had heard of an island in nearby Malaysia, which boasted of having both styles of existence – a tropical island paradise with a good-sized city as well. I decided to go and take a look for myself, so I packed my bags and boarded the ferry one last time and headed for Penang – the famed 'Pearl of the Orient'.

VIII

AN ANGEL IN WAITING

I ARRIVED IN Penang in Malaysia, feeling mentally and physically exhausted, and the thought of working at a resort hotel, with a supposedly slower pace, gave me hope that I could at least begin to recharge my batteries. In my dreams!

It turned out that I was totally naïve and deeply mistaken. The hotel team, and especially the kitchen brigade, gave me a warm enough welcome and they made me feel like I was a long-lost relative. Even so, I felt a little lost here on this small island – the famed 'Pearl of the Orient' – and was almost straightaway wondering if I had not made a mistake. A few of my friends called and asked what I was doing there. I had to confess that I may have made the decision in a moment of sheer madness.

Even after a couple of months, I still felt very lonely and out of place, and missed the company of my close friends. Getting ready for each new day was becoming increasingly harder, and swinging my legs over the edge of the bed when the alarm clock went off, more and more depressing. Fortunately, one fine sunny day (and most of them are hot and sunny here, anyway), the food and beverage manager asked me to join him for lunch. We sat eating and talking about the hotel operation and what needed to be done.

It was there, during a simple working lunch, that my life was to change forever in a single heartbeat. It was as if God himself had planned this detour to Malaysia, timing every second to perfection, and showing me once and for all the true meaning of my life.

My Caesar's salad was alright, a little bland perhaps and crying out for some more freshly grated Parmesan cheese. But then it happened. I looked up to see whose attention I could catch for the Parmesan, when I saw her. For a brief second, I was squinting as I tried to focus through blinding sunlight streaming right into my eyes. It made a direct hit on my face while brilliantly shining from behind her. A passing cotton wool cloud blocked the direct sunlight, dulling the glare, and there, through a ray of beautiful golden sunshine, I saw a woman with a perfect smile. For no reason at all, it just made my eyes well up with treacherous tears.

I sat there speechless, and as I watched her accomplishing her work at a breakneck speed, my conversation with the food and beverage manager ground to a halt. I couldn't focus on a thing the poor man was saying. Nothing could have got through to me at that moment, which I somehow sensed was going to decide the direction of my destiny forever. Everything became instantly clear – what was happening to me and the reason for my being here was a part of a bigger picture. Fate had brought me to work at this hotel which just moments before was a thorn in my side, but had now turned into my dream job.

I couldn't think of anywhere else I would rather be at that precise moment, as I gingerly raised my hand to get her attention. She came over and gave me the same patient, heavenly smile I had seen just seconds earlier. The smile that Beatrice radiated was one so natural and sincere that I knew it came from deep inside her heart and was not one practised to perfection in front of a mirror at home but was just, well … her.

Getting out of bed in the morning became rather easier now. There was a light, brisk spring in my step that had not been seen for some time.

The next day, I was looking forward to my lunch and to seeing once again that wonderful smile that was already becoming my lifeline and daily mental health tonic. I sat myself down and waited for the 'resident angel', whose every move seemed to have its own unique purpose which I swore was to drive me mad. I suddenly heard a commotion which seemed to be coming from the beachfront. The water sports guys were going berserk and wailing with all their might at an incoming parasailing guest, obviously a first time enthusiast, who was not listening to the simple instructions being screamed at him.

"Pull the lever!" shouted the water sports guys.

"Yee ha. Yee ha!" shouted the tourist, obviously overwhelmed by the experience.

"Pull the lever!" They shouted even harder from the ground.

"Yee ha!" whooped the parasailer.

"Pull the bloody lever before it's too late, you madman!"

"Yee ha!" he shouted back, in a final act of defiance before the ensuing smash and crunch sound of him tearing into a nearby tree. Then came the clouds of pollen flying in all directions and the shaken, half-dead leaves, the squawking of angry crows, disturbed from their barbed-wire nests, and finally the groans of self-inflicted pain from the amateur stuntman.

Everyone rushed to his aid, including me, though really I didn't know whether to laugh, or show some sympathy, or even remorse. The water sports team shouted up to him, realising that he was possibly injured and now absolutely stuck, perched on the top of an evergreen fir tree, like the proverbial Christmas fairy.

"Don't move, sir. We'll have you down in no time at all," reassured one of the guys, but whispered to his partner, "How in God's name are we going to get him down from there?"

They both stood, staring in deep thought, trying to come to terms with the challenge in hand. They scratched their heads for a second and off they went to start the ball rolling with their well-laid master plan. I sat down in one of the heavy wooden garden chairs and waited, trying to imagine what they were going to do. Suddenly they reappeared with a set of engineering ladders.

This is going to be good, I thought – complementary entertainment for the snoozing sun worshippers nearby, who were already starting to sit up and take notice.

The ladder was set up under the dangling tourist, who was looking rather dazed, but unfortunately, his escape route proved to be around five feet short. The sun worshippers and I sat back and waited for Plan B. The hapless parasailer continued to dangle.

By this time, the crowd was getting bigger and the poor victim's friends decided it was time that they took some positive action. Off they went, running to get their cameras! I wanted to tell them that they could take their time, and maybe even grab some lunch first, as this rescue operation was going to be a long haul. I decided not to, just in case our guys pulled off the save of the century.

At that moment, the sound of a small engine revving could be heard from around the corner. It was one of our engineering staff driving 'Genie' at full speed. The Genie is a set of electronically retracting ladders that are driven around on top of a small vehicle which is used for changing light bulbs in the high ceiling areas. Genie was driven slowly onto the beach and moved into position underneath the suspended guy. They started to raise Genie's ladder. But when extended to the fullest, even Genie was still around two feet short of the tips of his pointed toes.

Then came the smartest announcement of the day. "Unhook your safety belt and let yourself drop onto the top of the ladder," shouted one of the water sports guys. Luckily, after analysing a few technical drawings quickly scratched out in the sand, the chief engineer made an executive decision that may not have been the best idea.

"What do you think, chef?" he asked me, obviously getting desperate.

"Well, I would say that there are definitely not enough chocolate chips in these cookies, which makes the coffee just not taste right. I'll have to speak to the pastry chef straightaway."

He looked at me for a second without any expression at all, and finally offered his words of wisdom. "Why don't you just kiss my arse?"

"Well, I could," I started out, "but I don't think that will bring out the taste of the coffee either."

All hell threatened to break loose ... but then the boss arrived. What a total drag. He was clearly unimpressed with the whole debacle.

"Enjoying your coffee, chef?" he asked witheringly. He then turned his full attention to the technical experts, "What would be your next plan of action, gentlemen?"

"Well," answered the chief engineer, "we were thinking about waiting for a couple of hours until the tide comes in, floating a dinghy under him and asking him to jump when the water becomes deep enough. What do you think, boss?"

The boss just gave him an incredulous stare, not saying anything, obviously exasperated by the whole situation. "Do you have another plan, one that might take into consideration the safety of the guest as a starting point?" asked the boss, pointedly.

The chief engineer thought about it for a second, scratched his head and announced to howls of laughter from the gathered crowd of guests, "Actually not."

Feeling the need to take control of the situation himself, the general manager looked over to the water sports team and shouted, "Will you please climb up the tree right now and bring that chap down?"

The crowd erupted with cheers and loud applause for the simple logic and ingenuity of the great one.

Before the guys had climbed halfway up the tree, the general manager told the chief engineer to meet him in his office in five minutes. I was giggling to myself when he turned round to me and said, "Oh, and you might want to join us yourself, chef. That is, of course, if you have finished your coffee and can fit us into your obviously stretched schedule?"

I sat down again to take my last sip and to make sure the parasailer was lowered safely to the ground, which he was. As he reached terra firma, you would have thought he was a member of the Backstreet Boys and had just stepped onto the stage for a final encore. Relieved and shaken, but sporting enough, his ordeal over, he took a well-deserved bow. There were dozens of cameras clicking away as everyone took their final souvenir of the afternoon's pantomime. As for the general manager's choice words to the chief engineer and myself, they're probably best left unrecorded ...

I decided I just had to ask Beatrice out. Maybe just for a cup of coffee, to try to get her to talk to me a little. I knew she would be wary, and it might be a while before I could convince her to spend any of her free time with me. Who the heck was I anyway? Just this new guy around, and after all, she knew nothing of me.

I waited for the right moment when I was seated at a table in the restaurant by myself, and while I was feeling falsely confident, I signalled to her to come over. I looked to the right and then to the left as if to demonstrate that I was concerned about her privacy and reputation and didn't intend to give rise to any gossip. I then slipped my phone number into the meal bill folder, and whispered that I was too shy to ask her for her telephone number but that I wanted to give her the option of choosing to call me or not.

Inside, I secretly wanted to get on my hands and knees to beg her to call me that same day. Why wait a second? I silently implored her. But I thought better of it and decided patience was the necessary virtue here.

She took my number without any change in facial expression whatsoever and slipped it into her right-hand pocket nonchalantly, as if to say, 'Yeah? So what? Big deal!' and off she went. I waited for weeks for the call that was just not forthcoming, until one day, a note was placed under my door late at night. I opened the note with eager anticipation.

Nothing could have prepared me for its contents: 'Dear chef,' started the letter, 'I am looking forward to the day that you and I can make love together, and until that glorious day I remain secretly yours.' It was signed, 'You know who, don't you?'

I was so upset, shocked and disappointed, all in a single second, to think that 'my' angelic Beatrice could be this kind of girl. It was a big setback to my intentions. I sat there in my room, looking at the note over and over again, thinking out loud as I read it and trying to interpret its meaning. But this was no philosophical read-between-the-lines letter. Her intentions were quite basic and direct. I fell asleep with the note resting on my pillow in the same spot I had been reading it for the umpteenth time before I dozed off.

I next saw Beatrice while I was eating my breakfast without much appetite, and I tried to fit her outward personality with the note which I had read so many times the night before. The warm soulful smile, the reserved, calm body language, and the sincere, caring warmth of this wonderful woman just did not match what I had read. Sometimes things just did not make sense, I guessed, and wished that it could all be different.

That night my room phone rang. I was surprised to find no one at the other end – at least there was no one talking. I said, "Hello," and there was only a deathly silence, as if it was some kind of obscene call but without the obscenities.

"Hello?" I sounded out again, and still there was no reply. Frustrated, I hung up. Some crank call, I thought, feeling angry that the hotel operator would put these dummies through to my private quarters without screening the calls first. Annoyed, I called the operator and she told me that there had been no outside call.

The next day, some local members of royalty were due to visit the hotel and the security was tight and rigid, particularly as some media attention was deemed necessary to give the VIPs some very important 'face'. We were waiting in the lobby to greet the guests on their arrival with the usual amount of pomp and ceremony, including the red carpet spread out on the lobby floor. When we received the warning hand, waving from the scouting party stationed across the car park, we knew the VIPs were about to arrive. We all stood smartly to attention, waiting. Soon a white stretch limousine rolled up to the front door at a snail's pace and the media cameras at the entrance were readied.

As the chauffeur jumped out from his seat and went quickly round to open the passenger door, the photographers went into action, as if it were a scene from a movie set. The chauffeur tried the handle, then pushed and pulled to open the door and … nothing. He tried again, still to no avail. So he trotted back round to the driver's side, thinking that maybe he had forgotten to release the door security button by the steering wheel. His own door now appeared to be stuck, but he reached through the open window and pushed the button, giving a thumbs-up signal to the photographers and our grimacing general manager, as if to say, 'It's alright, folks, everything is under control now, just a minor hiccup.' Back he ran to the nearside door, pulled the handle, and … again, nothing. I had visions for a split second that he was going to start kicking, punching or even swearing at the door in the hope that it would become sufficiently intimidated to open by itself.

Instead, he tapped on the window and gestured to the VIP to wind down the glass, but by now the occupant was clearly not amused. The window duly lowered (very slowly, I might add) and the chauffeur spoke softly to the dignitary. He then turned sheepishly to the cameramen and media, asking them to turn off the cameras or point them away from the direction of the car. With the door still firmly jammed shut, he wound the window down to its maximum and the lady, in an elegant dinner ensemble, climbed out of the limousine window with the help of her trusty driver.

In total contrast to what one might have seen in the west, the local media acted as if they were disinterested or even unaware of what was going on. They gave her the all-important face, and then waited respectfully for the lady to arrange herself, checking in a small mirror as she stood by her vehicle. Then, with a nod from the chauffeur, we were back in line, as if a director had first announced 'Cut!' and then 'Action!' Everyone carried on with their greeting of the VIP as if nothing had happened.

I eventually returned to my room to find the phone ringing. I quickly picked it up, and once again there was deathly silence. Nothing was coming from the other end of the line. This time, though, I held on, not saying anything, and waited for the caller to get nervous or irritated. I was not going to be intimidated this time, I resolved. Sure enough, the caller decided to hang up first, and I felt glad I had shown that I was not intimidated by this nonsense.

I was not surprised when a few seconds later the phone rang again. I picked it up, expecting yet more silence, but this time I heard someone say: "Hi, chef, did you get the note that I left under your door the other evening?"

My mind was racing a mile a minute, trying to put a face to the voice, and then it suddenly hit me. It was the housekeeping boy who cleaned my room everyday! I had thought he just seemed to be an overly friendly kind of fellow. I mean, I never thought he was …

Acting dumb, I asked him, "What note?"

"You know," he replied, "the special one."

"Actually," I confessed, "I really only like girls, I'm afraid. I hope you understand."

"Oh … sure, chef, I won't disturb you again," he promised. "Can we keep this little secret to ourselves, do you think?"

"This will be our little secret so long as you understand the way I feel." Now it was my turn for some fun, so I threw in, "Who knows if circumstances were different … but unfortunately …"

He butted in, "Oh, I do, chef, I assure you, and I won't ask you again."

He hung up and that was that. I felt both sad and great at the same time. Sad for the poor guy who sounded very disappointed, if not upset, but great because it was not Beatrice who had sent me the note.

After a while, I started feeling like a real idiot and a heel. How could I have been so stupid to assume that a woman like Beatrice could ever have sent me such a forward note? I felt a jerk and had an uncomfortable and sleepless night, thinking how boring and self-assuming I had been over the whole matter. I had been invited to a friend's house for dinner on my next day off and thought how nice it would have been if Beatrice and I were an item. Visiting friends as a couple would have been such a pleasure. I realised that it had been a long time for me … too long.

My friend, Elvin, told me that Jenny, his wife, was doing the cooking for the dinner to which they had kindly invited me, and that she felt very scared, as she had never cooked for an executive chef before.

"What does one cook for an executive chef?" he asked with a nervous laugh. "She's been asking me every day for the past week – she's very nervous."

I explained to Elvin that, actually, anything home cooked was a blessing to me, and it always would be, as hotel food over the long term becomes tedious for most people, and besides, there was nothing like sharing good homely food, however simple, with friends or family.

Elvin said that Jenny would be mightily relieved to know that, and that the dinner would be basic, but they hoped I would enjoy the company. I told him that it sounded perfect and that I really was looking forward to a lovely evening.

On the appointed night, I showed up at Jenny and Elvin's house, looking forward to some tasty, wholesome food just like 'mama used to make', with maybe a nice glass of wine or two. I rang the doorbell and Jenny answered it with a smile.

As I stepped in through the doorway I was immediately hit by an incredibly strong smell, one which I could not place from anything I had experienced in the past. What the heck was it? I wondered. My hosts sat me down, offered me a cocktail and started off the conversation, wanting to know how my day had been. I actually wanted to be rude and ask them straight out what on earth was that smell, but decided against it. Asking in a more roundabout way seemed my best option, so off I went in pursuit.

"Do you have a dog by any chance?" I surreptitiously enquired.

"No, we really don't like animals in the house; we find them dirty and they make the house messy. Not our cup of tea at all, I'm afraid," said Elvin.

I carried on the conversation for a little while, talking about business at the hotel, but I was actually just waiting for another chance to drop another probing question.

"By the way, our children's club is marvellous," I proclaimed. "You might want to take your children there tomorrow. We have a nice party going on."

"The children are in England for a couple of weeks, visiting their granny, so don't worry, we have the house to ourselves tonight," came the reply.

By now I was lost for ideas. What could the terrible smell be? I thought. I started to feel queasy and needed something, anything, to settle my fast-turning stomach. Then a terrible thought came over me and my body involuntarily panicked, instantly tripling my heart rate. What on earth was I going to do if this unfortunate stench was, in fact, goodness forbid … the dinner?

What story on earth could I possibly come up with, that would get me out of the house without screaming and waving my arms around like an escaped lunatic? I had eaten a lot of things in my time, in some of the grimmest hole-in-the-wall places you could ever imagine, but nothing that I could recall had ever come close to matching the aroma of whatever 'delicacy' this was.

My hosts excused themselves to go and 'slip into something more comfortable' for dinner and that was when I seized the chance to take a quick peek in the kitchen. On the stove was a huge bubbling pot of something or other. Every few seconds, when it became too hot, the stock inside boiled over and doused the flames just until it gained strength to reboil again and repeated the same exercise. I tiptoed over to the 'witches' cauldron' of the dinner pot and tried to pick up the lid. I found it was hotter than hell, singeing my already fingerprint-less hands.

I sneaked another peek to make sure that no one was coming, grabbed the oven gloves and lifted the lid. The smell escaped out of the pot like a herd of stampeding bulls trying to escape the matador's weapons and went right up my wide-open nostrils. My eyes were already watery as I looked quickly into the pot, under the steamy camouflage that hid its contents. It was like a horror movie. I waved a little of the mist away with my other hand and couldn't believe what I saw.

"Oh, my God," I said out loud, trying to stop my knees from buckling.

Then, "Ah! You've uncovered our secret." The voice from behind startled me by saying.

"Err, I was just admiring the culinary delights of the evening."

"Is everything alright?" enquired my hosts.

"Everything's very nice. Thank you," I responded. "I've always wanted to try simmered pigs' snouts. I've heard they're wonderful, and I've yet to have the experience."

Of course, my appetite was by now absolutely non-existent. It had disappeared, perhaps forever, into the empty void in my gullet. I would surely never be able to eat again. This was going to be very tough, but I kept saying to myself, "You can do it, Saxon, you can do this thing."

We sat down at the table and Elvin began shovelling – I mean serving – the beautifully prepared nostrils out onto our plates. There was my portion: five snouty pieces, including nasal hair, just waiting for me to dig in and make a pig of myself, if you'll pardon the pun.

"Don't worry, there are plenty more if that's not enough; we should try to finish them all tonight as they don't keep, you know?" declared Jenny.

Don't keep! I'd have been surprised if they were not rotten already by the smell they were sending out around the house. Just then my host glanced across and saw my hesitation.

"Don't know how to eat them? Sorry, let me give you a few tips," Elvin said, grabbing a piece in his bare hands. "Alright, the first thing you should know is that no one is watching, so you don't have to worry about your P's and Q's. Just pick the fellow up with your fingers. Then you place the side of the nose into your mouth and suck all of the marrow out of the nostrils first, like so."

He slurped his piece of nostril appreciatively, and my stomach heaved. "That's the best part of the whole deal," he pronounced. "All the flavour is hiding right up there in those two crevices."

As he continued chomping I gathered my courage and plunged in and took my first bite. I had to smile, swallow and appear to be enjoying every morsel, or risk offending them and never being invited again. Now there was a thought! Never being invited back again to eat pigs' snouts … what a drag that would be. But if I made out that they were great, there was the possibility that they would invite me back next week. What's a chef to do? Insult and go in peace, or oblige and get another shot at the choking slime?

Somehow I managed to get through the meal in one piece, or rather, a very large piece, sitting like a dead weight in my tummy, impossible to digest in less than a fortnight. I gave my thanks, said my parting speech and rolled home, snorting to myself.

I staggered into my room and collapsed onto the bed, feeling absolutely wrecked. Then, of course, the wretched telephone rang again. Feeling like an anaconda snake that had just swallowed an animal twice its own size and wanted to lie vulnerably in the midday sun, I picked up the phone.

"Who is it?" I shouted down the handset. "Don't you have any manners at all? I have just eaten a dozen pieces of pigs' snout and have the worst case of indigestion in my life! Who the hell are you and what the hell do you want?"

There was a short, uneasy silence and then, a beautiful calming voice like opera music.

"I just thought that I would give you a call as you asked me to do. I have called quite a few times but I was too shy to say anything whenever you picked up the phone," said the caller. Astonished and mortified, I realised that it was my dream girl speaking to me on the other end of the line. All of a sudden, my stomach felt a whole lot better.

"So, anyway, how are you?" I asked in a lame tone.

"Oh, I'm doing fine," she answered, sounding as wonderful as ever.

There was an uncomfortable silence again and I knew that I would have to grasp the nettle here and just ask her out.

"Well, as you are on the line, I think that this would be a good time to ask you out to dinner. How do you feel about that?" I heard myself say. I felt like a teenager again, asking out my first date.

"I would be very happy to go out to dinner. I know some good places to eat, and they have specialities," was her encouraging reply.

"Specialities? As long as there are no pigs' snouts, I'm absolutely game."

And so the deed was done, and the ice finally broken.

A few days later, I was told that Margaret Thatcher, the then former British prime minister, was coming to town and would be staying at our hotel. The general manager asked me to design four imaginative menus for her to choose from because we wanted to entertain her in our 'fine dining' restaurant and show off a little of what we could do. I came up with the four menus and passed them to the boss who, of course, was not entirely happy with my ideas. Back and forth we batted the menus for weeks until everybody was eventually happy. We then had the menus carved in large pieces of tree bark by one of the local handicraft specialists and, I must say, they looked really good.

On the day of the great lady's arrival, everyone was excited and looking forward to the chance to show her what we were all made of on the culinary front. As the VIP car arrived, there seemed to be half the hotel's staff in the lobby, waiting to shake her hand, with the general manager, of course, first in line with his hands specially scrubbed and creamed.

"Good evening, Mrs Thatcher, welcome to our hotel. We have everything in order for your attention," beamed the boss.

"Why, thank you, young man."

"We are of course expecting you for dinner tonight, and have prepared four sets of especially creative menus for you to choose from. Will you be entertaining anyone this evening, ma'am?" the general manager enquired.

"No, I will not, and as it happens I will be eating out this evening and checking out tomorrow," declared Mrs Thatcher. "This is Penang after all, my dear chap! I couldn't visit this lovely island without going to eat at the famous hawker stalls now, could I?"

Well, yes, she's right, of course. Penang's portable food stalls out in the streets, by the side of the road, are truly famous. The food tastes absolutely great and some of the creations are unique to the island. But the rustic conditions were not exactly what we assumed would appeal to a former world stateswoman. But that was that, and 'Maggie' was gone without a look, much less a taste of the hotel's culinary delights.

Served us right, I guess, for assuming that we knew what was best for her and thinking that we had to protect her, from quite what I'm not sure, when maybe she just needed to be protected from us.

Fortunately, there was my new relationship with Beatrice to console me from the debacle with Maggie. After a short while, our romance really began to blossom and I knew I was falling in love with her. It was quite scary, actually, but at the same time it felt great.

There was a new chef in town, named Hugo, working at a hotel in the central area, and we arranged to meet for a drink in the pub in the basement of his hotel. The night went alright, the band was rocking away and before long it was time to go home. My drinking partner decided to leave at the same time as we both had to get up for work early in the morning. We were both over the safe driving limit and so I decided to take a taxi, advising Hugo to do the same.

He purported to be in great shape and said I shouldn't worry about him. I shrugged, waved to him, employed a driver and settled myself down in the car. As we set off, Hugo sped off in front us, doing double our speed, and I waved to him again as he passed by with a loud blow of his horn.

In Penang's beach resort area there are not many cars on the road late at night, so he must have thought he had nothing to worry about. The road was winding and hilly. It was pretty safe, but there was an uncomfortable drop if you were to get too close to the edge! About halfway home, on a steep incline, we passed the Pepper Estate at the top of the hill and came upon a large hole in the wooden perimeter fence, looking about the same size as my friend's car … Oops, I thought.

I asked my taxi driver to stop, stepped out of the car and looked down the hill to see Hugo's car down the embankment. I could hear the noise of clanking gears.

"Are you alright, my friend?" I shouted down the hill.

"Yes," he answered back, "but my bloody car won't reverse. I'm never going to get out of here."

I could see clearly that its front wheels were about two feet away from the rest of the car. Nearby was a small wooden hut and I could hear a major commotion going on inside. There were skid marks in the mud. It appeared that he had skidded, hit the hut, tore off the front wheels and careered down the embankment of the hill, coming to a halt when stuck in the deep mud. The occupants of the hut had obviously been shaken by the impact of the vehicle and were now very angry. I managed to put in a phone call to Hugo's hotel on my mobile phone and asked for the chief of security to come to help him out of the mess he was in.

When they arrived at the scene, the local chaps were shouting something in Chinese which I was sure was less than flattering. The chief security man explained that the people had been sitting having a peaceful game of mah jong when Hugo's car hit the hut and scared them all half to death. One of the guys had jumped off his stool with the impact of the car, and in the process knocked the game all over the room. As he was losing badly, the others felt he had done it on purpose and were unhappy that they could not now cash in on their anticipated winnings.

The security chief should have been in the diplomatic service. He came up with something that made everyone involved happy. At his suggestion, they calculated how much the other chaps would have won had the game continued, and came up with a figure they could all live with. Hugo had to come up with the cash to pay off the would-be winners, as well as cover the damage caused, sending everyone home content with the outcome. That is, except Hugo, of course, who would still have to organise a tow truck to lift his car up from the bottom of the embankment.

A few weeks later I joked with him, telling him that with all the money he had spent on those last couple of drinks, he could have bought a much newer and better car. I'm not sure he was particularly amused.

Mohamed, a member of my staff, invited me home to meet his family. It was supposed to be some kind of family reunion. I told them that I would love to come, but I insisted that they went ahead without me for dinner so that I would not intrude unduly on their family get-together, and that I would come along a little later for the after-dinner stories.

I had a large barbeque dinner at the hotel and set off to find the house which was somewhere in the nearby village, or kampung. It proved to be very hard to find and, as the time went by, I started to get worried that it was getting way too late. Eventually, I found the house and saw Mohamed standing on the porch, waving frantically at me. As I entered the house, I could see an elaborate dinner table, laden with all kinds of exotic food. Evidently everyone was still waiting to eat dinner with me present. They must have been starving. Not only that, but the large selection of sumptuous dishes on display would have made anyone excited to dive in, unless, of course, you had eaten a huge dinner already!

In fact, after living and working in such diverse culinary settings, if I had to choose a resting place based on which country offers the best overall dining experience, I would have to say Malaysia would definitely be my preferred 'backyard'. It is a very exciting crossroads of cuisines of Malay, Chinese and Indian origins. Over the years, different blends of these cultures have developed, inspiring the birth of 'Nonya' food which is a mixture of Malay and Chinese, 'Mamak' food which combines Malay with Indian, and 'Muhibbah' – a wonderful blend of all three.

The ingredients and utensils used in Malaysian cooking are very similar to those of Indonesia, but there are special touches. 'Agar agar', for example, is a setting agent used to make jelly-like desserts. Tamarind is a pulp which is squeezed out of pods and the juice used for flavouring dishes. Screwpine leaf comes from the pandan plant and the long grassy leaves are literally screwed into knots to bring out their flavour in the cooking. Some of the popular dishes here are similar to neighbouring Indonesian menus, but Malaysia has some famous dishes that are purely its own.

'Popiah' is a special form of spring roll, 'curry puffs' are an Asian version of the Cornish pasty, 'char kway teow' is fried rice noodles and there are umpteen variations on the highly acclaimed 'laksa' – a noodle soup with a spicy coconut milk gravy, variously claiming to hail from Penang, Siam, or even the homely Tanjung Bungah – a lesser outpost of the Penang beach area.

Diners can quench their thirst on the Indian style 'I tarik', a form of non-mechanical tea-milkshake, with a better froth than most Italian cappuccinos!

When dining out in Malaysia, it was not only the food that impressed me but also the warmth of the people who serve up this great and varied cuisine. Rarely will you be served in a rude or cold manner. It is just not the culture of the Malaysian people, and it is one of the aspects of the country that was, in due course, to creep up on me to such an extent that I wanted to make Malaysia my home.

On the evening of my invitation, however, I couldn't believe that they were still waiting for me and nobody had yet eaten. It was so late and I just felt awful. They, too, must have thought me so rude for keeping them all waiting as if I was some kind of royalty, but of course it would not be the Malaysian way to express this. This experience showed me how far Malaysian culture and its adherence to politeness and hospitality goes.

The worst part was that every time I finished a plate of food, it was quickly and liberally replenished. Refusing would have offended them, the inference being that it was not good, but by eating it all I was saying that it was great and I needed some more, thereby passing Mohamed's mother – the cook – the best compliment of all. How I managed to eat all the food I stuffed down me that night, I have no idea. It was pretty spicy too, so I knew the next day I was going to suffer, but what was a guy to do?

I was invited to Bangkok to witness the opening of a new hotel where my friend Simon was the executive chef. He asked me to take a few days off to come and help him with the ensuing battle. Simon was living in a rented apartment near the hotel with his new girlfriend, Lily. He invited me to stay with them and asked me to come along to the hotel every morning to see what was going on there. The traffic was incredible and everyone seemed to salute when you walked by them. You parked the car, the attendant saluted you. In the street, the policemen saluted you. You arrived at the hotel, the bellboy saluted you. The first time it happened, I turned round thinking that some general had just arrived behind me.

The infamous *Tuk-Tuks* were in and out, darting between every car, blowing their horns for no apparent reason, and there seemed to be few rules at all on the roads, except the basic one of every one for themselves. After a busy day at the hotel getting ready for the big event, Simon decided he would take me out on the town to show me a few of the attractions. He told me to take care because the Water Festival was on at the moment and some of the staff in the bars and pubs of Bangkok tended to get a little excited.

The Water Festival, or Songkran, which is celebrated from the 13th to 15th April, is when people celebrate the arrival of the rainy season, and I was surprised to find when we caught a taxi that the bottom of the car was full of water, especially when it wasn't raining outside. But I still didn't catch on to what I was in store for until we walked into a pub, at which point a member of staff standing inside the door threw a bucket of water right over us. It was so cold and there was so much of it that it soaked me right to my underwear. Something of a culture shock? What the heck was all this about? I thought to myself, while wanting to give the guy a kick in the butt.

We ordered two beers and everyone was having a good old laugh, like our drenching was a real hoot – which I guess it was, if you were not on the receiving end, that is. I, though, was a little less than impressed, especially when I reached into my pocket to find my wallet soaking wet and the bank notes all stuck together. My face dropped even further when Simon pulled out his wallet, which was all nicely wrapped in a plastic bag (was he a boy scout, or what?) and paid for the beer.

"This one's on me," he said with great amusement.

"The whole night's on you!" I growled. "Why didn't you tell me what was going to happen so that I could have wrapped my money up so very nicely also?"

"What, and spoil it all for you?" he said, jokingly. "The best part of this time of the year is when you watch someone else get soaked on their first occasion."

He, at least, was having a great evening.

I had to walk around for the rest of the evening soaking wet, and every time I sat down that horrible feeling came over me like I had wet my pants. The funny thing was that although it was well over thirty-five years since I had that particular experience, I could still remember what it felt like as if it was yesterday.

On the way home, we stopped at a red traffic light. It was very dark and surprisingly quiet. We set off again as the light turned to green, and about five minutes down the road there was a thundering crash as our windshield smashed, spraying small pieces of the shattered glass all over us. It was in my hair, my clothing and all over the seat but, luckily, not in my eyes.

Simon looked up, surprised for perhaps a split second, and then carried on talking and driving as if nothing had happened. I looked at him, alarmed as much by the way in which he just kept going and the fact that, incredibly, his conversation did not miss a beat, as by the incident itself.

All of a sudden he screamed out loud, "I know what just happened! It took a while for me to get it together but let me show you what's what before we go home."

The car screeched to a halt, then he turned round and we set off to retrace our tracks.

"There, look!" he proclaimed. "You know what I just did?"

"No, why don't you enlighten me so I can enjoy it as much as you?"

"When I set off after the traffic lights, I didn't see that the railway crossing was coming down and it hit our windscreen, and that's what smashed it," he explained.

Only then did I understand why the crazy guy was not as shocked as I was by the smashing of his windscreen, and that although he did not give the appearance, his mind must have been going a mile a minute trying to work out what had just happened, and with it the realisation that where there is a railway crossing, there is also the likelihood of a train not too far behind!

The next day, there was a hotel publicity stunt that leaves me incredulous even today. Simon's hotel was located close to another five-star hotel complex, separated only by a major dual carriageway, with a three-foot grass verge between the two roads. The publicity idea involved setting up a fine dining table for two, right in the middle of the road on the grass verge. The executive chefs from the two competing hotels had been invited to sit there in the middle of the rush hour traffic, and have lunch together as if they were in the finest restaurant in town.

Watching the waiters, dressed in black ties and tails, running across the road, dodging the cars moving at high speed, was really something, especially when carrying a champagne tray loaded with a bottle of bubbly, two cut crystal glasses and wearing white cotton gloves. This just took the biscuit.

The two chefs sat there as if this was their usual lunchtime routine, holding the delicate glasses up high and chinking them together as they took turns proposing the toast of the day. Media people were everywhere, taking photos and, no doubt, wondering to themselves if these people had escaped from a mental institution.

Later, on the way home, Simon told me the best stunt – his personal effort – was yet to come. It seemed he had not told his management yet and was not going to tell me either, because he wanted everyone to enjoy the surprise together.

"Are you sure that this is a good idea, mate? I mean, should you not clear it with your boss first?" I said, a little cautiously, remembering my Water Festival dousing.

"And spoil the big surprise for them? No way, man!" he said, clearly excited by the prospect. "Wow, I just can't wait to see their faces. It will be front page stuff, I promise you that!"

We retired for the evening and I left it at that, just waiting for the big surprise that we were all going to enjoy the following day. Grand openings are of major consequence for every hotel. The first impression is sent out far and wide, and balancing so many different elements gives the night much greater importance than any other party a hotel will ever throw. The launching hotel always invites the local big shots, the media and various dignitaries to show off their wares, so a hitch-free party is hoped – or should I say, prayed – for.

The next day dawned quickly, with everyone smartly on their toes, even after a universally sleepless night before. The party was going great and everything seemed under control. The general manager walked through the lobby, looking very calm indeed, and I had all but forgotten about Simon's big surprise.

People were arriving constantly, but Simon was nowhere to be seen. A couple of hours into the party, the band was playing, the food and drinks were flowing, and everything looked like a great success when, suddenly, a loud noise came from the back of the lobby.

Everyone turned round to see my friend Simon, the executive chef of this newly opened hotel, parading down the middle of the lobby, leading a baby elephant on a small-link chain. I swallowed hard for him, and tried to fathom his logic about this fateful career decision he had made so secretly. I glanced over to the boss to see a look of sheer horror on his face. He looked up into the air and closed his eyes as if to say a prayer. Yet all of a sudden, the guests started to clap and cheer, loving every minute of it and lapping it all up. Being in Thailand, Simon had gambled that bringing an elephant to the party, an animal loved and adored by Thai people, was going to be a great party popper, and fortunately for him and the hotel, he was right.

However, what had not been anticipated was that the elephant, standing right in the middle of the lobby with everyone cheering and the cameras flashing, would suddenly become nervous, because without warning it opened its bowels all over the brand new, very expensive, Persian carpet which had only been laid the previous day. Now, there was a huge pile of steaming dung for everyone to see and photograph at their leisure. Notwithstanding the country's love of elephants, it's not difficult to imagine what the headlines were the next day, and what the comments were from the hotel's competitors.

When Simon came home that night, he sat down, opened a beer, smiled forlornly and asked if I knew of any hotel looking for an enterprising young executive chef. C'est la vie!

When I left Bangkok, I really felt for the guy, but I knew that he would get another job soon enough. He was actually a very talented chef who just tended to go over the top at times, taking unnecessary chances when they were not his to take.

Back at my Penang hotel, I was looking forward to seeing Beatrice as we were going out to dinner, but there seemed to be a bit of commotion going on in the lobby.

"Chef, the Princess has arrived again," confided the concierge.

"Oh, yes?" I answered back, not knowing for a second who the heck they were talking about. "Which Princess?" I asked.

"Oh, I forgot you've never met her. Actually, she's not really a princess. She just likes to be called that. I think it makes her feel important, but seeing as she spends so much money in the hotel, who cares, right?"

The general manager told me later that the Princess would be taking dinner in the hotel that evening, and asked if it would be possible to organise 48 dozen oysters, to be served as pre-dinner cocktails. I wondered if it was dinner or an orgy she was planning. Who was actually going to eat these many oysters? I pondered.

When her guests started to arrive, I noticed that the table was only set for twenty-four people, and yet they had ordered these *48 dozen* oysters … hmm. Afterwards I got talking with the 'Princess' herself, and asked her what she was going to do with the collection of leftover oysters because 48 dozen would take quite some eating.

She replied, "These people are very good friends of mine and I want to impress them. I want them all to know that I am sparing no expense tonight and that they can all eat two dozen oysters each, if they choose."

"But, Princess," I started out, "now that we've opened the oysters, we will still have to charge you for them all, whether they are eaten or not!"

"Are you kidding, young man? Who cares?"

I was now getting the measure of our Princess.

As I watched her over the next few days, she threw private parties, engaged the private butler service and always paid her bills with a sack of cash in large bills. She had told a few of the staff during previous visits that she never settled bills with anything but cash.

"Using credit cards," she announced, "while spending a lot of money, makes people ask too many questions. It also makes it easier to be traced because of the receipts."

A smooth businesswoman indeed.

———◦∙◦∙◦———

We walked along a beach in Penang, had a drink in a small restaurant along the way and then decided to go and have some durian. The journey around the winding hills, looking for the elusive fruit, whilst sitting in the back seat of a taxi was, to say the least, harrowing. The driver, let's call him 'Speedy' for the sake of an argument, was a very friendly chap who just had to have what he considered a most interesting conversation with his customers, whilst driving at speeds any of his fellow Formula One drivers would have been proud of.

"You know," he proudly boasted, "the last time I came up here, I turned the car turtle." (Fondly known as turning the car upside down.) Turning round to face us and at the same time pushing his foot down with lead shoes to reach breakneck speed while manoeuvring 100-foot-drop corners, he calmly announced, "With a little bit of luck, we can avoid the same occurrence this time round."

With little confidence, I broke into a meek smile to try and cover up the feeling that I was going to die or at least vomit at any time, totally humiliating myself in front of my dream date, who was looking a little peeked herself. "Why don't you try to slow down a little there, big guy, the apples and pears won't go rotten, you know," I said sarcastically.

"What apples and pears? What the heck are you talking about?" he announced, puzzled by my comment about the upcoming fruit expedition. "This ain't London, you know, do you see any fog around here, any Yorkshire pudding or fish and chips on every street corner? Apples and pears …" and then he finished it off with a strange word I had not yet heard, it sounded something like 'boh dough', I recall.

"What does that mean?" I asked Beatrice.

"I did not hear what he said as the air conditioning is too loud," she said in a politically correct manner.

As I was sweating like an overweight sumo wrestler sitting in a hotter-than-hell sauna, I enquired, "What air conditioning?" and slowly received the message as she rolled her eyes at me. She would later explain to me that 'bodoh' meant stupid. Charming, I thought.

What with going round in circles combined with the feeling of sheer fright, I was almost going to lose my breakfast when I heard those golden words, "We are here." As we stopped and pulled over at the roadside, I was totally oblivious to where 'here' actually was. There was a small wooden hut constructed at the side of the road and a chap sleeping on a wooden rickety table made from tree branches and surrounded by four chairs.

"Wow, business must be great here, the fruit is so superb and fresh, everybody is lining up to grab some of it," I quipped with a smile.

"Shush," said Beatrice, giving me a nudge, "don't be so rude." The proud owner of the orchard woke up as Speedy gave him a shock by blowing his horn.

"Hey, Datuk, I have a couple of customers for you," he proudly announced. "That will be twenty ringgit," my friendly chauffeur said calmly.

"Twenty ringgit," I said in a high-pitched, you-must-be-nuts and shocked manner. "Anyway, where the heck do you think you are going?" I asked rather sheepishly. "Do you see any taxi stands around here, how on earth are we going to get back?" Mr. Speedy happily negotiated to wait without extra charge, which, I thought, was very polite and kind of him, until he announced that he was hungry and the sharing of our fruit might just clinch the deal.

Datuk had already gone walking through the jungle with his hands behind his back, looking down in the long grass whilst kicking, trying to find something. Surely, the durian would be rotten if it was lying on the moist ground, I thought. Not wanting to offend, I kept quiet and amused myself by looking at Beatrice and her lovely full lips and thought what it was going to be like when I kissed them. "Got one," shouted the orchard owner, he sounded so happy with himself and with his big find of goodness-knows-how-long-ago rotten fruit. As he emerged from the jungle and was making the short trek up to the hut, I saw in his hands the familiar and strangest looking fruit. I could imagine tourists thinking, what the heck is that? A large green funky-looking thing with spikes, their first reaction would probably be to ask how they were going peel this sucker.

"What do you have there, Datuk?" I asked, bemused. "The last time I saw something like that was in the *Aliens* movie," I hesitated for a second, "no, sorry, I think it was *Predator*."

"Don't be funny," said Speedy, "You might find yourself walking home."

"Safer ... and cheaper," I whispered to Beatrice. The durian was placed on the table with a *thud*; this was the first time I witnessed a fruit that if dropped would damage the table before it received even a single blemish. My new sweetheart explained to me that durian was somewhat of an acquired taste. Datuk bent down, reached under the table and emerged with a large knife. "I am sorry," I announced, "I did not mean anything if I offended you."

"Bodoh," said Speedy again, as they started to pry open the extremely thick skin with the tip of the blade. All of a sudden there was the usual offensive odour surrounding the table. Trying to be humorous, I smelt under my armpits to see if the smell was coming from me and then looked underneath my shoes to see if I had stepped in something. After acknowledging that the wonderful smell of fresh-picked roses was not my fault at all, I joked that the offending odour was in fact coming from the fruit. A thin blue-like haze was rising from the split skin.

"It's rotten," I shouted, "we will have to find another one, maybe one that is still on the tree and in better condition." Beatrice went on to explain that in fact that was how the fruit was supposed to smell and that the best ones have fallen from the tree by themselves, ensuring that they were totally ripe. Not wanting to let her know that I had in fact eaten it before, I acted dumb.

"You mean durian actually smells like that?" I asked in shock.

"Yes," was the one-word answer Beatrice offered me.

"And it's not rotten?"

"No," she countered.

"And we are going to pay good money for it and then eat it?"

"Yes, that's right. Will you please be quiet?" she pleaded. As the durian was laid on the table, everyone was unfortunately polite to offer the guest, yours truly, the first piece. So I took the smallest piece available and placed it in my mouth. My stomach, which by now was in a state of shock, dropped a subtle hint that it was less than impressed with the nourishment that I was offered by churning and tying in a solid gut-wrenching knot. I had tasted only once before this beautiful 'fruit' that smelt so bad and tasted so terrible with an unimaginable sickly and slimy texture. As it slithered down my throat, leaving a horrendous aftertaste, I managed to bear a thin tooth smile and throw out a single word: "Yummy," was all that I could muster. In a matter of minutes, the durian was finished, and I was offered another.

"Oh, no thank you, I could not eat a single delectable piece more," I announced, "I am totally full, stuffed actually." Then I held my breath and prayed that they would not purchase a second nightmare. Durian, I will give them both durian, I complained to myself. As we settled back in the car, I was dreading contending with Speedy, the winding road and the added disadvantage of having this lump of smelly, heavy and burp-promoting substance that was simmering around in my tummy like a volcano. "Speedy," I declared, "take us to a chemist as soon as you can. By the way," I pleaded, "do you have a plastic bag by any chance?"

On reaching town, I bought some Listerine to gargle with, which made me feel much more comfortable. With the smell and the bad taste in my mouth diminished, I diverted my attention back to concentrating on getting my sneaky kiss. As we sat on the now moonlit beach where the date had first started, I edged closer and put my arm around her shoulders. I looked into her eyes and they had 'kiss me' written all over them, so I did. As our lips locked together, she still had the durian smell on her breath that was rather off-putting. As I was about to drop a hint by offering her my new bottle of Listerine, I burped, sending my own version of deep-down in the stomach, after-dinner aroma into my date's face. Well, there you have it, my kiss had been and gone. Not very memorable, I am afraid, and that was that. Luckily, Beatrice forgave me; we are now both durian connoisseurs. I have fallen in love with durian over the years and constantly get looks of amazement as people see a '*matsalleh*' (foreigner) sitting down and digging in to a good durian where and whenever I can.

There are many species of durian; and did you know that it is an aphrodisiac? The only problem is after eating it and getting the necessary effect, nobody wants to come near you anyway, so the whole idea is rather redundant.

Bombaceae durio zibethinus (commonly known as the durian) has unfortunately quite a few calories; however, it has lots of protein, minerals, beta-carotene, vitamins B1, B2 and C, calcium and iron, and better still, has no cholesterol!

Durians from Thailand have more flesh, but with little taste; and the Malaysian version has less flesh, but a much better taste.

Congratulations, Malaysia, on producing a great version of this funky-looking thorny and stinky fruit!

A Japanese tourist went missing in the hotel and, after a few hours of searching, his family members became very worried and called the staff to help. We turned the place inside out until someone just thought about checking the most out of the way public toilets in the hotel. These were at the back of one of the restaurants, a little hidden and therefore not used very often by guests. When we went in to check, someone noticed that one of the cubicles was locked. Peeping under the door, we could see a guy sitting there with his trousers down around his ankles so we called out to him. No reply. We called him again, but still he didn't answer back, so we called security to come and pry open the door.

Unfortunately, when the door was finally opened we had found our missing guest, sitting on the throne with his eyes closed. It was just as if he had simply fallen asleep while sitting on the loo, but sadly, in this case, he had actually passed away. It was a very sad day at the hotel and for all concerned.

A few weeks later, a new executive assistant manager arrived. We had heard in advance that he was a very strict disciplinarian. What we thought we needed was an up-to-date manager. He was off to a racing start, almost from the word go, walking around, wreaking havoc and letting everyone know that he had arrived. When his shipment of personal effects arrived, I went to say hello and ask him if he needed any help to unpack and organise his office.

"No, I'm alright," he announced, "but while you're here, let me show you a few things that I picked up along the way."

He had a wonderful collection of woodcarvings with his name on, different brass golf pieces and that sort of thing, and I must say that after unpacking, his office looked very impressive indeed.

But after a couple more days of hell raising, he came in one morning to find his office had been completely sabotaged. The staff had got into his room in the middle of the night and thrown a bucket of, let's say, 'waste water' all over his prized possessions! When I found him, he was just sitting there, looking sadly at his souvenirs.

I decided on this occasion to spare him my 'Welcome to the zoo!' line.

Those he'd antagonised kept up the campaign in the ensuing weeks. They punctured his car tyres, and someone even threw a building brick through his car window. He was forced to adopt a less overbearing management style with the team and things eventually calmed down.

After Beatrice and I had been dating for a while, I decided it was the right time for my very first visit to Sabah, to introduce myself to my future in-laws. On announcing the master plan to visit the in-laws' village, Beatrice jumped out of her chair. "We can organise a Christmas party for all the people in my kampong."

"Hang on a minute, how many people are there in your village?" I was almost scared to hear the answer. I mean to say, feeding two or three thousand people had to cost a packet and on my salary at that time, I will tell you, it was a most daunting thought.

"Oh, there are lots," was not the answer that I was looking for, believe me.

"How many is lots?" I whispered to her.

"About fifty-two," she said enthusiastically.

"How many?!?" I asked in a shocked manner, expecting 5,200.

"Fifty-two," repeated Beatrice.

Well, I thought, this was going to be the cheapest Christmas party I could ever have hoped for. "Although we are short of money at this moment in time, I do believe that we can offer to hold a party for the entire population of your village, I will even throw in a couple of cases of beer for good measure," I announced, trying to conceal my relief. Beatrice booked and organised the trip, as she always does, and off we went. Arriving in the village named Papar, we were greeted with the biggest and heaviest tropical downpour that you could ever imagine, which stirred all the toads back to life and, unfortunately, all the mosquitoes too. Being eaten alive is not the most pleasant of experiences and not being able to sleep due to the loud croaking coming from the paddy fields did not help either. The day of the party was a monumental affair, to say the least, people came from miles around carrying pot luck food items to place on the table for everyone to enjoy. We worked all day to get everything ready and the time had come to enjoy ourselves. On discovering we had no ice, I offered to go and get it, so off we drove. The first thought I had was how dark it was getting. It was a moonless night, there were no lights to illuminate the road and driving slowly down the narrow path so you did not end up in the ditch was essential. Suddenly, we saw something in the middle of the road and slowed down. I thought it was a water buffalo having a nap before continuing on its journey. As we approached, we found that it was not a buffalo. Instead, it was one of the villagers, lying down motionless. He was not moving an inch and I was worried for the poor guy.

"Is he dead?" I asked, petrified.

"No," was her monosyllabic reply.

"Then what's wrong with him?"

"Tuak," Beatrice singled again.

"Tuak, what is that, a tropical disease or something?" I wondered out loud.

"No, it's tropical liquor, and he has had too much of it."

"Too much of it? He looks like he has had all of it. It's a wonder that there are any coconuts left, by the looks of him!"

I later nicknamed tuak 'gut rot' once I had tasted this delicate beverage. I will give you another red-hot tip. You do not want to drink this stuff whilst smoking – you may end up being blown to kingdom come!

As I stared at the drunken villager, out of the blue came the cavalry in the form of two of his mates. They picked him up and carried him off, having a good old laugh on his behalf as they went.

"How strong is that stuff?" I asked Beatrice.

"It's quite strong, but alright if you are used to it. Old man Bob is used to it – he's been drinking it all his life." If old man Bob was used to it, what would happen if someone was not used to it and drank it for the first time? We would be rushing him to the intensive care unit to have his stomach pumped … Or maybe even replaced.

"What is this stuff made from?" I asked Beatrice.

"Tuak can be made from the sap of palm trees or coconut trees, but is usually made from coconut tree sap. There are others as well, you know."

"Oh yes, well why don't you give me a heads up so that I can make sure I avoid the stuff at all costs?"

"Well," Beatrice started out, "there is bahar which is also made from the sap of palm trees, but is made with a different recipe. And then there is tapai which is made from rice." Different recipe? Maybe there is a recipe book I could buy and place on the drinks' list in my lobby lounge in our hotel.

I could not help but to ask her the golden question, "Do you like a tipple of this refined alcoholic beverage once in a while?"

Beatrice pulled her glasses down to the end of her nose and stared at me over the top of them. Her impression simply implied the articulate response she was expressing. 'Idiot' – would have been the best way to explain her thoughts, but as usual, her manners were way too polite to voice it.

When we got back from the shop it was time to get the party started. I decided to take a quick shower before I went down to the dinner table. I emerged from the bathroom about fifteen minutes later and everyone was sitting around, chit-chatting and looking at me with looks of anticipation on their faces. "What is going on?" I asked Beatrice.

"They are waiting for you to eat first before they start."

I thought to myself that I could not believe how polite the folks were in Malaysia, and then announced that they should all eat and enjoy themselves. I dipped my hand into a large bucket full of ice and grabbed a bottle of beer. As I turned round to speak to Beatrice, I could not believe the sight before me. There in front of me was old man Bob! Instead of being hungover for four days like I would have been after having my stomach pumped, he looked as if he had never touched a drop.

"Here in Sabah," he started out, "we like to consume this local beverage called tuak, have you ever tried it?"

"Before I answer that question, let me ask you one, do you have an identical twin?"

Beatrice came from nowhere, "Don't listen to him, Bob – he's a twit!" I tried to defend myself while looking around for help.

"To answer your question, Bob, not lately, no," I mustered.

"Well, let's have a shot together. Come, let's share a glass." He poured two glasses, walked towards me and handed me the one that was the most full. Very polite people, I thought, ... too polite.

"Why don't you have the full glass and I will have the short glass?" We swapped the glasses and I took my first sip. Now I have to tell you something that I shouldn't, but I can't help it. I have never tasted anything so vile in my entire life. As it passed down my throat and into my stomach, it dissolved every body part in its path like an ice cube in a microwave. "That's not so bad," I announced, whilst wincing badly. As Bob turned round to smile at Beatrice, I quickly poured the balance of the tuak into the paddy field next to me and pretended as if I had finished it. I could have sworn that I saw the paddy wilt instantly the tuak touched the water surrounding it. I probably contaminated the whole ecosystem of Sabah with that one thoughtless and selfish act.

"Wow, look at you," said Bob. "You have finished it all, but don't worry, there is plenty more where that came from, I will go and get you a top-up."

"Better not give me a top-up or I will throw up," I whispered to Beatrice.

"Just another drop to make them happy and then you can return to your beer," she pleaded.

"After another drop I am going to return to my bed. Hopefully not to a hospital bed!"

"Don't be such a baby!" Beatrice snapped. This was going to be a long night, I thought to myself, and a much longer day tomorrow if I kept on drinking this drain cleaner.

"Maybe we can place a few bottles in the boot of our car, just in case," I suggested.

"Whatever for?" asked Beatrice.

"Just in case we run out of petrol. We can pour it in the tank and use it to keep the car running for a few kilometres longer until we reach another gas station. Of course, we would have to keep it in a non-corrosive metal container. You know the one that does not dissolve if it comes in contact with metal-eating acid." I pointed out that this foul-tasting stuff had indeed been delivered to the village in a screw-top petrol can, which I thought was only appropriate since tuak was also a highly-flammable liquid. Beatrice rolled her eyes at my latest observation. Bob returned with another couple of glasses and I gingerly sipped on the cloudy substance until it was all but finished, trying to cause as little damage to my insides as possible along the way. As I was talking to old man Bob, his eyes glazed over and he started to fall backwards. I had downed two glasses of this rocket fuel myself which resulted in me not being as alert as I should have been and, thus, was not able to catch him. Bob just fell backwards right into the paddy field thereby squashing the toads. That was the end of my first and hopefully my last encounter with East Malaysia's version of toddy. Although I am sure that these home-grown Malaysian beverages create an enjoyable pastime, I have to say that they are a little bit out of my league in strength and I will stick to the conventional beer or red wine.

• • • • •

We had a very important wine sampling dinner booked in our fine dining restaurant and the theme was, believe it or not, Russian – a wine region with which I was not entirely familiar. As the food had to be authentic, I decided to try and find a local chef who had travelled in Russia. When I managed to locate a possible candidate, I interviewed him to see if I thought that he would be suitable for the occasion. This chef, Chinese by ethnic origin, conjured up some of the popular Russian dishes that he had seen during his travels and they tasted very good to me, so I hired him on the spot. After we agreed terms, we started to look at some ideas that we could propose to the main sponsor and organiser of the event.

A week later I was told that the sponsors had decided they were bringing a famous Russian chef out from Moscow, to make sure the function had exactly the right touch of authenticity they were seeking. It was very embarrassing to explain to my new Chinese friend, Wong, that I was no longer in need of his services, but he was very understanding.

Then the news trickled into my office, that the incoming Russian chef understood no English whatsoever, and if I would like to invite 'the local chap' to translate and generally help out in the kitchen on the night, that would be acceptable. So I had to call him again. He probably wanted to tell me to 'stuff it', but instead he was great about everything and told me not to worry; he would be there on the day.

Everything went to plan. The caviar and wines were delivered, the menu was agreed and the Russian chef was on schedule to arrive the night before the dinner. He was to check into the hotel and I was supposed to greet him in the lobby and take care of him for that night.

When he arrived, we shook hands, and as I was talking to him he looked a little, let's say, pickled. I surreptitiously checked my watch and it was only four o'clock in the afternoon, but his breath hinted at some kind of heavy liquor. His face was cherry red and I couldn't understand a single word that he was uttering, even though his mouth was going non-stop. Then, all of a sudden, up popped a word I could understand.

"Blah blah blah, blah blah blah ... Girls."

"Excuse me?" I replied, vaguely.

He just laughed, shook his head, picked up his bag, grabbed his key and off he went to his room.

Yuri, our Russian chef, was supposed to help me that night prepare the food for the following day, and I had told Wong, the local chef, that he didn't need to come over until the day itself. I was more than a little worried when I called Yuri's room later that evening for us to go to the kitchen, only to find that he had stepped out somewhere without leaving any sort of message. That night he was a total no-show.

The next morning, I really began to panic since there were some extremely big players attending this function, from top Russian companies, the Russian government, the Russian embassy and the Malaysian government. There I was, in my usual situation, back against the wall and my nuts in my hand (figuratively speaking), wondering what the heck I was going to do, when my phone rang.

"Hi, Mike, how is everything?" It was Wong, who despite having been treated as he had, was calling to see how the preparations were going.

"Wong!" I sighed in relief, "Am I glad to hear from you, my friend. Can you come over here as soon as possible to help me out? Yuri has gone AWOL."

"You're kidding," barked Wong. "I'm on the way." With that, he hung up the phone.

It seemed that no sooner had I stopped thinking how fabulous the guy was, he was knocking on my office door in full uniform with a bunch of chef's knives in his hand.

"Let's go, Mike, no time to lose," was all Wong said.

I simply couldn't believe it. What a lifesaver he was. It was at that moment I hit on an idea of how to repay him. I decided that as he would be the main stage chef, I would introduce him as my home-grown Russian guest chef. We went upstairs to the kitchen to start cooking and we were in the midst of things when in walked the organiser.

"Hi, chef, where is Yuri?"

"You tell me," I replied.

His face instantly turned pale. He looked stunned. "What are you saying?"

"Sorry, let me try again," I said, somewhat sarcastically since we were losing yet more time over the disappearing Yuri. "I have absolutely no idea where he is. But I do know that when he checked into the hotel last night, he mentioned the word 'girls' and I've not seen him since."

"Come, let us go and check his room upstairs. Can you get a key from the front desk?" he asked.

"Well, I think I can manage that, but while you're here, let me introduce you to Chef Wong. He is here preparing the food in the absence of Yuri."

"Yes, whatever. Let us go now!" He replied, totally brushing off any relevance Wong might have to the whole affair.

Lucky for me, Wong did not take offence – or more likely, did not show that he was offended. Otherwise he would have been out of the door and down the street as quickly as he came up it, but yet again he shrugged it off and just asked me where the blender was.

The organiser and I went upstairs and knocked on Yuri's door. There was no answer, so we knocked louder still. But to no avail. So we opened the door with the key and walked into the room. The place was a zoo. An empty vodka bottle – or two – lay on the floor, leftover pizza was smelling up the place, and there was lipstick on his pillow. Thank goodness his companion had already left. As we glanced around the room, we spotted Yuri, lying on the floor in-between the bed and the wall.

"Is he dead?" asked the organiser.

"How do I know? Why don't you go over and give the fellow a nudge or something?" I said helpfully.

Over tiptoed the organiser and nudged the chef … nothing. He nudged him again … still nothing.

"Chef, I tell you, he's snuffed it!"

"I told you, the guy's been drinking since before he arrived here …"

All of a sudden, Yuri stirred a little.

"Once more, sweetie, once more," he said, without opening his eyes.

"Hey, he learned three more words last night," I pointed out. "That's really great. If he stays here another ten years, he might be able to do an after-dinner speech!"

"Will you stop it, chef. What are we going to do now?" mumbled the organiser.

"I tried to explain to you downstairs that we have it all covered and you needn't worry. Wong is here and is fully capable."

With that, we went downstairs and left Yuri to sleep off his crazy night's activities and hoped that by evening he would at least be able to make some sort of appearance.

When the scheduled time for the function came and the guests started to arrive, as we put the finishing touches to the dinner, who should appear but Yuri, practically crawling into the kitchen on his hands and knees. The dinner actually went very well, and everyone was singing and dancing in the restaurant. Some of our regular guests demanded that I go outside to say hello and I decided to take Wong with me for some deserved exposure. As we entered the restaurant, everyone stood up cheering and clapping. Somehow the drunken Yuri story had already leaked out and they knew the truth. The local guests were especially excited and happy that one of their home-grown talents was responsible for the lovely meal so expertly prepared.

What eventually happened to Yuri, I do not know, but I was pleased that a superb local talent had been unearthed.

A few days later, Beatrice and I were having dinner in a local restaurant down the street, when our conversation drifted until there was a silent spell where neither of us was saying anything at all. I found myself staring at her while watching her eat. She did not seem to realise that I was watching her; she just carried on eating, totally oblivious to what was happening with me. I loved her facial expressions and the way that everything I tried to do to make her happy actually seemed to make her happy.

It was just lovely to have such a graceful woman sitting next to me because she wanted to be there and for no other reason than that. I found myself talking to an imaginary character in my mind, who was telling me how idiotic it would be to let this fine woman go. To make a mess of this relationship would surely end all chances of complete happiness. This was it, I felt, somebody was trying to tell me something. I knew that I had found my soul mate. But was I up to this? Had I really got over the past? Did I want to go through it all again? I looked down at the table, deep in thought, reluctant to say anything, trying to resolve if Beatrice was really meant to be my future life companion.

I looked up again and she was smiling at me. "Are you alright, Mike?" she enquired. "What are you thinking about? And why have you gone quiet?"

A multitude of questions flooded my mind. Was it not my turn for happiness? Did I not deserve her? Had I not been through enough already to merit some kindness now? I knew there was only one answer to all this and there would never be a better time to follow it up than right now. So I asked her.

"Beatrice, will you marry me?"

She looked at me, a fork in her half-open mouth, and she just became motionless. She was lost for words. Her silence made me feel that I had put her in an uncomfortable position and I immediately wanted to retract my proposal, to deliver it at a better time.

"I'm sorry, Beatrice, it just came out. Let's pretend that I never said it."

Beatrice turned her head away from me and my heart sank. Had I offended her and screwed this one up? I was feeling pretty disappointed with myself when she turned back to face me. She was weeping and I reached out for her hand.

"Beatrice, I'm really sorry. I never meant to upset you. Please forgive me?"

"Forgive you for what?" she said. "I can't imagine how I could be any happier than I am right at this moment. Mike, I'd love to marry you, and I hope it's soon. Every day we are not together is a day wasted for me."

My sensitive Beatrice had obviously been overwhelmed by the moment, but when she agreed to marry me, I thought I was just the luckiest guy in the world. After a truly memorable and romantic evening, we turned our attentions to the procedure for getting hitched. It was not going to be quite so simple. With me being a foreigner and wanting to marry a Malaysian citizen, we would have to get special permission to be married, and the first step was to register at the government registry office.

When we had a day off together, we decided to go to the registry office to start the ball rolling. We arrived to find the doors firmly closed for lunch. There was no alternative but to hang around outside in the hot sun until the office eventually opened again for business.

A good lunchtime *'makan'*, or meal, is sacrosanct in Malaysia, and while the office was closed, an incredibly long line had formed and it moved very slowly. Everyone seemed to have long, complex and challenging questions to put to the officer in charge. I saw him looking at us from time to time through the corner of his eye, but he never signalled us to approach his desk. As there was no numbered ticket service in operation, we were at his mercy. Eventually, with everyone else dispatched, he lifted up his finger, signalling for us to approach him.

"What may I do for you today?" he asked.

"We understand," I began, "that you have the forms we need to fill out."

"Forms for what?" he asked, a little brusquely, before leaning back in his chair with his arms outstretched.

I pointedly looked towards the top of the door where a very large sign announced, 'Marriage Registry Office', but thought for a second before saying anything. I was trying to fathom if it was a trick question of some kind, perhaps designed to see if I was of sound mind.

"The forms for marriage," I finally answered. "You see we would like to get married."

"Oh, I see, just wait a minute," came the reply. With that, he bent over and rummaged around under the table, pulling out about three different forms for us to fill in.

Well, that was easy enough, I thought. Then I took a closer look and noticed that they were all in the local language, Bahasa Malaysia. I did not speak it but thankfully Beatrice did. She sat calmly down to read the forms and translate for me. After a while, she suggested we take them home to fill out.

Just as well, as it took us weeks to complete all the forms, carefully trying not to make any mistakes. They required a lot of information about Beatrice's parents and, as she was from Sabah in East Malaysia, she was constantly on the phone, collecting the information needed. Finally, the mail arrived carrying the much-awaited photocopies of her official papers, and then it was time to make a return visit to the office with the completed forms. We had our own *makan* first this time before we joined the queue.

"Let's have a look, then," invited the inspector. "Hey, this should be over here and that should be over there, and why did you write that there? That should be on the next page. I'm sorry, these will have to be filled out again," he declared.

Now this really made me feel useless. I now knew how terrible and debilitating it must feel for people who cannot read or write. He gave us back a new set of forms and off we went to tackle the job again.

Fortunately, we were in no hurry as we had planned not to get married for another five months or so, and it was a good job, I must say, because it was beginning to feel it would take that long to get the paperwork sorted. A few days later we returned with the forms once again.

As before the inspector looked them over very slowly. "Yes, that's good. Yes, good. That's alright," he said, in a more optimistic tone. Just as I thought for a second we were going to make it, however, he announced, "Wait a minute … are you from Penang, Beatrice?"

"No, I am from Sabah. Why?"

"Well, if you are from Sabah you cannot get married here," said the inspector, "unless, of course, you officially change your address from there to here."

I just couldn't believe what I was hearing. Was this real?

"How does one do that?" I asked him, wondering what was coming next.

"Well, there's another form for you to fill out, and I have one somewhere here," he replied, as he delved back under the table, resurfacing with yet another piece of the rainforest.

We left the office with another form, also in Bahasa, for us to fill in, seeming as if we were going backward instead of forward. Beatrice stood outside the office, staring at the ground and looking terribly despondent. I tried to reassure her.

"This is just a minor setback and nothing could possibly put me off marrying you. I love you with all my heart and there is nothing more important to me than this. Please believe me when I say that nothing will stop me from marrying you."

We filled out the change-of-address form and re-presented it, with the necessary documentary evidence, at the office the next day. This time a lady was sitting behind the desk and she gestured for Beatrice to approach with the form, which was amazingly given a clean bill of health.

She then asked, "Where are the four photographs?"

"What photographs?" asked Beatrice, disbelievingly.

"Yes, we do need four photos," said the official. "You can get them anywhere … passport-size, please."

So off we went again, running around looking for an instant-photo booth. We found one, only to return to find the office closed for the remainder of the day. Another step backward but we were both determined not to let this bureaucratic marathon beat us. Through dinner that evening, I joked about the experience, trying to make light of it, but the joke really started to wear thin when we returned again the next day with the photos, only for that same official to announce, "Oh dear, I'm afraid that we need black and white ones. Did nobody tell you?"

By this time I was spewing lava. We went looking everywhere until we finally found a studio that would take the photos, but we would have to call back the next day to collect them. So back we went again to collect the photos, and then to the registry office. Everything was handed over, and we waited with bated breath.

"Yes, everything is in order. You can come back tomorrow for the signed document notifying the office upstairs of your change of address," the official pronounced.

"Could you not call them for us today and just inform them verbally that the forms are on their way so we can continue with the other elements of the process?" we enquired, to no good effect.

"No, I'm sorry, this is not allowed. You will have to return here tomorrow."

So that was that. Another afternoon blown and another night of forced humour over dinner.

On our next day off, we returned together with the original forms and the letter officiating Beatrice's change of address from Sabah to Penang, and handed them to the original fellow at the Marriage Registry Office.

The inspector's response was not what we'd bargained for.

"I'm sorry," he said, "but unfortunately, you will have to fill out the application forms again because Beatrice has changed her address."

As he bent over to pick up the new set of forms, I must say, I really wanted to let go with some choice verbals. Knowing that nothing would be accomplished by this, I managed to swallow deeply, smiled and said as politely as I could, "That is wonderful. You have been very helpful. We will be back next week."

We took back the old forms with the new ones, so that we could copy what we needed and off we went. A week later, we walked into his office, for what seemed like the umpteenth time, with everything at the ready and handed them to him. He looked at us and smiled.

"Good afternoon, you two, I wondered when I would see you again." After a period of studied silence, he then chimed, "No, this should be here and that should be there. But I tell you what, I have some correcting fluid here. Why don't I change it for you?"

I smiled at him warmly and told him that he was a gentleman and a scholar, and he got down to work.

"Alright," he announced a good while later, "you have to go over to the Penang Court House to get one of our lawyers to stamp and sign these forms to formally declare everything to be correct."

Of course, silly us, we had not thought to bring the originals of all our documents because we had shown them to this chap and the others so many times already, which meant we had to return home first for the passports, birth certificates, etc. At the court house, we found yet another waiting area, this time with a line that would scare any would-be criminal well and truly onto the straight and narrow. We waited for ages until finally an officer called us to approach the window.

"May I see all the papers and documents, please?" she began. She looked rather fierce, and I thought for a second that I was approaching Checkpoint Charlie or was playing a role in the movie *Midnight Express* – or was it just my jaded view of officials by that point? After turning every page and scrutinising every word as if it was likely to be a forged document, she eventually looked up, smiled and said, "Well, I guess congratulations are in order."

I couldn't believe it. Was that finally it? I was so happy to know that it was over and I had seemingly earned the right to marry the girl of my dreams.

"What do we have to do now?" I dared to ask, sensing that the officer was in a better mood.

"Now you go back to the Marriage Registry Office, and they will tell you what to do next."

Since it was already late in the day and I had to be back at work, it was the following week before we could go back to the registry officer whom we had first seen.

He looked at us and laughed, "You have some good news, do you?"

"Yes, we have come to make our appointment for the big day," we said joyfully.

We still had plenty of time left as the day we wanted was now four months away, in early June. We had planned it down to the precise day, inviting our overseas guests and telling them of our exciting news.

"Not so fast," the inspector added, "you have something else to do."

"You are kidding. What else?" I snarled, which seemed to take the officer a little by surprise.

"Because you are both from out of the state, you have to get the permission of the Governor of Penang to be married here."

After pointless remonstrations, off we went with all the documents in a bulging brown envelope, and our tails between our legs, to pay a call on the Governor, whose office was, of course, across town in the rush hour traffic. As seemed our fate, the Governor's office was closed when we got there. I considered throwing myself down on the marble floor and just sobbing, but decided against adding to Beatrice's humiliation and dejection.

Instead, we made an appointment for our first available day off, but unluckily for us it was going to be another two weeks before it coincided with the Governor's schedule. Back at his office on the due date, we had to line up to gain a security pass before being shown into the Governor's office to meet the dignitary himself. I must say, though, how thoroughly charming and hospitable he was, and my initial thought was that we had finally hit the jackpot and it was at last all over.

We were amazed that he asked us exactly the same questions that everyone else had asked previously. Seemingly, every office conducts itself in the same manner, as if it is uniquely responsible for collecting the evidence themselves. Then he dropped the thunderbolt and asked us for our passports. Since all the forms had been verified by countless numbers of people already, I had assumed that we would not need them. I asked the Governor if we could return after lunch with everything that he would need. He looked at his watch and told us to return to his office within one hour. We raced home, grabbed the passports and got ourselves back with seconds to spare.

Finally, the Governor agreed that everything was in order and signed the newly stamped copy of our forms for us to return them to the registry office one last time. Almost two months later and hundreds of dollars lighter, like in the game of Monopoly, we had finally got back to 'Go'.

"Well, is that it now, inspector? Are we done here?" we dared to enquire.

"Yes," he replied. "Congratulations, that's the whole thing in the bag. Now the most important question … when would you like the big day to be?"

"Well, it is now early March and we were thinking of June sometime. What dates do you have left?" we asked, pleased with ourselves that we had come through the administrative maze.

"Oh, that's not possible, I am afraid," he answered.

"What do you mean?" I asked, too scared to want to know the straight answer. I held my breath for a second and waited.

"Actually, you see, once the forms have been signed by the Governor, they have a shelf life of only one month," he explained.

"What are you saying?" we probed.

"Well, if you do not get married within the next thirty days, the paperwork becomes null and void and then you have to reapply!"

"Why the heck did you not tell us this? Why did you not ask us when we first arrived when we wanted to get married, before we went through this whole rigma-role?" I asked him, dumbfounded and rapidly losing my cool.

"You never asked me how long the papers were good for," he answered with his usual warm smile.

So, with no real alternative, we had to make an appointment on the spot to get married within the month, changing all our previously laid plans. And that was exactly what we did.

The big day quickly came round and we arrived at the registry office to find our friend, the same inspector we had come to know so well, bending under his desk, rummaging for forms, and when he raised his head up to see us he beamed a huge warm smile.

"Well, good morning there. How nice it is to see you all dressed up and ready to go," he said, in greeting.

There were people everywhere and lots of well-dressed couples holding hands and gazing into each other's eyes, enjoying every second of their day.

"What number are we?" I asked the inspector.

"For all your efforts, you wonderful couple are first."

Exactly on time, he announced that there would first be a general presenta-tion to which all the couples were to attend before starting their respective official proceedings. They then led us into a small hall where we all sat together, wondering what would happen next. I whispered to Beatrice, "They probably want to tell us about the birds and the bees, or maybe give us some marriage counselling to save us all the pain later on down the road."

She laughed in my ear and sat closer, giving me a tight hug.

A gentleman walked into the room, looking very serious and rather fierce in a dinner suit. "My name is Mr Teng," he started, after clearing his throat. "I represent …"

"Here goes," I whispered to Beatrice, "it's going to be insurance …"

"Well, actually … I own a leading bridal and photographic shop here in Penang, and they allow me on each wedding day to explain to you young couples what packages we have on offer at my showroom …"

I could not believe it! Here we were at what I thought would be a solemn and private ceremony, only to be given a lousy sales pitch from someone I had no interest in at all. I was totally nonplussed by this, but when I looked across at Beatrice, I was amazed to find her so excited. She was almost beaming with anticipation, and I knew that we would have to go to Mr Teng's studio to take a series of photos to help her remember this day forever. His sales pitch worked – and I suspect not just with us.

After the presentation, we were called in to meet the Registrar, and what seemed like little more than five minutes later, it was all over. We stepped out of the Registrar's office as a married couple.

"Michael!" called our friend, the inspector, as we came out. "Can you do me a favour? The next couple do not have any witnesses. Could you and Beatrice step back inside and do it again for someone else?"

So back inside we went, to sit in the witnesses' chairs, masquerading as old experienced hands, showing them where to sign on the dotted line, and so on.

Afterwards, and for our own benefit, we had a lovely quiet blessing of our marriage in a nearby church, before going for a celebratory lunch with six of our closest friends. As we sat down to eat, a beautiful bunch of roses were delivered to Beatrice, which I had organised earlier, adding to the romantic tone of our first meal together as a married couple.

When our friends had departed, I took Beatrice to visit the bridal studio down the street. We decided which photography package we wanted and made an appointment for the picture session. For some crazy reason I thought that we would show up, sit around for a while, take the shots and be back home for lunch. However, just to be on the safe side, we made an appointment to have dinner with friends that evening at six o'clock, giving us time to go home, take off all the make-up and change our clothes before dinner.

We were asked by the studio to show up at the hair salon first, so that they could prepare Beatrice for the photos while I slipped away for a morning coffee. I dropped her off at nine o'clock and went next door for my wake-up brew.

I returned half an hour later to find her 'not quite ready, yet'. So off I went for a walk round the block, returning at ten o' clock to find her 'not quite ready, yet'. So off I went to have another coffee, by now getting 'quite wired' with all the caffeine I was drinking. When I returned an hour or so later, she was almost ready.

Anyway, we eventually took the first photographs at closer to twelve-thirty, and I was enormously cheesed off. I couldn't believe how slow these 'creative people' were, and how the hell was I to fake a grin now, never mind a large toothy smile that was supposed to show that I was the happiest man on earth. I gamely struggled through, without food or water, until four-thirty in the afternoon, and I can tell you, my smile muscles were killing me.

The photographer finally said, "Alright, that's it." At this point Beatrice and I ran into the cubicles, and started to drag all the clothes off that he had dressed us up in, and tossed them on the floor.

"Now!" he shouted out. "We are going to go around town to take the outdoor shots in the garden and by the waterfall."

I peeped over the top of the cubicle door and asked him with the straightest face on the earth, "Of course, you are joking, right? And I can tell you now, it isn't funny, not one bit, my friend."

But he wasn't. So off we went around town to take the other half of the shots that would finish off a long and extremely boring day with the intended bang. Then all of a sudden we were finished, and off to meet our friends for dinner in a casual restaurant, covered in make-up and wearing a black tie and dinner dress, as we had no time in the end to go home and change. A rib and chicken combo surprisingly tastes exactly the same when you are wearing a tuxedo as it does when you wear jeans and a T-shirt, but the service does improve.

A few days later, the pictures from this marathon photo shoot were delivered to the hotel, and I left them in our room and went back to work. I returned later to find Beatrice quietly sobbing to herself, holding the photo album.

"Darling, what's the matter?" I asked. "I thought they looked quite good."

I felt awful to see her so distraught, looking at something that was supposed to capture our very special moment. "We can go and take them again. I don't care how much they are going to cost," I said. "I just want you to be happy. So come on, wipe your eyes and we'll call them now to set up another appointment."

Beatrice looked up at me with an extremely surprised expression, as if she couldn't understand, or believe, what she was hearing.

"Mike, these photos are the most beautiful I have ever seen, and to think they are of you and me makes me feel I am the luckiest woman alive. I am already as happy today as I will ever be."

I had obviously not understood the importance these pictures had for Beatrice. For the next few days, each time I went home, I would find her just staring at the album with a look of joy on her face that I could not fully explain. How could I have underestimated how much they meant to her? Instead, I had been waiting, long-faced for just a few short hours while she got ready for her once in a lifetime event. Even today, long after the taking of the photos, I still often find her looking at the pictures with her eyes all welled-up, and I am overawed by the amount of pleasure they give her.

After the official ceremony, there was, of course, a bigger gathering of friends for our wedding reception a few weeks later. We decided to hold this very special event in a nearby competitor hotel – much to the shock of everyone that I told – but we wanted to ensure that most of our friends at the hotel where we lived and worked could also enjoy the party with us. None of us wanted to be worrying about the end result on this particular occasion!

We checked into the hotel which was organising the function to find two wonderful hearts on our bed, shaped from orchid flowers, plucked, we guessed, from the gardens that very morning. I sat on the balcony and a strange thought passed through my mind. I felt comforted to know that I was the one relaxing and someone else had to do the running around and worrying for once. I smiled ruefully to myself that they also had the added pressure of knowing that the wedding was for another executive chef, and even worse, the executive chef from the competitor hotel down the beach!

I could just imagine the briefings that had been going on in that kitchen. But everything seemed to be well organised, and we were able to relax before the party began. Being something of a worrier by nature, however, although it was not me sweating downstairs, I was still sweating inside, just that little bit.

By the time the moment came for us to take the short journey downstairs in the lift to the glittering ballroom, we had already made numerous trips back to our own hotel to pick up forgotten items!

As we arrived at the ballroom our friends made a human arch at the entrance for us to walk down, and they were all standing there with their hands behind their backs. As you can imagine, I was thinking what they concealing? Confetti, rice, perhaps, or even something else kitchen-related? My mind boggled and I thought ruefully of the numerous pranks I had either played, or witnessed, over the years.

We began to walk through the arch and suddenly all the arms were thrown into the air, tossing hundreds and hundreds of freshly picked, perfumed red rose petals. It was a lovely moment and made us both feel very special indeed.

The reception started off well and most of my friends from the food side of things at my hotel were already starting to get on a roll with their, 'Yum Sing's', the local version of toasting at a celebration – or literally translated, 'Bottoms up'. The traditional chanting before the toasting is another intriguing piece of the local culture. Everyone gathers around the table of the person who is the centre of attention, on this occasion Beatrice and myself, and holds their drinks in the air with their right hand. Then everyone, at the top of their voice, starts chanting, and it goes something like this:

"Yummmmmmmmmmm … (holding the note, and screaming as loud as you possibly can, for whatever reason nobody knows, and when you have absolutely no air left in your lungs and feel as if you are almost going to faint, you finish off with) … Sing!!!"

It is only practice that enables you to empty your lungs to such an extent that there is only the exact amount of air left to struggle with the spluttering of the 'Sing' part. On that note, everyone finishes the drink in one shot to prove their stamina. If anyone is not able to manage to finish their drink right down to the last drop, they are barracked so badly they decide to either sit down quietly or challenge the big mouth making fun of them to one more Yum Sing and then it starts again.

"Yummmmmmmm … Sing!!!" You know the rest.

The problem is at your wedding party, you may be expected, as the hosts, to visit every table individually for their own private Yum Sing. The guests need, of course, only to do it once but depending on the amount of tables at your function, it is a different story for the hosts. Fortunately, my master plan was already in place, and the waiter of the hotel followed me around with my own bottle of brandy, pouring large measures each time into my glass, as if to prove my manhood to all the guys.

After finishing, I staggered over to my table and sat down next to my wife, and she said, "You're such a man, darling. Don't you feel sick?"

"Of course not," I declared, "I can take it!"

"How was the coloured water you were drinking?" she enquired with a broad smile.

I couldn't believe that she thought I would stoop to such a low trick, so I confided. "It was cold tea, actually," and we both broke into peals of laughter.

She had got to know me all too well in a short time, and was well aware of my pathetic tolerance to serious drinking.

Another surprise on the local wedding scene is the dummy wedding cake, which, when I saw one for the very first time, knocked the socks off me. The hotel provides a splendid, multi-tiered wedding cake made out of a base of Styrofoam but decorated on the outside with real icing, giving an authentic-looking but altogether inedible cake. The caterers will secretly cut another real, albeit smaller, cake into bite-sized pieces behind the scene, and wrap it in beautiful boxes to give to the guests on their departure. The dummy cake is only for photographs and there is even a ready-made incision in the Styrofoam base for the happy couple to insert the decorative knife as if they were cutting the real thing.

On my own wedding day it felt bizarre to be standing there in front of this huge, beautiful, but wholly Styrofoam cake! Happily, the wife of a dear friend of mine had made a truly wonderful cake at home and brought it along as her contribution to the occasion. Everyone was very complimentary, saying how great it tasted!

Beatrice and I decided it was time to slip away as we were exhausted after a very long day. We returned to our room for the night most young lovers dream of

– their wedding night. As we lay on top of the bed, speechless and trying to catch our breath after a fast and action-filled day, we both drifted off into a sound sleep. The big night that comes but once a lifetime (or maybe twice) would have to wait until tomorrow.

Fortunately, that night there were no rats in my bed, merely strange sounds coming up from the garden. I could have sworn it was a gaggle of merry chefs, shouting up at our window …

"Yuuuummmmmmmmm … Sing!!!"

Exercise

Exercise can help your sleep by improving your general health, changing your brain temperature, and relaxing your body. It also has the potential to disturb your sleep by arousing you, or contributing to disturbed sleep caused by cramps, aches, and pains.

Goal

To create a routine that includes both regular and routine exercise programmes (exertion, as explained below, for about 20 minutes three times a week) and, more importantly, an active lifestyle, with at least 30 minutes of physical activity every day.

Action

- If you haven't exercised for some time or if you don't feel well, you should check with your doctor before starting an exercise programme. He or she may want to give you a physical examination and make recommendations. Even modest exercise could be dangerous if done incorrectly.
- Start off slowly. You don't have to run marathons to get some benefit. While experts generally support the benefits of 20 minutes of vigorous exercise about three times a week, any step towards that goal is beneficial. Your usual doctor, health centre or local gym should be able to give you a programme that gradually increases the intensity of your exercise.
- Find an exercise that you enjoy. You'll be more likely to stick with it and make it a constant part of your life.
- An active lifestyle may be even more important than intermittent all-out exercise. Avoid sitting for long periods; get up, stretch, and preferably take a short walk (even if just along the corridor and back) every 20 minutes or so. Use the stairs rather than the lift, and try to walk all or part of the way to work.
- Avoid engaging in moderate or heavy exercise within two hours of your bedtime. It increases your body temperature and heart rate, both of which interfere with your ability to go to sleep.
- Make sure that you exercise safely. Do the appropriate warm-up and cooling down routines, stretches, etc. Again, your doctor or other professional advisor should be able to tell you where to get advice.

- If you are walking, jogging or cycling, use a safe route and make sure that you can be seen by motorists.

IN CONCLUSION

We've tried to cover as many different topics as we could in the limited space available. There is much more that could be said about sleep disorders, but you should probably take those questions to your doctor.

The ultimate goal of *The Sleep Solution* is to:

> **Accept nothing less than refreshing, restorative sleep and the bright, alert wakefulness that results from it.**

CHAPTER 8

Sleep resources

GLOSSARY

Advanced sleep phase syndrome: A condition in which the biological clock is earlier than the usual clock. This leads to a pattern of needing to go to bed earlier, and waking up earlier, than is usual or than the sufferer wants to.

Antidepressant: A medication used to treat depression.

Apnoea: Literally, 'want of breath'. Lapses in breathing as you sleep. These may result from an obstruction in the upper airway, or a loss of stimulation to breathe.

Bi-level positive airway pressure: (e.g., BiPAP ®) A device to help breathing. The machine forces room air into the upper airway at two pressure levels, one for inspiration and one for expiration.

Bright-light therapy: The use of bright lights for two or three hours at the right time of day to attempt to reset the biological clock.

Bruxism: Grinding or clenching of teeth.

Circadian: 'About a day', usually used to refer to a biological rhythm.

CPAP: Continuous positive airway pressure. A device to help breathing which forces room air into the upper airway at a positive pressure to prevent it from collapsing.

CSA: Central sleep apnoea. Sleep apnoea in which the brain does not appear to send the proper signals for co-ordinated breathing.

Delayed sleep phase syndrome: A condition in which the biological clock is later than the usual clock. This leads to a pattern of needing to go to bed later, and waking up later, than is usual or than the sufferer wants to.

Delta sleep: NREM sleep stages three and four. See **Slow-wave sleep**.

Drug holiday: One or two days a week on which stimulants (for example) are not taken, in order to maximize their effectiveness at other times. Drug holidays should be arranged only through consultation with your doctor.

First-night effect: The phenomenon in which the first night's sleep in a strange place is significantly more disturbed than usual. Some insomniacs have a 'reverse first-night effect' in which their sleep is better for one or two nights under different circumstances.

GER: gastro-oesophageal reflux. Acid backing up from the stomach into the oesophagus.

Hypopnea: A short episode of restricted breathing, either as a result of an obstruction or reduced stimulation from the brain.

Insomnia: Difficulty in getting to sleep and/or, maintaining sleep, or waking too early.

LaUP: Laser-assisted palatoplasty. A surgical procedure used to treat snoring and mild apnoea.

Lights out, lights out time: The time when you stop doing wakeful things and start to try to fall asleep.

Long-sleeper: Someone whose only problem with sleep is requiring more time asleep than most people.

Main sleep period: The longest and best-consolidated sleep period. For most people, this is their night-time sleep.

Microsleeps: Short episodes of sleep during wakefulness that last a few seconds or so. The sleeper perceives them as brief lapses in consciousness.

Nap therapy: The use of short (usually 10- to 30-minute) naps to combat excessive daytime sleepiness. A common pattern is to take a nap before driving a motor vehicle, or working. Nap therapy may be a sufficient treatment itself, or may allow the dosage of stimulants to be reduced.

Narcolepsy: A rare disease usually beginning in the sufferer's teens or twenties in which excessive daytime sleepiness is often, but not always, associated with sleep-onset ('hypnagogic') hallucinations, sleep paralysis, and cataplexy (sudden weakness when the sufferer is feeling strong emotion).

Nightmare: A frightening dream, usually occurring during REM sleep, the details of which are usually remembered by the sufferer.

Night terror: A frightening episode, sometimes with screaming, characterized by a lack of mental imagery, and believed to arise during NREM sleep. Sometimes the patient is unaware that the episode even took place.

NREM sleep: Non-rapid eye movement sleep. Also known as **Quiet sleep**.

OSA: Obstructive sleep apnoea. A pause in breathing caused by a narrowing or obstruction of the airway.

Parasomnia: Major activity that occurs during sleep, usually at a transition from deep sleep to an arousal. Examples include sleep-walking, sleep-talking, and REM sleep behaviour disorder.

PLMS: Periodic limb movements of sleep (periodic limb movement disorder). Kicking or twitching movements of the legs that occur every 30 seconds or so for periods of the night.

Prone: Lying front down, back uppermost.

PSG: Polysomnography, the name for the primary study of sleep in a sleep disorders centre, meaning 'many measurements of sleep'.

Quiet sleep: One of the two main types of sleep. Also known as non-REM sleep. Consists of stages one, two, three and four. Stages three and four are together known as **Delta sleep**.

Rebound insomnia: Insomnia that returns when a sleeping-pill is stopped, and which may be even more severe than the original problem.

REMS or REM sleep: Rapid eye-movement sleep.

REM sleep behaviour disorder: A disorder of REM sleep in which the patient appears to be acting out his or her dreams.

Reverse first-night effect: Some insomniacs experience an improvement in their sleep for one or two nights under different circumstances. Compare this with the usual 'first-night' effect in which the first night's sleep in a strange place is significantly more disturbed than usual.

RLS: Restless legs syndrome. An unpleasant situation, usually in the legs, that is worse in the late evening or at night, and when the sufferer is immobile. Movement usually relieves the feeling for a short time, but more complete relief comes only with sleep.

Short-sleeper: Someone who truly needs less sleep than most people to function well. Many people believe themselves to be short-sleepers but are not.

Sleep drunkenness: Confusion and lack of co-ordination when waking up, particularly after a nap.

Sleep efficiency: The percentage of time spent in bed (starting from lights-out time) that is spent asleep.

Sleep inertia: The difficulty in becoming fully alert after waking up.

Slow-wave (Delta) sleep: One of the deeper or deepest stages of sleep in which the brain EEG shows large, slow waves. This stage tends to occur in the first half of the night.

Somnambulism: Sleep-walking.

Somniloquy: Sleep-talking.

Supine: Lying on one's back.

Unwelcome sleepiness: Sleepiness that interferes with your wakefulness, rather than helping you to get to sleep.

UVPPP: Uvulopalatopharyngoplasty. A surgical procedure for sleep-related breathing problems.

USEFUL ADDRESSES

Sleep Matters
Medical Advisory Service
PO Box 3087
London W4 42P

British Snoring and Sleep Apnea Association
The Steps
How Lane
Chipstead
Surrey CR5 3LT

The Narcolepsy Association
South Hall High Street
Farningham
Kent DA4 0DE

Royal Collage of Psychiatrists
17 Belgrave Square
London SW1X 8PQ

National Back Pain Association
16 Elmtree Road
Teddington
Middlesex TW11 8ST

BOOKS AND ARTICLES

This list is by no means complete, but contains some of the more helpful or interesting books that have been published over the last few years.

General

Ancoli-Israel, S, 1996, *All I Want Is a Good Night's Sleep*, Mosby-Year Book, paperback, ISBN 0815148437, 142 pages.

Inlander, CB & Moran, CK, 1998, *67 Ways to Good Sleep*, Random House, hardcover, ISBN 051718138X.

Insomnia

Hauri P & Linde S, 1990, *No more sleepless nights*, John Wiley & Sons, revised edition, ISBN 0471149047, 284 pages.

Chopra, Deepak, 1996, *Restful Sleep: The Complete Mind/Body Program for Overcoming Insomnia*, Crown Publications, paperback, ISBN 0517884577.

Digeronimo, T et al., 1997, *Insomnia: 50 Essential Things to Do*, Plume, paperback, ISBN 0452276365, 192 pages.

Snoring, Sleep Apnea and other Breathing Problems

Johnson, TS & Halberstadt J, 1992, *Phantom of the night, Overcome sleep apnea syndrome and snoring — win your hidden struggle to breathe, sleep and live.* New Technology Publishing, ISBN 1882431022, 172 pages.

Pascualy, RA & Soest, SW, 1996, *Snoring and Sleep Apnea, Personal and Family Guide to Diagnosis and Treatment*, Demos Vermande, 2nd edition, paperback, ISBN 0939957825, 238 pages.

Lipman, DS, 1997, *Snoring from A to Zzz: Proven Cures for the Night's Worst Nuisance*, Spencer Press, paperback, ISBN 0965070816, 256 pages.

Restless Legs Syndrome

Wilson, VN, 1996, *Sleep Thief, restless legs syndrome*, Galaxy Books, hardcover, ISBN 0965268209.

Complementary Medicine/Natural Remedies

Hoffmann, D, 1997, *Herbs for a Good Night's Sleep: Herbal Approaches to Relieving Insomnia Safely and Effectively. Understand Your Sleeplessness - And Banish It For ever!*, Keats Publications, paperback, ISBN 0879837934, 96 pages.

Lavery, S, 1997, *The Healthing Power of Sleep: How to Achieve Restorative Sleep Naturally*, Firesdie, paperback, ISBN 0684833522, 160 pages

Goldberg, B, 1998, *Alternative Medicine Guide to Sleep Disorders*, Future Medicine Publications, paperback, ISBN 1887299203.

Narcolepsy

Utley, MJ, 1995, *Narcolepsy: A funny disorder that's no laughing matter*, published by the author.

Dreams

Empsom, J, 1994, *Sleeping and Dreaming*, Harvester Wheatsheaf, 2nd revised edition, paperback, ISBN 0133021181.

McPhee, C, 1997, *Stop Sleeping Through Your Dreams: A Guide to Awakening Consciousness During Dream Sleep*, Henry Holt (Paper), paperback, ISBN 0805025154.

Shift work

Morgan, DR, 1996, *Sleep Secrets for Shiftworkers & People With Off-Beat Schedules*, Whole Person Associates, paperback ISBN 1570251185, 176 pages.

Children's Sleep

Guilleminault, C, *Sleep and its disorders in children*, 1987, Raven Press, ISBN 0881672785, 316 pages.

Technical and Professional

Kryger MH, Roth T, & Dement WC, 1994, *Principles and practice of sleep medicine*, WB Saunders, 2nd edition, ISBN 0721642179, 1,067 pages.

National Commission on Sleep Disorders Research, *Wake Up America, 1994, A national sleep alert.* US Government Printing Office, 302 pages.

Chokroverty, S, 1994, *Sleep Disorders Medicine*, Butterworth-Heinemann, ISBN 075069002X, 504 pages.

Morin, CM, Insomnia, 1996, *Psychological Assessment and Management*, Guildford Press, Reissue edition, paperback, ISBN 1572301201, 238 pages.

The Epworth Sleepiness Scale on page 47 is reprinted by permission. The original publication was: Johns MW, 1991, A new method of measuring daytime sleepiness: The Epworth Sleepiness Scale. *Sleep* 14:540-545.

WEBSITES

The Internet is the fastest growing source of information and ideas. Even if you don't have a computer at home, many libraries are now catering for public access.

You'll be able to find most of the useful information on the Internet from two main websites. *The Sleep Solution* site is at:

http://www.thesleepsolution.com

This site complements this book. It connects you with the widest range of sleep solutions that you'll find anywhere.

If you just want to know what's out there in cyberland, try the SleepNet:

http://www.sleepnet.com

It's designed to provide comprehensive links to sleep sites of all sorts.

INDEX

G

gasping, 209

gastro-oesophageal reflux, 35, 154, 155, 196

getting to sleep, 109-12, 174-5, 189-94

grinding teeth, 219

groaning, 218-19

grogginess: on awakening, 41
and napping, 91, 168
oversleeping, 166

grunting, 218-19

guests, 189

H

hallucinations, 30-1, 222

headaches, 197

health checks, 43, 89, 139

health problems, 139-41

heart: breathing problems, 29
diet and, 155
heart attacks, 34, 129

heartburn, 100, 154-5, 196

holidays, 167

homoeopathy, 139

hormones, 25

hotels, 188-9

hypnic (hypnagogic) jerks, 212

I

insomnia, 43
causes, 27-8

rebound insomnia, 134
sleep restriction therapy, 109-11, 174, 231
sleeping-pills, 134-6, 228-9
symptoms, 53

insufficient sleep syndrome, 28, 53, 204

irritability, 35

J

jerks, 212-13

jet-lag, 167

joint pain, 197

junk food, 83

K

K-complexes, 19

L

larks, 23, 113

lavatory visits, 195

legs: cramps, 213-14
periodic limb movement disorder, 30, 54, 118, 213
restless legs syndrome, 30, 44, 54, 118, 214-15

leisure activities, 87-9

Leonardo da Vinci, 16

lethargy, 32-3

letting go, 87

light, 100, 105, 225
biological rhythms, 113-15

If you have enjoyed *The Sleep Solution*, you may be interested
in the following titles also published by Vermilion:

One-Minute Stress Management
by Dr David Lewis   0 7493 1214 9

The Stress and Relaxation Handbook
by Jane Madders   0 09 181514 2

The Complete Guide to Stress Management
by Dr Chandra Patel   0 09 181366 2

Tired All The Time
by Dr Alan Stewart   0 09 181290 9

Fatigue
by Xandria Williams   0 7493 2066 4

To obtain a copy simply telephone
TBS Direct on 01206 255800